Islamist

D0000111

What were tł
and the man
the cause of Islamist terrorism relat
Middle East? The assumption that ....
the two phenomena was widely accepted in the post-2001 period and
appeared to inform Western foreign policies in the region, but does the
premise really stand up to scrutiny? Through detailed research into
the activities of both radical and moderate organizations across the
Middle East, such as the Muslim Brotherhood, Hamas, Hizbullah and
the GIA, and via interviews with key personnel, Katerina Dalacoura
investigates whether repression and political exclusion pushed Islamist
entities to adopt terrorist tactics. She explores whether inclusion in
the political process had the opposite effect of encouraging Islamist
groups toward moderation and ideological pragmatism. In a challenge
to the conventional wisdom, she concludes that Islamist terrorism is
not a direct consequence of authoritarianism in the Middle East, and
that there are many other political, strategic and social factors that
generate radicalism or inspire moderation.

Katerina Dalacoura is Lecturer in International Relations at the
London School of Economics and Political Science. She is author
of *Islam, Liberalism and Human Rights, Third Edition* (2003) and
*Engagement or Coercion: Weighing Western Human Rights Policies
towards Turkey, Iran and Egypt* (2004). She has published in many
journals, including *Review of International Studies, Millennium,
International Affairs, Democratization*, and *International Studies
Notes and International Relations*.

Islamist Terrorism and Democracy in the Middle East

KATERINA DALACOURA

The London School of Economics and Political Science

CAMBRIDGE
UNIVERSITY PRESS

CAMBRIDGE UNIVERSITY PRESS
Cambridge, New York, Melbourne, Madrid, Cape Town,
Singapore, São Paulo, Delhi, Tokyo, Mexico City

Cambridge University Press
32 Avenue of the Americas, New York, NY 10013-2473, USA

www.cambridge.org
Information on this title: www.cambridge.org/9780521683791

First published 2011

Printed in the United States of America

A catalog record for this publication is available from the British Library.

Library of Congress Cataloging in Publication data
Dalacoura, Katerina.
Islamist terrorism and democracy in the Middle East / Katerina Dalacoura.
p.   cm.
Includes bibliographical references and index.
ISBN 978-0-521-86518-0 (hardback) – ISBN 978-0-521-68379-1 (paperback)
1. Terrorism – Middle East.   2. Terrorism – Religious aspects.
3. Islamic fundamentalism.   4. Islam and politics.   5. Democracy – Middle
East.   6. Middle East – Politics and government.   1. Title.
HV6433.M5D35   2011
363.3250956–dc22   2010047275

ISBN 978-0-521-86518-0 Hardback
ISBN 978-0-521-68379-1 Paperback

To Greta and Marcos

Contents

Acknowledgements

Writing a book, particularly an academic book of this kind, is a long, hard and lonely business. During this time I incurred numerous debts, only some of which I can acknowledge here.

Part of the research for the book was funded by the United States Institute of Peace in 2007. Its grant enabled me to take time off from teaching and to travel to the Middle East region for fieldwork. However, the opinions, findings and conclusions or recommendations expressed in this publication are my own and do not necessarily reflect the views of the United States Institute of Peace.

Engaging with my excellent students at the LSE and my colleagues in the International Relations department has provided intellectual stimulation and food for thought in the creative process. From outside the LSE, I am especially grateful to Charles Tripp, Margot Light and Bob Springborg for their support. Hugh Roberts, Ewan Stein and Amnon Aran read chapters of the manuscript and usefully commented on them. I am thankful for their time and effort. I can acknowledge but never repay the debt I owe to my teacher, colleague and friend, Fred Halliday, who passed away in April 2010 as the book was nearing completion.

The book benefited from the suggestions of the anonymous reviewers who commented on drafts of the initial proposal and on the manuscript at various stages. I thank them (in particular 'Reviewer B') for engaging with my work. Marigold Acland, commissioning editor at Cambridge University Press, was excellent throughout the process. My research assistant, Alex Edwards, and Rashmi Singh at the LSE, were extremely helpful, as were Valerie Grove, Philip Davies, Vijee Natarajan and Joy Mizan in the final editing process. I owe a special note of thanks to all those who received me and talked to me in my various trips to the Middle East. I hope I have not misrepresented their views or betrayed their confidence.

Finally, I owe a note of personal thanks to my family and friends, here in Britain and in Greece. The unflinching love and support of my husband, Spyros Economides, is my mainstay. In the past few years, two wonderful individuals, Greta and Marcos, have appeared in our lives and now share our home with us. 'The book' has taken a fair part of their mummy away from them, so it feels completely right to dedicate it to them.

Introduction

The Book's Central Question and Rationale

The attacks against the United States of 11 September 2001 stunned the world and left a shocked American public wondering 'why do they hate us?' In the debate that followed in US public policy and academic fora, a consensus quickly formed that the terrorism of al Qaeda – and Islamist terrorism more generally – was the product of a democratic deficit in the Middle East. Not everyone agreed that this was the *only* cause; many argued that Islam itself, poverty and social anomie, or resentment towards US policies in the Middle East were also possible answers. However, there were few detractors of the proposition that brutal authoritarianism in the Middle East was a key reason behind the renewed threat of Islamist terrorism now confronting the world.

The causal links appeared self-evident. Being excluded from political processes deprived Islamists of the opportunity to peacefully express their views and pursue their political objectives. It prevented them from becoming socialised in the norms of negotiation and compromise, the ordinary give-and-take of politics. Isolation forced some of these individuals and groups to take up arms. Repression, in the form of imprisonment, torture and persecution of themselves and their loved ones, exacerbated feelings of alienation from their respective societies and governments and sowed hatred in their hearts. Regimes encouraged virulent anti-American rhetoric in place of dissent and exported trouble-makers to assure internal stability.[1]

---

[1] This argument was made in relation to the Egyptian and Saudi Arabian regimes in particular because Egyptians and Saudis were most prominently involved in the 11

The idea for the book developed as I considered these connections between democracy and terrorism. They appeared obvious and commonsensical, but were they borne out by the facts? The phenomenon of terrorism outside the Middle East – in Asia, South America, Africa and even more so in Europe and the United States – seemed, at first glance at least, unrelated to issues of democracy or the lack thereof. Was the presumed link between the lack of democracy and Islamist terrorism yet another instance of Middle East or Islamic 'exceptionalism', the view that the concepts and modes of analysis of social science do not apply either to the Middle East region or the Islamic religion as they do to the rest of the world?[2] The book aims to investigate the alleged causal relationship between the lack of democracy in the Middle East region and Islamist terrorism and to draw (or allow the reader to draw) well-informed theoretical and policy conclusions based on this investigation.

I have set myself a limited task: not to take on the broader question 'what causes Islamist terrorism?' but to isolate one suggested explanation, the lack of democracy, and test it using concrete case studies from the Middle East. My focus excludes non-Islamist terrorism – for example leftist or nationalist – which has also been rife in the Middle East. With the partial exception of al Qaeda, it also excludes Islamist terrorist movements from beyond the Middle East region but in other ways, and more specifically in its wide range of case studies, the book aims for breadth. Excellent work on the linkages between (the lack of) democracy or political participation and Islamist terrorism (although sometimes under a different label, for example 'rebellion' or 'extremism') has been published in recent years. It includes monographs by Jennifer Noyon,[3] Jillian Schwedler[4] and Muhammad Hafez.[5] However, these works focus on a small number of cases. At the inevitable cost of covering the material in relatively less depth, I aim to provide a fuller, albeit

September 2001 attacks. Josh Pollack, 'Saudi Arabia and the United States, 1931–2002', *Middle East Review of International Affairs (MERIA)* 6 (3) September 2002.

[2] The George W. Bush administration also appeared to consider the Middle East as 'exceptional' in that, as Thomas Carothers pointed out, the democracy drive was 'almost absent from the main pillars of Bush policy toward the rest of the world', that is, outside the Middle East. Thomas Carothers, 'Debating Democracy', *The National Interest*, 90, July/August 2007, p. 9.

[3] Jennifer Noyon, *Islam, Politics and Pluralism: Theory and Practice in Turkey, Jordan, Tunisia and Algeria*, London: Royal Institute of International Affairs, 2003.

[4] Jillian Schwedler, *Faith in Moderation: Islamist Parties in Jordan and Yemen*, New York: Cambridge University Press, 2006.

[5] Mohammed M. Hafez, *Why Muslims Rebel: Repression and Resistance in the Islamic World*, Boulder, CO: Lynne Rienner, 2003.

not exhaustive, view of the relationship between democracy and Islamist terrorism in the entire Middle East region.

US Democracy Promotion in the Middle East after 11 September 2001

Investigating the relationship between authoritarianism and Islamist terrorism has important policy implications for US foreign policy in the Middle East. In the post-9/11 period this policy was driven, at least rhetorically, by the assumption that actively promoting democracy in the region would encourage widespread political reform and democratisation, and in doing so ultimately serve US interests.

The idea of the United States as a beacon of democracy has always been a powerful (albeit controversial) element in US foreign policy, and its implications have been continually contested. During the Cold War, US foreign policy in the Middle East was driven primarily by the *realpolitik* aims of containing the Soviet Union, securing petroleum supplies and ensuring the survival of Israel.[6] The end of the Cold War and the perceived victory over the Soviet Union changed this to some degree: The foreign policy of the two consecutive Bill Clinton administrations (1993–2001) was influenced by liberal internationalist values both globally and, to a lesser extent, in the Middle East, where a combination of idealistic and pragmatic considerations brought about greater attention to 'democracy promotion'. Given the 'democratic peace theory', whereby democracies do not go to war with one another, democracy was seen not only as a good in itself but also a means of resolving conflict in a region plagued by dissent and war. The results of this shift were limited, however, as the main 'driver' of policy throughout the 1990s remained the desire for stability by way of supporting pro-Western, if authoritarian regimes.[7]

This changed dramatically after 9/11. As previously noted, in the search for the cause of the attacks unanimously attributed to al Qaeda and Osama Bin Laden, the argument that Islamist terrorism was the outcome of a democratic deficit in the Middle East quickly gained currency. Although this view was widely shared by many across the political spectrum, both in policy circles and among prominent commentators,

---

[6] US support for Israel cannot be reduced solely to *realpolitik* considerations, of course, and sometimes even clashed with them.

[7] The literature on the democratic peace theory is enormous, but Russett's classic study is still worth consulting. Bruce Russett, *Grasping the Democratic Peace: Principles for a Post-Cold War World*, Princeton, NJ: Princeton University Press, 1993.

its greatest impact on US foreign policy occurred as a group of so-called neo-conservatives gradually became the dominant element in the first administration of George W. Bush (2001–5). The neo-cons agreed with others across the political spectrum that the lack of democracy led to Islamist terrorism. However, they were unique in the aggressive manner in which they proposed to remedy this, and introduce democracy in the region, via the United States' newly launched 'war on terror'. They were also extreme, as we shall see below, in making democracy promotion instrumental to pursuing their own interpretation of US interests, not only in combating terror but also in ensuring US ascendancy and a newly found sense of mission across the globe.

Soon after the attacks of 9/11, a spate of policy initiatives on promoting reform in the Middle East were launched by the Bush administration. Announced in December 2002, the Middle East Partnership Initiative (MEPI) was the flagship democracy-promotion programme, embodying the new approach and diverting more funds to democratic reform. The Greater Middle East Initiative (which became Broader Middle East and North Africa Partnership Initiative [BMENA]) was announced in June 2004 at the G8 summit in Atlanta, Georgia. It included Pakistan and Afghanistan in the targeted 'broader' Middle East area and aimed to involve US allies as well as local partners in promoting democracy. A number of parallel initiatives such as the establishment of Radio Sawa ('Together') and al Hurra ('The Free') television station targeted 'hearts and minds' in the Middle East in an attempt to create favourable attitudes towards the United States and imbue them with US values. Assuming a causal connection between economic and political liberalization – a long-standing tenet in US foreign policy – the Bush administration announced its intention to conclude free trade agreements with individual Arab states, and eventually did so with Jordan, Morocco, Bahrain and Oman. It also envisioned the creation of a free trade area in the region by 2013.[8]

Such concrete policy initiatives were reinforced through traditional and public diplomacy. Members of the Bush administration made the US intention to encourage democracy in the Middle East clear on several occasions. One of the main themes in President Bush's National Endowment of Democracy speech in November 2003 was democratic

---

[8] Tamara Cofman Wittes and Sarah Yerkes, *What Price Freedom? Assessing the Bush Administration's Freedom Agenda*, Saban Centre for Middle East Policy, Analysis Paper 10, September 2006, p. 6.

reform in the Middle East. Secretary of State Condoleezza Rice suggested a role for 'transformational' diplomacy ('hands-on efforts by US
envoys globally to promote and build good governance and rule by the
people') in affecting change in the region.[9] In contrast with previous
practice, it was expected that US embassy officials on the ground and
US administration officials visiting the Middle East would give democracy and human rights more prominence in their contacts with regional
governments. There was also an expectation – though this was not
always explicit – that the United States could make economic and even
military aid conditional on progress towards reform.[10]

The Bush administration, driven by its neo-conservative ideologues,
pursued its democracy promotion policies while at the same time violating international legality and ignoring its own human rights treaty
obligations.[11] The most extreme instance of this discrepancy was its
decision to invade Iraq, which was in part presented as another means
of pursuing democracy in the region. While the 2003 Iraq war followed
on from the 2001 intervention in Afghanistan, it was very different in
purpose and rationale. The reasons behind it, real and purported, are
complex and will not be discussed at length here. Briefly, however, the
United States and its coalition partners argued that they and their allies
were threatened by the government of Saddam Hussein because it was
in the process of acquiring weapons of mass destruction (WMDs) which
could potentially be made available to terrorist groups. An extended
interpretation of pre-emptive self-defense (far beyond the conventional
and accepted definition of pre-emption as a response to imminent attack)
was therefore offered by the Bush administration and its coalition partners as the main justification for the invasion. A parallel, albeit intermittent, argument was also made, based on the view that democratic change
in the region would benefit the United States by draining the recruitment
pool for Islamist terrorists. Rapidly and forcefully transforming Iraq
into a democracy would produce a 'tsunami' of political reform in the

---

[9] Guy Dinmore, 'Critics of "Utopian" Foreign Policy Fail to Weaken Bush Resolve',
Financial Times, 13 January 2006. See also Justin Vaisse, *Transformational Diplomacy*,
European Union Institute for Security Studies, Challiot Paper 103, June 2007, http://
www.vaisse.net/BiblioJustin/Livres/Justin_Vaisse_Transformational-Diplomacy_
Chaillot-Paper_103_July_2007.pdf, accessed 18 January 2010.

[10] For instance, small-scale conditioning of aid to Egypt was used by Congress to promote tentative steps in democratization in 2005. Cofman Wittes and Yerkes, *What
Price Freedom?*, p. 26.

[11] Kenneth Roth, 'The Wrong Way to Combat Terrorism', *The Brown Journal of World
Affairs*, 14 (1) Fall/Winter 2007, pp. 263–72.

Middle East and serve as a model or beacon for the transformation of other authoritarian regimes in the region along democratic lines.[12]

Initial reaction in the Middle East to the announcement of US policies of democracy promotion was derision and incredulity, both at a popular level and among political commentators and officials.[13] As Tunisian human rights activist Moncef Marzouki argued, this reaction exposed the serious credibility gap in US policy.[14] A common response from the region, as well as from critics in the West and elsewhere, was that the United States was being hypocritical, and that the rhetoric on democracy hid ulterior motives which would ultimately prevail and ensure uninterrupted US support for Middle East dictators. Very soon, the critics were vindicated. The United States hailed the democratic reforms of its friendly regimes such as Jordan, Bahrain and Qatar as substantial, whereas in fact they were shallow, limited and easily reversible. Despite its profound authoritarianism, Tunisia was described as a 'stable democracy'[15] and its president, Zine el Abidine Ben Ali, feted by Bush shortly after the latter's 'forward strategy for freedom' speech.[16] By contrast, democracy was used as a 'stick' with which to beat US rivals such as the Syrian and Iranian regimes and the Palestinian Authority.[17]

A second reaction was furious indignation at both the US presumption of being an agent of democracy in the region and its attempt to interfere in the internal affairs of regional states. The impossibility of separating the message from the messenger – with its long history and continuing involvement in the region on the side of Israeli suppression of Palestinian rights and authoritarian Middle Eastern states – thus became quickly apparent in the post-9/11 politics of democracy promotion.[18]

[12] Marina Ottaway, Thomas Carothers, Amy Hawthorne and Daniel Brumberg, *Democratic Mirage in the Middle East*, Carnegie Endowment for International Peace, Policy Brief 20, October 2002.

[13] Marina Ottaway, 'The Problem of Credibility', Thomas Carothers & Marina Ottaway (eds.), *Uncharted Journey: Promoting Democracy in the Middle East*, Washington, DC: Carnegie Endowment, 2005, pp. 173–92.

[14] Moncef Marzouki, 'The US Project for Democracy in the Greater Middle East – Yes, But With Whom?' (Arabic), *Al Hayat*, 23 February 2004; quoted in Gilbert Achcar, 'Fantasy of a Region that Does Not Exist: Greater Middle East: The US Plan', *Monde Diplomatique*, April 2004.

[15] Human Rights Watch, *World Report 2002*, New York: Human Rights Watch, 2002, p. 405.

[16] Neil Hicks, 'Our Friend the Autocrat', *Washington Post*, 16 February 2004.

[17] Katerina Dalacoura, 'US Democracy Promotion in the Arab Middle East since 11 September 2001: A Critique', *International Affairs*, 81 (5) 2005, p. 969.

[18] Ibid., p. 973.

Critics pointed out that on its own home ground (which in effect included Guantanamo Bay, despite its special legal status), the United States was sacrificing civil liberties in the 'war on terror' and that this was extended to its allies in the Middle East region who increasingly used 'terrorism' in the post-9/11 climate as an easy way of assuring US support for their repressive policies.[19]

A third criticism of US democracy promotion policies was that despite the lofty statements and the grand policy initiatives of the post-9/11 era, they were short on substance and lacking in fresh ideas. Critics were quick to point out, for example, that the projects proposed by MEPI did not differ much from those of the 1990s. Likewise, many of the components of BMENA were already present in pre-existing US (and European) programmes.[20]

However, despite their limitations and flaws, and the negative local reactions, US democracy promotion policies – or at least the rhetoric – caused lively debate in the region on the need for, and possible direction of, reform.[21] A wide range of political actors, including Islamist groups, took part in this debate. For instance, the Muslim Brotherhood in Egypt responded to the proposal for the Greater Middle East Initiative (later BMENA) of the G8 in March 2004 by issuing its own reform programme.[22] Another outcome of US attention to democracy was a brief and narrow opening of political space in some Middle Eastern states. For example, US pressure led to unprecedented public discussion in Egypt about whether it was right that Hosni Mubarak should again run as presidential candidate, and for the first time an alliance of opposition parties began to voice demands that he stand down. This marked the beginning of the Kifaya ('enough') movement which came to life in 2004–5.[23] Although a campaign against foreign interference had

[19] Mhand Berkouk, *US-Algerian Security Cooperation and the War on Terror*, Carnegie Endowment Web Commentary, June 2009, http://www.carnegieendowment.org/publications/index.cfm?fa=view&id=23276, accessed 18 January 2010.

[20] International Crisis Group, *The Broader Middle East and North Africa Initiative: Imperilled at Birth*, Middle East and North Africa Briefing, June 2004; and Marina Ottaway and Thomas Carothers, *The Greater Middle East Initiative: Off to a False Start*, Carnegie Endowment Policy Report 29, March 2004.

[21] Thomas Carothers, *A Better Way to Support Middle East Reform*, Carnegie Endowment, Policy Brief 33, February 2005. See also Human Rights Watch, *World Report 2002*, p. 392.

[22] Official website of the Egyptian Muslim Brotherhood, http://www.ikhwanonline.com/Article.asp?ID=5172%26SectionID=356, accessed 26 October 2009.

[23] Issandr Amrani, 'Mubarak's Last Stand?', *Middle East International*, 742, 21 January 2005.

been sweeping the country, external pressure was also a major factor in Mubarak's decision to amend article 76 of the Egyptian constitution to allow multi-party presidential elections for the first time.[24]

The year 2005 was the high point of the Bush administration's democracy-promotion policies in the Middle East. In that year, there was a 'tentative sense' that a twilight might be descending on authoritarian governments, with the aforementioned changes in Egypt, and also Lebanon (where a so-called 'Cedar Revolution' precipitated a Syrian withdrawal from the country), municipal elections in Saudi Arabia, elections in Iraq and the Palestinian Occupied Territories and the granting of the vote to women in Kuwait. The US commentator Thomas Friedman argued that the invasion of Iraq 'triggered the first real "conversation" about political reform in the Arab world in a long, long time'.[25] For others, the Iraqi election of 2005 suggested that 'democracy is indeed an idea whose time has come for the Arab world'.[26]

However, far from causing substantial and far-reaching change, the results of US democracy-promotion policies in the Middle East proved to be a flash in the pan. In response to BMENA, a number of ostentatious conferences named 'Forum for the Future' brought together Middle East and G8 governments and civil society representatives. In the 'Conference on Democracy' held in Yemen in January 2004, 600 delegates of Middle East governments, NGOs and international organizations assembled to discuss reform. A meeting at the Bibliotheca Alexandrina in Egypt in March 2004 produced the Alexandria Statement, but despite the furor surrounding these events, their net effect on reform was questionable. They were government-led affairs which aimed to co-opt civil society activists, not give them space to assert their demands. The pro-reform statements produced on these occasions were general enough to render them innocuous. In the sharp words of the late Egyptian liberal activist Said el Neggar, rather than raising real problems in specific countries, the documents' authors 'wanted to tackle the reform question in a diplomatic way that would not offend the authorities'.[27]

---

[24] Paul Schemm, 'Grand Gesture', *Middle East International*, 745, 4 March 2005, pp. 19–20.

[25] Thomas Friedman, 'At Least Iraq's Got the Arabs Talking', *International Herald Tribune*, 20 February 2004.

[26] Editorial, 'The People of Iraq Speak', *Daily Telegraph*, 14 February 2005.

[27] Said el Naggar, 'The Alexandria Statement', *al Wafd*, 25 April 2004 (unofficial translation from the Arabic by Robert Springborg and Ahmed Ezzelarab).

On the ground, too, the reality of change was limited. There occurred no liberal–Islamist convergence in favour of reform, nor widespread and sustained movement in this direction.[28] Kifaya remained an elite affair, incapable of denting authoritarianism in Egypt. As I have already suggested, governments responded to perceived US pressure with moves which appeared substantial but were in fact merely cosmetic, designed to deflect criticism by giving the appearance of reform. One example was the previously mentioned constitutional amendment of the Egyptian presidential election the impact of which, paradoxically, was to divert political debate and silence critics without permitting true pluralism in the presidential race.[29] Elections in Saudi Arabia and other Gulf countries caught the headlines in the West and gave the appearance of reform to the outside world but for the most part were extremely circumscribed events often to elect (segments of) powerless national assemblies or weak municipal authorities which could barely affect the authoritarian structures of Gulf states. The Cedar Revolution quickly gave way to the hard reality of confessionalism in Lebanon. Despite the elation accompanying the Iraq elections of 2005, the impact of the Iraq war on the Middle East region was actually a *retreat* of reform movements. One example of this was Iran where the insecurity created by the US interventions in Iraq and Afghanistan allowed conservative clerics to further depoliticize and demobilize the population, at least in the short run.[30]

The final nails in the coffin of US democracy promotion in the post-9/11 Middle East were hammered in by the electoral successes of anti-Western Islamist forces. The election in December 2005 of eighty-eight Muslim Brotherhood (nominally independent) candidates to the Egyptian parliament and the subsequent resounding electoral victory of the Islamic Resistance Movement (Hamas) in January 2006 in the Palestinian Occupied Territories rammed home to the United States that freer elections in the Middle East could mean gains for Islamist anti-Western opposition movements.

Disillusionment led to a subtle yet real change of tone in Washington, which commentators quickly started to describe as a 'backlash' against

---

[28] Amy Hawthorne, 'The New Reform Ferment', Thomas Carothers and Marina Ottaway (eds.), *Uncharted Journey: Promoting Democracy in the Middle East*, Washington DC: Carnegie Endowment, 2005, pp. 57–77.

[29] Author's interview with Hishem Kassem, journalist and political activist, Cairo, November 2007. I take this issue up again in the Conclusion.

[30] Hadi Semati, 'Democracy in Retrograde', *Los Angeles Times*, 24 September 2004.

democracy promotion.[31] Leading neo-conservative thinker Robert Kaplan, for example, now suggested that pursuing 'normality' had become more important than 'democracy' in the Middle East.[32] Realist, liberal and other critics of the neo-conservative project reasserted their positions. The opinion that democracy cannot defeat terrorism and that democracy promotion endangers long-held US interests in the Middle East region was restated forcefully.[33] Others pointed out that spreading democracy was a 'gift' to Iran's government, a long-standing antagonist of the United States.[34]

By 2006, with the United States clearly backtracking from its commitment to democratic change, authoritarian Middle East regimes – sensing that the United States was back to 'business as usual' – began reversing the tentative reforms and clamping down on the limited democratic openings they had allowed over the previous two to three years. As soon as the United States signalled it had lost faith in democratization, there was crackdown on dissent.[35] The stalling of democracy in the Arab world – and in particular the cases of Egypt, Jordan, Qatar, Yemen and Saudi Arabia – was also helped by economic booms which stifled demands for political reform.[36] Freedom House reported in 2006 that there was 'freedom stagnation' and growing 'pushback' in the Middle East and beyond.[37]

The Book's Argument and Methodology

US democracy promotion policies in the Middle East came full circle with the end of the second Bush administration in January 2009. However,

[31] Amira Howeidy, 'Democracy's Backlash', *Al Ahram Weekly Online*, 785, 9–15 March 2006, http://weekly.ahram.org.eg/2006/785/eg3.htm, accessed 18 January 2010. See also Thomas Carothers, 'The Backlash Against Democracy Promotion', *Foreign Affairs*, 85 (2) 2006, pp. 55–68.

[32] Robert Kaplan, 'We Can't Force Democracy: Creating Normality is the Real Mideast Challenge', *Washington Post*, 2 March 2006.

[33] F. Gregory Gause III, 'Can Democracy Stop Terrorism?', *Foreign Affairs*, 84 (5) 2005, pp. 62–76; see also the remarks attributed to Gause in: *Democratizing the Middle East?*, The Fares Center for Eastern Mediterranean Studies, Tufts University, Occasional Paper 2, 2006, pp. 41–6.

[34] Ted Koppel, 'Gifts for Iran: Look What Spreading Democracy Can Do', *International Herald Tribune*, 22 July 2006.

[35] Howeidy, 'Democracy's Backlash'.

[36] Hassan Fattahm 'Drive for Democracy Stalls in Arab World', *International Herald Tribune*, 10 April 2006.

[37] Freedom House, *Freedom in the World Report 2007*, www.freedomhouse.org/template.cfm?page=15, accessed 18 January 2010.

the debate over the Middle East democratic deficit, its association with terrorism, and the role of the West, particularly the United States, is ongoing and will remain with us for a long time to come. The present study contributes to this debate by exploring the underlying assumption of US democracy promotion in the Middle East since 9/11, namely that Islamist terrorism is caused by the pervasiveness of authoritarianism in the region. It does so first of all by situating Islamist terrorism within the broader context of terrorism studies and linking it to the general discussion of democracy and terrorism (Chapter 1).

The argument developed in the main body of the book (Chapters 2–6) is that there is *no* necessary causal link between authoritarianism in the Middle East and Islamist terrorism. To demonstrate this, the study takes a broad view of the Middle East, incorporating Iran, Turkey and North Africa but excluding Pakistan and Afghanistan. It traces the emergence and evolution of those Islamist movements deemed relevant to the research question over the last thirty years or so, bringing in earlier histories when necessary.

The case studies in this work are individual Islamist movements, as opposed to the entirety of Islamist actors within a particular country. I opted for this way of organising the material because, more often than not, each country contains a variety of Islamist movements which are organisationally discrete from and even hostile to one another. However, the drawback of this method is a somewhat artificial analytical separation between movements which are otherwise interconnected in vital ways because they operate within the boundaries of the same state and society. For example, a movement may be able to abandon terrorist tactics and become more moderate when its more radical members 'migrate' to another movement within the same country or even abroad. I have tried to compensate for this methodological problem and avoid artificial dichotomies between movements on a case-by-case basis, by bringing in all the movements I consider necessary to provide a complete picture of events. So, for example, to understand the Algerian Groupe Islamique Armé (GIA), I discuss the Front Islamique du Salut (FIS) and the Armée Islamique du Salut (AIS); to understand the Egyptian Gamaa Islamiya, I bring in the Muslim Brotherhood, and vice versa.

The book explores the relationship between authoritarianism and Islamist terrorism thematically. In Chapters 2–4, I divide Islamist terrorism into three categories or types: transnational Islamist terrorism, such as al Qaeda's; Islamist terrorism associated with national liberation movements, such as Hamas and Hizbullah; and Islamist terrorism associated with domestic insurgencies against existing regimes, such as the GIA in Algeria and Gamaa Islamiya in Egypt.[38] The first category, of transnational Islam, where terrorists' grievances and victims transcend borders of multiple states, 'has implications for two or more countries' through its perpetrators, victims or audience. The third category of domestic terrorism deals with Islamist movements operating within national boundaries and is 'homegrown and home directed, with consequences for the venue country, its institutions, citizens, property, and policies'. The second category related to national movements lies somewhere in between, in that it operates domestically but targets an 'outside' oppressor.[39] The dichotomies between these three types of Islamist terrorism sometimes appear forced or even artificial. For instance, transnational terrorism can be an outgrowth or 'spill over' of domestic terrorism. Again, I have tried to compensate for this methodological problem on a case-by-case basis, by bringing out the complex relationships of individual Islamist movements with the wider Islamist 'scene' in their country and region.

The second part of the book (Chapters 5–6) explores the relationship between authoritarianism and Islamist terrorism on the other side of the metaphorical coin and asks whether political participation – albeit in non-democratic or partially democratic systems – encourages moderation. Moderate Islamist movements in opposition and in government are two distinct categories. I enquire whether and how participation in political processes caused modification in ideas and practices amongst Islamist groups, even if they remain in opposition to existing regimes. Under this category, I analyse the Jordanian Muslim Brotherhood/Islamist Action Front, the Egyptian Muslim Brotherhood and the Tunisian Nahda movement. I pose similar questions about the responsibilities of governing: Have they forced Islamist movements to make ideological compromises and adopt more moderate positions in response to the citizenry's demands and the practical requirements of exercising authority? Here, the case studies are the Turkish Welfare and Justice and Development parties and the Islamic Republic of Iran.

---

[38] Here, I have modified the categorisation put forward by Najib Ghadbian in 'Political Islam: Inclusion or Violence?', Kenton Worcester, Sally Avery Bermanzohn and Mark Ungar (eds.), *Violence and Politics: Globalization's Paradox*, New York: Routledge, 2002, pp. 95–6.

[39] B. Peter Rosendorff and Todd Sandler, 'The Political Economy of Transnational Terrorism', *Journal of Conflict Resolution*, 49 (2) April 2005, p. 172. See also Paul Wilkinson, *Terrorism versus Democracy: The Liberal State Response*, 2nd edition, London and New York: Routledge, 2006, p. 4.

To address its central question, the study examines the motives which drove the leaderships of some Islamist movements – and not others – to adopt terrorist methods. Were these related to the weakness of democratic institutions, the violation of civil rights, repression and/or lack of political participation, or did they lie elsewhere? Conversely, the decision by non-violent Islamist movements to avoid such methods is placed under the microscope. To ascertain such motives, part of the research was carried out by interviewing participants in Islamist movements and their observers in their respective countries of operation.[40] But the large number of case studies and the need to capture the long-term development of movements over a number of decades meant that have I relied mostly on secondary sources in the languages (English and French) which are directly accessible to me.

Key Terms and Concepts

To develop the book's argument, I need to define its key terms and concepts at this early stage. I have used the definition of terrorism as 'a political act, ordinarily committed by an organized group, involving the intentional killing or other severe harming of non-combatants or the threat of the same or the intentional severe damage to the property of non-combatants or the threat of the same'.[41] Terrorism's definition is marred by acrimonious debates, for example, on whether states as well as non-state actors should be legitimately described as terrorist actors.[42] These debates are so fraught and politicised that the term occasionally appears more of a hindrance rather than an asset to academic analysis. The solution, however, is not to drop the term altogether but to use it with caution and precision. For instance, it is important to underline that terrorism is a *means* or method used to achieve political objectives and does not refer to the objectives themselves.[43] Contrary to the widespread belief that 'one man's terrorist is another man's freedom fighter' – which

---

[40] I was unable to do any primary research on the al Qaeda case study. It was also impossible for me to visit and carry out research in Iran.

[41] C. A. J. Coady, 'The Morality of Terrorism', *Philosophy*, 60 (231) 1985, p. 52. I include political assassination, in so far as it involves the killing of civilians for political purposes, under this definition of terrorism. This is particularly relevant to the discussion of Iran in Chapter 6.

[42] Daniel Byman, *Deadly Connections: States that Sponsor Terrorism*, New York: Cambridge University Press, 2005.

[43] Gordon Graham, *Ethics and International Relations*, Oxford: Blackwell, 1997, pp. 122–5.

confuses means and ends – there is no logical contradiction in describing, as I do in this study, cases where a national liberation movement is *also* a terrorist actor.[44]

Distinguishing terrorism from other forms of political violence is a constant challenge which sometimes appears insurmountable. For instance, rioting or the wilful destruction of property, when they have a political purpose, are not normally described as terrorism, even though they target the property and sometimes even the lives of non-combatants. It is particularly difficult to separate terrorists from 'radicals', 'militants' and 'extremists', especially in the case of Islamism. The existence of gray areas, however, does not mean that we should discard the terms nor that it is impossible to separate terrorism from other forms of political violence. There *is* something exceptional about the indiscriminate targeting of civilians, which often includes the frail and vulnerable such as the very old and the very young. Indeed, I would argue that triggering emotional shock and aversion by such indiscriminate targeting is an integral part of the terrorist's purpose and objective.

A final but major source of problems with the definition of 'terrorism' derives from the gray area between the conditions of war and peace. Indiscriminately targeting civilians is wrong in both, but in peacetime it is labelled 'terrorism' whereas in wartime it is a violation of the principle of discrimination or non-combatant immunity. This would not have been a problem, except that there is often fundamental disagreement between the parties in a conflict on whether it should be called a war or not. I am confronted with this almost intractable problem in numerous instances in the course of this study, for example, when discussing national liberation movements such as Hamas and Hizbullah which claim to be *at war* with Israel; or determining whether the Algerian conflict in the 1990s should be described as a civil *war*. One alternative would have been to avoid the term 'terrorism' altogether and concentrate on the act of indiscriminately targeting civilians without naming it one way or another. Although it has benefits, I have not opted for this solution because, in my

---

[44] If an actor or movement is described as 'terrorist', this does not mean it cannot also have other descriptions. On this issue, I disagree with the argument by Harmonie Toros and Jeroen Gunning who claim that 'labelling a group or person as "terrorist" limits our understanding of them as *only* the perpetrators of terrorist acts'. This is not, in my view, necessarily so. Harmonie Toros and Jeroen Gunning, 'Exploring a Critical Theory Approach to Terrorism Studies', Richard Jackson, Marie Breen Smyth and Jeroen Gunning (eds.), *Critical Terrorism Studies: A New Research Agenda*, Abingdon, Oxon: Routledge, 2009, p. 97.

view, the term 'terrorism' does retain conceptual and analytical value. I have also long abandoned hope of finding a precise set of criteria for distinguishing between the conditions of peace and war. Therefore, in each instance where I am faced with this dilemma, I develop analytical rules of thumb which, I hope, draw sufficiently on international law (and common sense) to convince the reader.

'Islamism' is also a key term in this study. I use it interchangeably with 'political Islam' and define it as a political ideology which employs an interpretation of Islam as a blueprint for building the ideal society.[45] Islamism is a complex and multi-faceted phenomenon and many of its strands follow multiple and divergent routes: For instance, the reformist Salafi tradition, which originated in the late nineteenth century, but is in recent times more closely associated with hard-line and puritanical Islamic thought, has given rise to movements which are political and apolitical, violent and non-violent, for and against the established order.[46] The view that violence and terrorism are inextricably linked to and stem from Islamism as an ideology (and even from Islam as a religion) is widely held, even if not always explicitly asserted, let alone substantiated. In contrast, an important assumption of my argument is that not all Islamists are real or potential terrorists or terrorist sympathisers, and that, far from being monolithic, Islamism can evolve in different and widely divergent ideological directions under the influence of specific factors and conditions.[47]

It follows that 'Islamist terrorism' is but one variant of Islamism (and, I would also emphasise, is but a small minority in a wide range of movements). 'Islamist terrorists' are those individuals or movements who pursue Islamist objectives using terrorist methods, as defined here. Contrary to current practice, and unless I am quoting others, I eschew the term 'jihadism' because it inaccurately associates *jihad* exclusively with violence. I do not use Islamist terrorism interchangeably with Islamist radicalism, extremism, militancy or fundamentalism, although sometimes context or the particular case I am referring to permits me to do so. Although all Islamist terrorists are radicals/extremists/militants/fundamentalists,

---

[45] Some Islamist movements, such as Tablighi Jamaat – which I discuss briefly in Chapter 2 – claim to be apolitical and have not been associated with violence. They therefore lie in a gray area between religious and political movements or between Islam and Islamism.

[46] Wendy Kristianasen, 'Who is a Salafist?', *Monde Diplomatique*, February 2008.

[47] I have developed this argument more fully in *Islam, Liberalism and Human Rights: Implications for International Relations*, London: I. B. Tauris, revised edition, 2003.

the reverse does not necessarily hold. The strict and puritanical ideas of any of the latter are not inevitably translated into use of or support for violent methods, let alone terrorism. In other words, many radical/extremist/militant/fundamentalist organisations – such as Hizb ut Tahrir, discussed below – are non-violent. Others, such as Hizbullah since the mid- to late 1990s, are violent but, arguably, not terrorist.

Islamism, or political Islam, comprises a spectrum of interpretations, with the hard-line positions at one end and Islamist liberalism, defined as the thorough and genuine reconciliation of Islam with liberal principles, at the other. In between these extremes lies an infinite range of ideological possibilities. As already stated, in order to address its core research question on the relationship between democracy and terrorism, the book's second part examines the reasons behind the emergence of Islamist moderation. The criteria of Islamist moderation are widely discussed in the literature on political Islam. An important distinction is between moderation in tactics and objectives.[48] For a movement to be defined as moderate it must eschew terrorist or violent tactics. If objectives are sub-divided into political (democracy and pluralism) and social (the position on women's role in society, the status of non-Muslims, freedom of expression and conscience), a moderate Islamist movement must demonstrate some acceptance of at least the former.[49] A willingness to pursue relations with and openness towards the West is also sometimes taken as a criterion of moderation, but I do not include it.[50] For the purposes of this study, I follow Gudrun Krämer's two-pronged definition of moderate Islamist groups as 'those Islamic groups and activists who formally declare their respect for, and commitment to, pluralism and the democratic principle and renounce the use of violence in achieving their objectives'.[51] I will also occasionally refer to these movements' social

---

[48] Carrie Rosefsky Wickham, 'The Path to Moderation: Strategy and Learning in the Formation of Egypt's *Wasat* Party', *Comparative Politics*, 36 (2) 2004, p. 206.

[49] Gudrun Krämer, 'The Integration of the Integrists: A Comparative Study of Egypt, Jordan and Tunisia', Ghassan Salamé (ed.), *Democracy without Democrats? The Renewal of Politics in the Muslim World*, London: I. B. Tauris, 1994, pp. 208–9.

[50] This is the (implicit) view of Amr Hamzawy, who argues that engagement with Islamists must be limited to movements which renounce violence and 'are willing to cooperate with the West'. See Amr Hamzawy, *The Key to Arab Reform: Moderate Islamists*, Carnegie Endowment for International Peace, Policy Brief 40, July 2005, p. 7.

[51] Gudrun Krämer, 'Cross-Links and Double Talk? Islamist Movements in the Political Process', Laura Guazzone (ed.), *The Islamist Dilemma: The Political Role of Islamist Movements in the Arab World*, Reading, Berkshire: Ithaca Press, 1995, p. 42. A similar term to 'moderate' is 'mainstream' Islamists, defined by the Institute for Public Policy Research as 'those Islamist movements that engage or seek to engage in the legal

worldviews and objectives, although they are not strictly speaking part of my definition of 'moderation'.

Strictly speaking, because the book is concerned, not with the objectives, but with the methods Islamist movements use to achieve them, and in particular the use or avoidance of terrorism, its second part should have focused on 'non-violent' or 'non-terrorist', not 'moderate' Islamists. Although they may be more accurate, these terms are awkward and inelegant, as well as somewhat limiting. Moreover, moderation in tactics or methods often, though not always, goes hand in hand with greater openness to political pluralism and democratic principles (though not necessarily in social mores, as we shall see). It is important to add a caveat, however, that such openness does not necessarily entail a profound or complete espousal of democratic principles and political culture. Islamist 'moderates' are not Islamist liberals or democrats, although they may have taken a crucial step in this direction.[52] Furthermore, if 'moderate' is defined as 'avoiding extremes; temperate in conduct or expression',[53] it is obvious that 'moderation' is an inherently imprecise concept, always relative to context and in particular to the other available currents of Islamist thought and action. An Islamist movement which may seem moderate in a country ridden by war and extremism such as Afghanistan would not seem so in the more sedate Moroccan setting, and so on.

Finally, the term 'democracy' can be defined generally as 'the rule of the demos, the citizen body: the right of all to decide what are matters of general concern'. Essential components of democracy include free and fair elections which provide effective choice and offer the people's representatives the right to legislate and oversee government decisions and practices. Democracy also crucially depends on the protection of basic civil, political and social rights.[54] We cannot speak of democracy being

---

political process of their countries and that have publicly eschewed the use of violence to help realise their objectives at the national level, even when they are discriminated against or repressed.' Alex Glennie, *Building Bridges, Not Walls: Engaging with Political Islamists in the Middle East and North Africa*, London: Institute for Public Policy Research, 2009, p. 9.

[52] The term 'post-Islamism' is sometimes used to describe what I would describe as Islamist liberalism. I avoid the term 'post-Islamism' because it implies that there can be no reconciliation between Islamism and liberal or democratic values because once these values have been espoused, Islamism has been 'overcome'. I take up this point again in my discussion of the Justice and Development Party in Chapter 6.

[53] R. E. Allen (ed.), *Concise Oxford Dictionary of Current English*, Oxford: Clarendon Press, 1990.

[54] 'Democracy', Alan Bullock and Oliver Stallybrass (eds.), *Fontana Dictionary of Modern Thought*, London: Fontana/Collins, 1977, p. 161.

either 'present' or 'absent'. In each political context, the blend of democratic and undemocratic elements varies and there are as many democratic systems as there are political settings. But the essential, underlying principles of democracy – accountability, tolerance, respect of fundamental freedoms – are universally valid and not culturally specific. To put it simply, there are varying *degrees* and applications of democratic freedoms within discrete political systems, but not different *kinds* of democracy.

Investigating whether democracy helps to offset the emergence of Islamist terrorism in the Middle East is, strictly speaking, an impossible task: We cannot observe the impact of Islamist participation in democratic systems because there are no full democracies in the region. There are different levels of authoritarianism, of course, and the harshly repressive systems of Saudi Arabia or Syria are very different from the 'milder' autocracies of Morocco and Jordan. The Israeli and Turkish systems, although more democratic than any others in the region, are flawed in major ways – in the case of the former because of the ongoing occupation of Palestinian territories, in the case of the latter, until at least very recently, because of the continuing political power of the army and other legal and constitutional impediments. In Iran, where authoritarian structures co-exist with democratic institutions in a particularly dynamic mix, categorisation is much more difficult. However, although we cannot talk of fully fledged democracies in the region, some political systems are more inclusive and pluralist than others.[55] Political participation can also be possible in non-democratic regimes.[56] In line with these distinctions, the present study investigates *political* as opposed to democratic participation as a likely cause of moderation.[57]

Political participation is broadly defined as 'activity by private citizens designed to influence governmental decision-making'.[58] It can be

---

[55] The distinction between a democratic versus a pluralist and inclusive process is made by Schwedler. See Schwedler, *Faith in Moderation*, pp. 20–1.

[56] Ellen Lust-Okar and Saloua Zerhouni (eds.), *Political Participation in the Middle East*, Boulder, CO: Lynne Rienner, 2008.

[57] The idea that including a movement in the political process causes it to moderate its ideological positions – the 'inclusion-moderation hypothesis' – is widely studied in political science and specifically in the literature on democratic transitions and rational choice theory. Its most common formulation is 'that institutions shape political behaviour by creating constraints and opportunities, which in turn structure the choices available to political actors'. However, as Jillian Schwedler further notes, in-depth studies on the inclusion-moderation hypothesis are lacking and evidence is often anecdotal. Exactly how inclusion leads to moderation is not thoroughly examined. Schwedler, *Faith in Moderation*, pp. 11, 15 and 21.

[58] Samuel Huntington and Joan Nelson (eds.), *No Easy Choice: Political Participation in Developing Countries*, Cambridge, MA: Harvard University Press, 1976, p. 4, quoted

mobilized or autonomous, state-driven or society-driven. It takes three forms: political participation within the limits of the authoritarian state through populist or corporatist structures; political participation through informal social networks; and participation through oppositional political institutions autonomous from state control, such as political parties and civil society organisations.[59] I discard the first and second forms of political participation in the analysis that follows. Participating, say, in labour unions fully controlled by the state or extracting state resources through patronage networks are hardly instances of political participation.[60] Instead, I focus on the third form of political participation, namely through political parties and civil society organisations, despite the admittedly very limited role they play in Middle East authoritarian systems. More specifically I concentrate on the following as instances of political participation by Islamist movements: the contestation of elections for political office, either as independents or organised in political parties; taking part in professional association and student body elections and politics;[61] involvement in civil society associations; participation in public policy debates;[62] cooperation with other oppositional (non-Islamist) groups.[63] In some cases, such as Egypt or Jordan, electoral participation has limited goals and possibilities, mostly as a means of accessing resources through patronage; in others, such as the Palestinian case after the January 2006 elections, participation can truly challenge ruling elites.[64] There is a view, which I will take up again in the Conclusion, that incumbent regimes introduce greater inclusiveness not to facilitate a transition to democracy but to block it. However, irrespective of its ultimate objective, permitting some degree of political participation allows us to study its effects on Islamist movements.

in Holger Albrecht, 'The Nature of Political Participation', Lust-Okar and Zerhouni (eds.), *Political Participation in the Middle East*, p. 17.

[59] Ibid., pp. 20 and 28.

[60] I disagree with Laila Alhamad who describes such participation as political. Laila Alhamad, 'Formal and Informal Venues of Engagement', Lust-Okar and Zahouni, *Political Participation in the Middle East* (see especially p. 36).

[61] Vickie Langohr, 'Of Islamists and Ballot Boxes: Rethinking the Relationship between Islamisms and Electoral Politics', *International Journal of Middle East Studies*, 33 (4) 2001, p. 591.

[62] Such participation is not easy to pinpoint or quantify but it is important in encouraging the rethinking of ideological positions.

[63] Janine A. Clark, 'The Conditions of Islamist Moderation: Unpacking Cross-ideological Cooperation in Jordan', *International Journal of Middle East Studies*, 38 (4) 2006, pp. 539–40.

[64] Ellen Lust-Okar, 'Taking Political Participation Seriously', Lust-Okar and Zerhouni (eds.), *Political Participation in the Middle East*, p. 7.

In this work, I also consider the take-over of government or the state as a form of political participation. This is controversial because running a government or state is different from participating in politics in an oppositional role. Nevertheless, it is still a form of political participation and can even be seen as its culmination – being in government is, after all, the pinnacle of politics and the objective of all political actors. Islamist movements which take over governments or states have already spent a period in opposition, however briefly. But they are further transformed as they assume the responsibilities of government and are forced into the compromises and concessions of principle that it requires.

If the concept of 'democracy' and political participation in the Middle East needs unpacking, so does its opposite: the 'lack of democracy' or 'authoritarianism'. For the purposes of this study, I borrow Mohammed Hafez's dual emphasis – which he uses in the different context of analysing Muslim rebellions – on institutional exclusion from the political process and repression. The former refers to situations where a movement is 'prohibited from influencing public policy through institutional channels'[65] and the latter to any action taken by the authorities which 'raises the contender's cost of collective action'.[66] Repression can take a variety of forms including restrictions of rights to freedom of association and expression, mass and arbitrary arrests and executions, 'disappearances' and the use of torture.[67]

---

[65] Hafez, *Why Muslims Rebel*, p. 28.

[66] Charles Tilly, *From Mobilisation to Revolution*, Reading, MA: Addison-Wesley, 1978, p. 100, quoted in ibid., p. 71.

[67] Ibid., p. 71. Hafez distinguishes between 'pre-emptive and reactive' and 'selective and indiscriminate' repression, but I do not do so in the course of this study.

Terrorism, Democracy and Islamist Terrorism

Islamist terrorism has dominated the field of terrorism studies since the attacks of 11 September 2001.[1] Its proper analysis, however, is bedevilled by Middle Eastern and Islamic 'exceptionalism', which either implicitly or explicitly assumes an inherent association between terrorism and the Middle East as a region and/or Islam as a religion. Such exceptionalism removes Islamist terrorism from the wider context of terrorism studies and places it in a separate and unique category. Recent developments in the field, such as the focus on 'new terrorism' – which has become increasingly linked with Islamism since 2001[2] – have reinforced the idea

---

[1] Andrew Silke, 'Contemporary Terrorism Studies: Issues in Research', Richard Jackson, Marie Breen Smyth and Jeroen Gunning (eds.), *Critical Terrorism Studies: A New Research Agenda*, London: Routledge, 2009, p. 43.

[2] 'New terrorism' initially referred to technological and organisational shifts in terrorist groups; many of these innovations were not by Islamist groups. However, since 2001, the unrelenting focus on al Qaeda has reinforced the link between 'new' terrorism and Islamist terrorist movements and even presented the shifts as something essentially 'Islamist'. I owe this clarification to Dr. Rashmi Singh, Centre for the Study of Terrorism and Political Violence, University of St. Andrews. Another view is that the 'new terrorism' is networked, not hierarchical. Kegley describes 'new terrorism' as: borderless, lethal (aimed at mass casualties rather than publicity), novel in that its scope and the destruction it causes is unprecedented, carried out without state sponsorship, technologically sophisticated, carried out by transnational networks of fanatical extremists, outside previously accepted legal and moral norms, driven by hatred and 'predicated on the *realpolitik* principle that the power to destroy is equal to the power to change and control'. Charles Kegley (ed.) *The New Global Terrorism: Characteristics, Causes, Controls*, Upper Saddle River, NJ: Prentice Hall, 2003, p. 4. See also Walter Laqueur, *The New Terrorism: Fanaticism and the Arms of Mass Destruction*, New York: Oxford University Press, 1999.

of a close association between Islam and terrorism.[3] The present chapter bucks this trend. It situates Islamist terrorism within the wider global and historical context of terrorism studies and suggests that we must use social-scientific conceptual tools to analyse it. De-mystifying Islamist terrorism in this way constructs a foundation for understanding the causes of its emergence and development in the Middle East region – the task of subsequent chapters.

One instance of the combined effects of Middle Eastern and Islamic 'exceptionalisms' is the automatic or facile association between the Middle East and Islamist terrorism. Islamist terrorism may be most visible at present, but for the greater part of the post–World War II period, the Middle East was, and in some cases remains, more closely associated with terrorism of the ethno-nationalist and left-wing ideological types. In Turkey, the Revolutionary People's Liberation Party/Front (Devrimci Halk Kurtuluş Partisi/Cephesi, DHKP-C, formerly Dev Sol), a Marxist anti-Western group, and the Kurdistan Workers' Party (Parti Karkerani Kurdistan, PKK), a leftist Kurdish nationalist organisation, have been active for decades and are still prominent today. In the Palestinian context, the secular nationalist organisation Fatah was a protagonist in terrorist violence in the 1970s and 1980s. An array of extremist leftist, secular, nationalist movements belonging to the Palestinian rejectionist front opposing negotiation with Israel, such as the Abu Nidal organisation, the Popular Front for the Liberation of Palestine (PFLP) and the Popular Front for the Liberation of Palestine – General Command (PFLP-GC), were also notorious for their terrorist methods. Clearly, terrorism in the Middle East has also been employed by Christians and Jews, not only Muslims. The Irgun and the Stern Gang used terrorist tactics against both Arabs and British in the years leading up to the establishment of the state of Israel.[4] Kach (Kahane La-Knesset) is an extremist Jewish nationalist group described as terrorist by the US State Department, and is illegal in Israel. Some of the Palestinian terrorist leaders, such as Georges

---

[3] The following studies explore the link between religion and terrorism: Mark Juergensmeyer, *Terror in the Mind of God: The Global Rise of Religious Violence*, Berkeley, Los Angeles and London: University of California Press, 2003; Bruce Hoffman, *Inside Terrorism*, New York: Columbia University Press, 2006; Jessica Stern, *Terror in the Name of God: Why Religious Militants Kill*, New York: HarperCollins Publishers, 2003.

[4] For a fascinating discussion of terrorism in the context of the Zionist struggle, see Ian S. Lustick, 'Terrorism in the Arab-Israeli Conflict: Targets and Audiences', Martha Crenshaw (ed.), *Terrorism in Context*, University Park: The Pennsylvania State University Press, 1995, pp. 517–33.

Habash, head of the PFLP, were Christians. A number of Armenian anti-Turkish organisations such as the '28 May' Armenian Organisation and the Armenian Secret Army for the Liberation of Armenia (ASALA) also employed terrorist methods. In other words, even though Islamist terrorism is the focus of this study, we must not forget the wider context of the terrorism phenomenon in the Middle East.

The argument in this chapter proceeds in two parts. In the first section, I explore the links between the phenomenon of global terrorism – beyond the Middle East – and democracy or the lack thereof. I draw on a dense and complex body of academic literature to argue that democracy is not an 'antidote' to terrorism and that some of the characteristics of a democratic system can even encourage it. Having thus provided the general framework for the book's argument, I proceed, in the chapter's second section, to examine Islamist terrorism. I introduce a typology of the causes of terrorism and then focus more narrowly on the causes of Islamist terrorism. The purpose of this discussion is to introduce the conceptual tools for the rest of the study by placing the democracy factor alongside other possible explanations of Islamist terrorism.

Terrorism and Democracy[5]

Even a cursory examination of the literature on the causes of terrorism shows that 'no single explanation for terrorist behaviour is satisfactory',[6] and that '[t]he endeavour to find a "general theory" of terrorism, one overall explanation of its roots, is a futile and misguided enterprise'.[7] However, even with this important proviso in mind, it is still possible to isolate each of the proposed explanations of terrorism and test them separately. The central purpose of the book is to investigate whether a convincing case can be made that Islamist terrorism in the Middle East has political causes stemming from non-democratic or authoritarian structures. Before turning to Islamist terrorism, however, I investigate the links between democracy and the broader terrorism phenomenon.

A substantial body of opinion in the terrorism literature champions the view that democracy hinders its emergence and undermines its appeal.

---

[5] This section was written with the help of Rashmi Singh.
[6] Martha Crenshaw, 'The Logic of Terrorism', Walter Reich (ed.), *Origins of Terrorism: Psychologies, Ideologies, Theologies, States of Mind*, New York: Woodrow Wilson Centre, 1990, p. 24.
[7] Walter Laqueur, *No End to War: Terrorism in the Twenty-First Century*, New York: Continuum, 2003, p. 22.

The rationale behind this view is summarised succinctly by Brynjar Lia and Katja Skjølberg:

Based upon freedom, openness and popular participation, democracies tend to enjoy greater legitimacy among their populations – hence dissatisfaction rarely reaches a level of serious threat to the existence of the regime itself. In addition, democratic systems have various alternative channels for expression and influence through which potential frustration and dissatisfaction can be directed. With the presence of such virtues, one would expect a high level of state legitimacy and a low level of terrorism in democratic regimes.[8]

Jan Oskar Engene's study of patterns of terrorism in Western Europe confirms this thesis; he asserts that the occurrence of terrorism is systematically related to low measures of freedom and democracy.[9] Ted Robert Gurr suggests that most terror campaigns in democratic societies are doomed to failure because the violence inherent in terrorism offends the public and engenders a backlash amongst potential supportive constituencies, while simultaneously increasing general support for strong counter-terrorism measures by the authorities.[10]

Equally, the literature highlights the causal links between authoritarianism and terrorism. Authoritarian regimes may in the first instance appear well placed to prevent both domestic and transnational attacks inside their borders but they can 'export' the problem, for example by sponsoring terrorism abroad and assassinating exiled dissidents. Having successfully controlled opposition and armed activities domestically, authoritarian regimes can become exposed to protest attacks against their interests abroad.[11] Repressing terrorist and insurgent groups on their territory may run the risk of transforming them into transnational terrorist organisations, attacking targets abroad. Conversely, political liberalisation in authoritarian states can reduce the prospects of terrorism 'spilling over' as it allows for the repatriation of opposition groups based abroad and encourages the channelling

---

[8] Brynjar Lia and Katja Skjølberg, *The Causes of Terrorism*, Kjeller, Norway: Norwegian Defence Research Establishment, 2004, p. 34.

[9] Jan Oskar Engene, *Patterns of Terrorism in Western Europe, 1950–1995*, Bergen, Norway: University of Bergen, 1998, unpublished PhD Thesis.

[10] Ted Robert Gurr, 'Terrorism in Democracies: When it Occurs, Why it Fails', Charles W. Kegley Jr. (ed.), *The New Global Terrorism: Characteristics, Causes, Controls*, Upper Saddle River, NJ: Prentice Hall, 2003. Gurr asserts that in a democracy, support for terrorist groups will only be maintained over time among distinctive minorities such as the militant Catholics in Northern Ireland and Basque activists in Spain.

[11] Dennis Pluchinsky, 'Terrorism in the Former Soviet Union: A Primer, a Puzzle, a Prognosis', *Studies in Conflict and Terrorism*, 21 (2) 1998, p. 119.

of militant protests and armed campaigns against national institutions into peaceful activities.[12]

The preceding arguments on the relationship between democracy and terrorism merit consideration and, clearly, there are no definitive answers to such questions in social science. However, I demonstrate in subsequent paragraphs that, on the weight of the evidence, democracy is not a certain antidote to terrorism.[13] Western Europe, seat of the world's most mature democracies, witnessed the emergence of a wide variety of terrorist movements in the post–World War II period, some of which have plagued its politics ever since. These movements were either ideological (mostly on the extreme left), or ethno-nationalist in their objectives. Examples of the former include the Greek 17 November Group established between 1973 and 1975, the Italian Red Brigades founded around 1970 and the German Red Army Faction (Baader Meinhof), which began operations around the same time. The latter included the National Front for the Liberation of Corsica (Fronte di Liberazione Nazionale Corsu, FLNC) founded in 1976, the Basque Homeland and Liberty (Euskadi ta Askatasuna, ETA) established in 1959, and the Provisional Irish Republican Army (PIRA) which split from the IRA in 1969–70 in Northern Ireland.

Apart from the obvious point of terrorism being widespread, and sometimes intractable, in European democracies, widely available statistical evidence also suggests that there is no identifiable causal relationship between democracy and terrorism. The US State Department's Annual 'Patterns of Global Terrorism' report shows that, between 2000 and 2003, '269 major terrorist incidents around the world occurred in countries classified as "free" by Freedom House, 119 occurred in "partly free" countries, and 138 occurred in "not free" countries.' These numbers 'simply indicate that there is no relationship between the incidence of terrorism in a given country and the degree of freedom enjoyed by its citizens'.[14]

---

[12] Dennis Pluchinsky, 'Middle Eastern Terrorist Activity in Western Europe in 1985: A Diagnosis and Prognosis', Paul Wilkinson and A. M. Stewart (eds.), *Contemporary Research in Terrorism*, Aberdeen University Press, 1987; Omar A. Lizardo, 'The Effect of Economic and Cultural Globalisation on Anti-US Transnational Terrorism, 1971–2000', *Journal of World-Systems Research*, 12 (1) 2006, http://jwsr.ucr.edu/archive/vol12/number1/pdf/jwsr-v12n1-lizardo.pdf, accessed 25 January 2010.

[13] I borrow the phrase from Thomas Carothers, 'Democracy: Terrorism's Uncertain Antidote', *Current History*, December, 102 (668) 2003, pp. 403–6.

[14] Gregory Gause III, 'Can Democracy Stop Terrorism?', *Foreign Affairs*, 84 (5) 2005, p. 66. These figures exclude the 11 September 2001 attacks and Palestinian attacks against Israel.

In fact, democracy may not only fail to stymie terrorism but can positively *encourage* it, for a number of reasons. One is that the open nature of democracies inadvertently provides a hospitable environment for terrorism.[15] Democracies permit the freedoms of movement, information and assembly which may allow terrorist groups to organise and remain undetectable for long periods of time. Other analysts associate semi-authoritarian or semi-democratic countries with the greatest risk of experiencing terrorism and violent conflict.[16] Brynjar Lia and Åshlid Kjøk argue that terrorist groups generally establish support networks and organise attacks from 'safe havens' provided by democratic states, then targeting authoritarian states from which they have been evicted or democratic states of whose foreign policies they strongly disapprove.[17] In contrast to democracies, most highly authoritarian states are less exposed to terrorism. Dennis Pluchinsky's study of terrorism in the former Soviet Union noted, for example, that there were 'few reported incidents of political terrorism carried out in the Soviet Union'.[18] In 2003, the World Terrorism Index produced by the London-based World Markets Research Centre classified North Korea as the country least exposed to international terrorism.[19]

William Eubank and Leonard Weinberg go even further in establishing a positive link between democracy and terrorism. They demonstrate statistically that terrorist attacks occur most often in the world's most stable democracies, and that both victims and perpetrators of terrorist acts are citizens of stable democratic countries (in contrast to insecure democracies and partial democracies).[20] According to the authors, elements in the 'internal dynamics of democracies make the use of terror tactics attractive to their own citizens'. Terrorists may represent a sizeable,

---

[15] Paul Wilkinson, *Terrorism and the Liberal State*, Basingstoke: Macmillan, 1986, p. 103.

[16] See, for example, Harvard Hegre, Tanja Ellingsen, Scott Gates and Nils Petter Gleditsch, 'Toward a Democratic Civil Peace? Democracy, Political Change and Civil War 1816–1992, *American Political Science Review*, 95 (1) 2001, pp. 33–48; Tanja Ellingsen and Nils Petter Gleditsch, 'Democracy and Conflict in the Third World', Ketil Volden and Dan Smith (eds.), *Causes of Conflict in the Third World Countries*, Oslo: PRIO, 1997.

[17] Brynjar Lia and Åshlid Kjøk, *Islamist Insurgencies, Diasporic Support Networks and Their Host States*, Kjeller: Norwegian Defence Research Establishment, 2001.

[18] Pluchinsky, 'Terrorism in the Former Soviet Union', p. 119.

[19] 'Global Terrorism Index: Key Findings' *Guardian.co.uk* www.guardian.co.uk/world/2003/aug/18/alqaida.terrorism1, accessed 25 January 2010.

[20] William Eubank and Leonard Weinberg, 'Terrorism and Democracy: Perpetrators and Victims', *Terrorism and Political Violence*, 13 (1) 2001, p. 155.

discontented, excluded minority, 'whose preferences have lost out or are no longer seriously considered in the normal democratic struggle over the formation of public policy'.[21] This view is shared by Paul Wilkinson, for whom terrorists in democratic societies are 'desperate people' because they know that the legitimacy and support their government enjoys renders any peaceful challenge to it futile.[22] The democratic system can, on occasion, turn into a tyranny of the majority, so terrorism emerges in cases where the principle of majority voting is repeatedly perceived as a systematic assault on a minority and their wishes.[23] Christopher Hewitt similarly argues, with reference to the US political context, that sustained outbreaks of terrorism 'are associated with the existence of a substantial body of sympathizers and supporters' but the timing of each outbreak appears to coincide with the decline of popular mobilization rather than with its highpoint. He suggests that the failure of direct action tactics – picketing and clinic blockades – galvanizes some individuals into resorting to terrorism.[24]

Research on the links between terrorist groups and political parties by Leonard Weinberg draws similar conclusions on a positive link between democracy and terrorism. Weinberg asks whether political parties abandon peaceful means and turn to terrorism as a result of failing to do well in democratic processes, which in turn creates a sense of futility about achieving their objectives. Although the author, by his own admission, undertook no systematic effort to assemble data on the electoral performances of the parties related to terrorist groups, he 'has the impression but cannot prove that the more common experience has been for the terrorism-related parties to fare poorly at polls'. There are notable

---

[21] Ibid., pp. 161 and 163.

[22] Wilkinson, *Terrorism and the Liberal State*, p. 94.

[23] For example, Katja Skjølberg's study of ethnic violence in Western Europe finds that ethnic terrorism is more likely in the less proportional democracies than in open proportional systems, suggesting that the threshold for using violence depends on the existence of alternative channels of influence. Katja Skjølberg, 'Ethnic Pluralism, Legitimacy and Conflict: Western European Separatism 1950–95', Paper presented at the ISA Conference, Los Angles, March 2002, www.svt.ntnu.no/iss/fagkonferanse/IPkvant/Skjolberg.pdf, accessed 7 January 2010.

[24] Christopher Hewitt, 'The Political Context of Terrorism in America: Ignoring Extremists or Pandering to Them?', David Rapoport and Leonard Weinberg (eds.), *The Democratic Experience and Political Violence*, London: Frank Cass, 2001 p. 339. Referring to the classic study of James C. Davies, *When Men Revolt and Why*, New York: Free Press, 1971, Hewitt notes that 'the resort to violence is most likely to take place when members of a group have their hopes and aspirations raised, but then become disillusioned with the political process' (p. 340).

exceptions, however, such as the Tamil Tigers, a movement well-known for its use of terrorist methods and in particular suicide bombings: It was set up in 1978 when the Tamil United Liberation Front was the single largest opposition party represented in parliament.[25]

Martha Crenshaw's classic study of the causes of terrorism highlights other possible positive links between democracy and terrorism. She argues that terrorism, more often than not, represents the strategy of a minority who may act on behalf of a wider constituency without necessarily consulting with it. Thus it is pursued by a disaffected minority elite who believe that prevailing conditions allow no other means to effect change.[26] Terrorists 'perceive an absence of choice'.[27] Paradoxically, terrorism may be the sign of a stable society or even – as Luigi Bonanate suggests – a 'blocked' society, 'incapable of answering the citizens' requests for change but nevertheless capable of preserving and reproducing itself'.[28] So terrorism is not a sign of a society's imminent collapse but of a phase of self-perpetuating immobility. In this interpretation, 'the appearance of terrorism becomes an indicator that the society in question is only apparently democratic'[29] in that it distorts democratic rules into mere formal rituals which are not converted into substantial representation. Bonanate concludes that 'terrorism appears wherever the masses lose their role as protagonists of history'.[30]

Finally, a very different reason for linking democracy positively to terrorism is suggested by Robert Pape (whose exclusive focus is suicide

---

[25] Leonard Weinberg, 'Turning to Terror: The Conditions under Which Political Parties Turn to Terrorist Activities', *Comparative Politics*, 23, (4) July 1991, p. 432. Rapoport and Weinberg discuss the close association between elections and violence (their focus is wider than terrorism). Elections are linked to violence and even seem to encourage it because they raise the political stakes and encourage desperate measures by those who feel they are in danger of losing out in the political process. The authors state that elections can both provoke violence and bring peace. In case of the former, violence is provoked due to various causes but the bulk, if not all of these, are politically motivated by the fear of losing out. They compare elections with heredity, as both are processes of succession, and illustrate how the different nature of each gives rise to two different patterns of violence. David C. Rapoport and Leonard Weinberg, 'Elections and Violence', Rapoport and Weinberg (eds.), *The Democratic Experience and Political Violence*, pp. 15–50.

[26] Martha Crenshaw, 'The Causes of Terrorism', *Comparative Politics*, 13 (4) 1981, p. 384.

[27] Ibid., p. 396.

[28] Luigi Bonanate, 'Some Unanticipated Consequences of Terrorism', *Journal of Peace Research*, 3 (16) 1979, p. 205.

[29] Ibid., p. 197.

[30] Ibid., p. 209.

bombings, not terrorism generally). He argues that the central objective of every suicide campaign from 1980 to 2001 was to coerce a foreign government into removing their military forces from what the perpetrators see as their homeland, and that 'the target state of every modern suicide campaign has been a democracy.'[31] The reason is that, more than other types, democratic governments are vulnerable to pressures from their publics in unique ways. Terrorists use the psychological and emotional impact which the destructive method of the suicide bombing (purportedly) has on the larger population to 'get at' their leaders and force a rethinking of their policies.

Clearly Pape's assessment of the character and responses of a democratic citizenry contrasts sharply with Gurr's belief, mentioned earlier, that terrorist campaigns fail in democratic societies because of the backlash they create among their publics. Such ambivalence, however, characterises many other studies in the field of democracy and terrorism. One example is Quan Li's work on transnational terrorism. Li uses a quantitative methodology to further the debate, as he describes it, between those who argue that greater democratic participation reduces the number of transnational incidents in a country, and those who argue that countries with greater institutional constraints on their governments experience more such incidents. His conclusions are mixed. Using a multivariate analysis for a sample of 119 countries from 1975 to 1997, he shows that although 'democratic participation reduces transnational terrorist incidents', democracy 'is demonstrated to encourage *and* reduce transnational terrorist incidents, albeit via different causal mechanisms' (my emphasis).[32]

One of Li's findings is that 'countries going through regime changes are vulnerable to more transnational terrorist attacks, while countries with stable regimes tend to experience fewer incidents'.[33] A number of analysts agree that the process of democratisation itself, particularly when the transition is protracted, can cause internal conflict and civil war.[34] For example, Michel Wieviorka argues with regard to ETA that

---

[31] Robert Pape, 'The Strategic Logic of Suicide Terrorism', *American Political Science Review*, 97 (3) 2003, p. 350. See also Robert Pape, *Dying to Win: The Strategic Logic of Suicide Terrorism*, New York: Random House, 2005.

[32] Quan Li, 'Does Democracy Promote or Reduce Transnational Terrorist Incidents?', *Journal of Conflict Resolution*, 49 (2) April 2005, p. 294. For the entire article, see pp. 278–97.

[33] Ibid., p. 287.

[34] See, for example, Jack Snyder, *From Voting to Violence: Democratization and National Conflict*, New York: W. W. Norton, 2000.

'the armed struggle was never so deadly as in the years following the transition and the changeover to democracy in Spain'.[35] As the prevailing power structures are modified, established elites may challenge the threats to their political status by stirring up ethnic, religious or socio-economic disturbances to intimidate opponents, create a climate of fear and prevent further reform. This is especially so in countries where most economic and social opportunities are available only through state-controlled institutions.[36] Focusing on transnational terrorism, Brian Lai arrives at similar findings. He notes that democracies as well as states 'undergoing incomplete regime transitions' are likely to experience more transnational terrorism than semi-democratic and authoritarian regimes, suggesting that the decisive factor is the opportunity afforded by democracies to organise attacks, rather than the availability of legal channels of protest. He also finds some evidence that regime transitions provide incentives for groups to increase levels of terrorist violence. These findings lead to the conclusion that 'failed democracies that do not become consolidated authoritarian states are likely to experience tremendous amounts of terrorism'.[37]

The Causes of Islamist Terrorism

I argued in the book's Introduction that terrorism is a method of achieving political objectives and that, in analysing the terrorism phenomenon, means and ends must remain conceptually distinct. We can differentiate between terrorist movements on the basis of objectives and distinguish, for example, between ethno-nationalist, ideological and single-issue terrorist movements.[38] Objectives, in turn, must be carefully

---

[35] Michel Wieviorka, *The Making of Terrorism*, Chicago and London: University of Chicago Press, 1993, trans. David Gordon White, p. 169.

[36] Eubank and Weinberg, 'Terrorism and Democracy: What Recent Events Disclose', *Terrorism and Political Violence*, 10 (1) 1998, pp. 108–18; Lars-Erik Cederman, Simon Hug and Andreas Wenger, 'Democratization and War in Political Science', *Democratization*, 15 (3) 2008, pp. 509–24; Lutz Krebs, Dominic Senn and Judith Vorrath, 'Linking Ethnic Conflict and Democratization: An Assessment of Four Troubled Regions', NCCR *Working Paper* 6, 2007, www.nccr-democracy.uzh.ch/publications/workingpaper/pdf/WP6.pdf; Judith Vorrath and Lutz Krebs, 'Democratization and Conflict in Ethnically Divided Societies', *Living Reviews in Democracy*, 1, 2009, www.lrd.ethz.ch/index.php/lrd, both accessed 7 January 2010.

[37] Brian Lai, 'Explaining Terrorism Using the Framework of Opportunity and Willingness: An Empirical Examination of International Terrorism', Research Paper (unpublished), Department of Political Science, University of Iowa, April 2004.

[38] Paul Wilkinson, *Terrorism versus Democracy: The Liberal State Response*, London and New York: Routledge, 2006, 2nd edition pp. 20–1.

distinguished from the *causes* of terrorism. I offer my categorisation of the latter in the list below:

Ideational causes:

1. Psychological: Terrorism as a consequence of a disturbed personality.
2. Millenarian: Terrorism as a consequence of apocalyptic worldviews.
3. Religious and/or cultural: Terrorism as a consequence of a particular worldview.
4. Ideological: Terrorism as a consequence of a set of ideas for reforming society.

Material/structural causes:

5. Social: Terrorism as an outcome of marginalisation and alienation.
6. Economic: Terrorism as an outcome of economic deprivation, relative deprivation, desperation and poverty.
7. Political: Terrorism as an outcome of political exclusion and repression.
8. Strategic/instrumental: Terrorism as an outcome of the calculation that it is the best or only available means of achieving an objective.

Describing strategic/instrumental causes as 'structural' is controversial. In contrast to social, economic and political causes, strategic and instrumental explanations highlight the role of the *agent* in deciding to use terrorist methods. However, structural factors – mainly structures of power – also play a role in constraining and determining the decisions of the agent.[39]

Building on Martha Crenshaw's sharp distinction between terrorism as socio-pathology and as an expression of a political strategy,[40] I argue that psychological and strategic/instrumental causes (the first and last on the just mentioned list) lie at opposite analytical poles and produce widely divergent interpretations of the terrorism phenomenon.[41] Otherwise the

[39] The ambiguity between agency and structure in relation to strategic/instrumental explanations runs through my entire argument in this study.

[40] 'Editor's Note', Martha Crenshaw, 'The Logic of Terrorism: Terrorist Behavior as a Product of Strategic Choice', Reich (ed.), *Origins of Terrorism*, p. 7.

[41] For examples of analyses focusing on the psychological approaches see Judy Kuriansky, *Terror in the Holy Land: Inside the Anguish of the Israeli-Palestinian Conflict*, Westport, CT: Praeger Pulishers, 2006; David Lester, Bijou Yang and Mark Lindsay, 'Suicide Bombers: Are Psychological Profiles Possible? *Studies in Conflict and Terrorism*, 27 (4) 2004, pp. 283–295. Compare to analyses focusing on tactical/strategic approaches: Martha Crenshaw (ed.), *Terrorism, Legitimacy and Power: The Consequences of Political Violence*, Middleton, CT: Wesleyan University Press, 1981; Ehud Sprinkzak, 'Rational Fanatics', *Foreign Policy*, 120, 2000, pp. 66–73.

boundaries between the various causes of terrorism tend, in practice, to be blurred. For example, it is difficult to disentangle social from economic factors (hence my frequent use of 'socio-economic' as a category of explanation in this study). Depending on one's analytical approach, religion and culture may be sometimes impossible to set apart from ideology, as in the case of Islamism which I defined in the Introduction as a political *ideology*. The conceptual dividing lines between the various causes of terrorism are all the more difficult to maintain because different motivations sometimes characterise the members of a single movement. For instance, a group's leaders can be rational and calculating in their choice of tactics and objectives whereas the followers are driven by a millenarian ideology or may even be psychologically disturbed individuals. Nevertheless, the categories on the previously mentioned list are useful as rough general guides, and I use them throughout the course of the study.[42] More immediately, in the remainder of this section, I use them as the framework for outlining the debate on the causes of Islamist terrorism.

Many observers of Islamist terrorism see its causes as primarily ideational. Islamist terrorism is driven by the ideas of Islam as a religion – and occasionally as culture – or Islamism as a political ideology (refer to 3 and 4 on the list above). Their argument is that the precepts of Islam, including the Koran, contain an intolerant view which enables or encourages terrorism's emergence; that the core principles of Islam as a religion or Islamism as a political ideology are *inherently* prone to terrorism; and that the causes of Islamism and Islamist terrorism overlap. Such views have become widespread in recent years although – in academic writings at least – they are rarely expressed openly. Nevertheless, they are there implicitly. The passage that follows, by Walter Laqueur – a widely read author who straddles the academic and popular literature domains – is a

---

[42] There are, of course, other ways of distinguishing between the various causes of terrorism. One is Martha Crenshaw's differentiation between 'pre-conditions, factors that set the stage for terrorism over the long run, and precipitants, specific events that immediately precede the occurrence of terrorism'. The former include modernisation, urbanisation, social 'facilitation' (social habits and historical traditions that sanction the use of violence against the government); and/or the government's inability or unwillingness to prevent terrorism. Direct causes can comprise concrete grievances within an identifiable subgroup of a larger population, the lack (or perceived lack) of opportunity for political participation particularly when combined with inefficient government repression; and government actions such as unexpected or unusual use of force in response to protest or reform attempts. Crenshaw, 'The Causes of Terrorism', pp. 381–5. Although not directly relevant to my argument Crenshaw's distinction is useful to bear in mind.

good illustration of subtly but surely linking Islam with fundamentalism and terrorism and so deserves to be quoted at length:

Endorsements for nearly anything can be found in the holy writs of the major religions, and the Koran is no exception. In Sura 2, verse 256, it says that there should be no religious compulsion, but adherence to this rule is a rare exception in Islam. On the whole, violence is sanctified in Islam if it is carried out against infidels or heretics "in the path of Allah." On the philosophical-religious level, there is no room for nonbelievers in the Islamic system, even if minorities are temporarily tolerated. The faithful live, at least in theory, in a permanent state of war with the non-Islamic world, and this will change only if and when the nonbelievers have accepted the one true faith. Over the last thousand years, political realities have mitigated these absolutes, except for the fundamentalists, for whom the basic outlook of the faithful is the same as it always has been. But pacifism is still no virtue in Muslim eyes. In brief, the Islamic fundamentalist attitude toward violence is that the final aim justifies the means. There was a school of thought in the 1930s that drew parallels between Nazism and political Islam, particularly Islam's fanaticism, sense of mission, and use of violence against political enemies. In some respects these parallels were misleading, but in others they were striking. Radical Muslims exhibit hostility toward all those who are different, a free-floating rage, and a tradition of violence that favors the appearance of terrorism.

Popular Western perception equates radical Islam with terrorism. While many fundamentalists do not support terrorism, the perception is still more accurate than the apologist's claim that Western fears are "mythical" in character, based on unfounded apprehensions, prejudices, and insufficient knowledge about Islam. There is, of course, no Muslim or Arab monopoly in the field of religious fanaticism; it exists and leads to acts of violence in the United States, India, Israel, and many other countries. But the frequency of Muslim- and Arab-inspired terrorism is still striking. In twenty armed conflicts proceeding at present in the world, Islam is involved in sixteen, or 80 percent. Of the thirteen United Nations peace missions in action at the present time, nine concern Muslim countries or interests. The proportion of Muslim involvement in terrorism could well be of a similar magnitude. A discussion of religion-inspired terrorism cannot possibly confine itself to radical Islam, but it has to take into account the Muslim countries' preeminent position in this field. It has to devote more time and space to investigating Muslim and Islamic terrorism than other such movements simply because other such movements are less numerous, less effective, and politically less important. [43]

In contrast to Laqueur, I take seriously the view that there is no inherent interpretation of Islam. If Islam can be variously interpreted – and only very specific, extremist interpretations of Islam, or Islamism, give rise to terrorism – the important question which logically follows is *why* such

[43] Laqueur, *The New Terrorism*, pp. 129–30.

interpretations have at times prevailed over others in Middle Eastern societies. Ideas, in this instance, particular understandings of Islam or Islamism, may *justify* and reinforce the decision of a Muslim individual or movement to use terrorist methods, but they do not *explain* them. They are the symptom rather than the cause.[44] The debate within Islam about its interpretation is crucial and must continue, because it will be a driving force behind the future direction of the faith. To understand how and why individuals and movements opted for readings of Islam that favoured terrorism in the first place, however, we must draw on structural factors and explanations (numbers 5–8 on the list above). It is to these I now turn.

Social factors, particularly the frustrations and alienations of modern life, are often presented as key explanations of Islamist terrorism. Terrorism is seen as the product of the widespread misery and helplessness in many Middle Eastern societies. Social dislocation and uncertainty – a frequent outcome of rapid urbanisation – make migrants particularly vulnerable to terrorism's appeal. These social reasons are also meant to explain why wealthier or middle-class elements in Middle Eastern societies – not just the poor and downtrodden – are attracted to terrorism. For example, following 9/11, some analysts pointed to the emptiness of the day-to-day lives of Saudi youth, who do not have to work for a living and are otherwise not usefully employed, as the cause of their vulnerability to the appeal of 'higher' causes and becoming a 'martyr'.[45] For others, existential crises caused by material factors and a world full of daunting free choices produce mindsets conducive to terrorism.[46] Alongside social factors, analysts also highlight economic factors, arguing that either absolute or relative economic deprivation drives individuals or groups to desperate measures, including terrorism. The Middle East's many failures

---

[44] The example of the debate on Middle East school curricula which followed the attacks of 11 September 2001 illustrates my point. At the time, criticism was directed at the obscurantist and intolerant interpretations of Islam in educational systems of countries such as Egypt and Saudi Arabia which, it was argued, were decisive in creating the mindset of the Islamist terrorist. Washington started devoting considerable sums and effort to reforming these curricula. But the question which arguably was even more important, in terms of analysis and explanation as opposed to policy, was why and how these interpretations found their way into school curricula.

[45] John V. Whitbeck, 'Life and Death in Saudi Arabia', *International Herald Tribune*, 3 June 2004.

[46] Michael J. Mazarr, 'The Psychological Sources of Islamic Terrorism', *Policy Review*, 125, 2004, www.hoover.org/publications/policyreview/3438341.html, accessed 29 February 2010.

in economic development – if not necessarily absolute poverty – seem obvious explanations for Islamist terrorism.[47]

Socio-economic explanations of Islamist terrorism are closely connected to political explanations, the core focus of this study. Similarly to political and public policy commentators – whom I discussed in the Introduction – academic analysts draw a clear causal link between authoritarian structures and Islamist terrorism. Although not referring to terrorism as such, Gudrun Krämer states that 'revolutionary violence and clandestine underground work found wider acceptance only after previous attempts at non-violent struggle and integration had been suppressed by the government in power'.[48] An important academic monograph advocating a causal link between authoritarianism with Islamist terrorism is Muhammad Hafez's *Why Muslims Rebel*[49] (though Hafez's focus is rebellion and he uses the term 'anti-civilian violence', rather than terrorism). His two main case studies, among others, are the Muslim rebellions in Egypt and in Algeria in the 1990s. Hafez critiques socio-economic and psychological approaches and suggests, drawing on a social movement theory approach, that they must be complemented by looking at *political process* to explain why a movement becomes rebellious. He explicitly links Muslim rebellions to institutional exclusion and indiscriminate and reactive repression.[50]

Finally, strategic/instrumental explanations maintain that some Islamist movements rationally calculate that terrorist tactics will maximise the chances of achieving their objectives, either defensive or

---

[47] The Arab Human Development Report of 2002 showed that the incidence of dire poverty is lower than in any other developing region. But it also catalogued a number of economic failings in the Arab 'core' of the region. Arab Human Development Report, 2002, www.nakbaonline.org/download/UNDP/EnglishVersion/Ar-Human-Dev-2002.pdf, accessed 29 March 2010. See also the Arab Human Development Reports of subsequent years.

[48] Krämer 'The Integration of the Integrists: A Comparative Study of Egypt, Tunisia and Morocco', Ghassan Salame (ed.), *Democracy without Democrats?: The Renewal of Politics in the Muslim World*, London: I. B. Tauris, 1994, p. 204.

[49] Muhammad M. Hafez, *Why Muslims Rebel: Repression and Resistance in the Islamic World*, Boulder, CO: Lynne Rienner Publishers, 2003. I have already discussed Hafez's work in the Introduction.

[50] Analysts who are not Middle East specialists but nevertheless make reference to the region in their work also make similar arguments. For Larry Diamond, 'one of the main sources of terrorism is chronically bad governance'; he points particularly to corruption as being a cause of popular anger and frustration. Larry Diamond, *Winning the New Cold War on Terrorism: The Democratic-Governance Imperative*, Institute for Global Democracy, Policy Paper 1, 2002, www.911investigations.net/IMG/pdf/doc-267.pdf, accessed 11 August 2010.

offensive. This rational calculation derives from an assessment of the existing power structures which are constituted, in the eyes of these movements, by the dominant regional and global role of the West, particularly the United States, and the firmly established position of incumbent pro-Western regimes in the Middle East region. A major proponent of this approach in the academic literature is Richard Pape, whose work was mentioned in the previous section. Pape argues that suicide terrorism, including its Islamist variant, follows a 'strategic logic' in that it is not random, irrational or purely fanatical but is based on a strategic calculation (at least at leadership level) of how to attain maximum benefits. It has a double purpose: to gain supporters and coerce opponents. Pape argues that liberal democracies are particularly vulnerable to being coerced into changing their policies under the impact of suicide terrorism.[51]

Before concluding this discussion on the causes of Islamist terrorism, a final theoretical note on social movement theory is in order. This theory views terrorist organisations as parts of larger social movements, driven by similar dynamics as their larger, legalised counterparts.[52] In his work on Islamist activism, which includes references to Islamist terrorist movements, Quintan Wiktorowicz argues that sociopsychological, economic and political strain explanations of Islamic activism (including terrorism) are inadequate because they do not explain why ubiquitous grievances and structural strains elicit movements in some cases and not in others. In contrast to the view that 'a particular set of grievances, translated into religious idioms and symbols, engenders mobilization', the social movement theory approach suggests that resource availability, framing resonance and shifts in opportunity structures, are inextricably linked to the mobilization processes and ultimately account for social movements more effectively. 'Resource mobilisation theory' asks which intermediary variables – resources and mobilising structures – translate individualised discontent into organised contention. The availability of the mosque as a focus for mobilization, and informal networks of association, as well as more formal professional and student associations, NGOs and political parties, explain the robustness of Islamic activism.

[51] Pape, *Dying to Win*. See also Shaul Shay, *The Shahids: Islam and Suicide Attacks*, Somerset, NJ: Transaction Publishers, 2004; Bruce Hoffman and Gordon McCormick, 'Terrorism, Signalling and Suicide Attacks', *Studies in Conflict and Terrorism*, 27 (4) 2004, pp. 243–81.

[52] Jeroen Gunning, 'Social Movement Theory and the Study of Terrorism', Jackson, Smyth and Gunning (eds.), *Critical Terrorism Studies*, p. 160.

Ideational factors including social interaction, meaning and culture also play a role in a process of meaning construction called 'framing', whereby a movement draws upon indigenous cultural symbols, language and identities (including, presumably, Islam) to enhance mobilisation. Finally, the opening or closing of political space creates or eliminates 'political opportunity structures' which allow for or prevent collective action by Islamist social movements.[53]

In the chapters that follow, I link the analysis of Islamist terrorist and moderate Islamist movements with the political-opportunities structures in their respective settings. I also make reference to the ability of Islamist terrorist movements to mobilise resources and (albeit not explicitly) to 'framing', in the sense of exploring the role of ideational contexts. However, in my view, social movement theory is not the most useful explanatory framework for understanding Islamist terrorism. This is for two reasons. First, it fails to account for important aspects of the phenomenon, most critically why certain ideational frames are preferred over others from a very wide menu of options. In trying to account for Islamist terrorism, reference to 'cultural master frames' is especially problematic, given the contested nature of culture in this as any other setting. Secondly, social movement theory focuses on the processes whereby the various underlying causes (grievances or strains) are translated into the emergence of Islamist terrorism. This is an interesting 'how' question but it does not address the critical question of 'why' the particular method of terrorism is chosen and why an extreme interpretation of Islam – one that is conducive to terrorism – is preferred by some Islamist movements. It cannot explain, for example, why some mosques become hubs of terrorist operations whereas others remain centres of non-violent, even apolitical activities. It does not give reasons why a literalist or puritanical interpretation of the Koran is chosen over a liberal or progressive interpretation. For answers to these questions, we must revert to a combination of social, economic and political factors, and investigate how they interact with ideas and ideologies in pushing some Islamist movements towards extremism, including terrorism. My analysis, therefore, will rest on a grievance- or strain-based approach, as outlined on my list of terrorism causes in the beginning of this section.

---

[53] Quintan Wiktorowicz, 'Introduction: Islamic Activism and Social Movement Theory', Quintan Wiktorowicz (ed.), *Islamic Activism: A Social Movement Theory Approach*, Bloomington: Indiana University Press, 2004, pp. 1–33.

Conclusion

The chapter's two sections pursued distinct aims. The first demonstrated that there is no simple or consistent pattern of causation or an identifiable and consistent relationship between democracy (or lack thereof) and terrorism. There is a strong body of opinion which sees democracy as an antidote to terrorism. I disagree: democracy not only fails to prevent terrorism but may in fact encourage it. This is for many reasons, including that in democracies, disaffected minorities, perceiving an absence of choice, are pushed to desperate measures and, more straightforwardly, that democracies are easier prey to terrorist activities because of their openness. By the same token, terrorism is more easily contained by authoritarian systems, although they in turn may only appear to resolve the problem by their oppressiveness while pushing it under the carpet or exporting it for others to deal with. Finally, there is some evidence that both stable democracies and stable authoritarian systems are less vulnerable to terrorism than transitional or semi-democratic, or semi-authoritarian, regimes. I will be drawing on various aspects of this general analysis as I discuss the Middle East cases in the chapters that follow, and will return to it in the Conclusion.

The second section offered a list of the various causes of terrorism and considered the causes of Islamist terrorism more specifically. A widespread position is that ideas, and specifically the precepts of Islam (either in themselves or because they are interpreted in a hard-line and puritanical fashion), are an essential part of the explanation for the emergence of Islamist terrorism. This view is either wrong, in so far as it interprets Islam as immutable, or begs the question why the precepts of Islam are interpreted in ways which are conducive to terrorist acts. For fuller answers on the causes of Islamist terrorism, we must turn to material or structural factors. I briefly outlined socio-economic and political approaches, which maintain that the key factors behind Islamist terrorism are social alienation or economic deprivation or authoritarian and repressive structures. I highlighted strategic/instrumental explanations which claim that terrorist methods are used by some Islamist groups because they most effectively allow them to achieve their aims. This discussion remained purposefully open-ended. Its objective was to lay out the various approaches which will constitute the study's conceptual tools. Chapters 2–4 will focus primarily on the political explanations of Islamist terrorism and demonstrate that democracy or the lack thereof are not the main causal factors behind Islamist terrorism. In the course of the discussion, and especially in the concluding sections of each chapter, I will also juxtapose political with socio-economic and strategic/instrumental explanations. Chapters 5–6 will employ similar categories to analyse the shift *away* from Islamist terrorism in the direction of ideological moderation.

Finally, I outlined the merits and limitations of social movement theory in accounting for Islamist terrorism and explained why, although it nicely complements my list of causes by focusing on process, an emphasis on grievance must drive the analysis of the case studies in Chapters 2–6.

2

Transnational Islamist Terrorism: Al Qaeda

The lethal attacks on the US embassies in Kenya and Tanzania in August 1998 and against the Twin Towers in New York and the Pentagon complex in Virginia on 11 September 2001 catapulted al Qaeda onto the global scene and made it the most prominent Islamist terrorist actor of recent times. This prominence has led to a tendency to associate Islamist terrorism exclusively with it. It has also led to the widespread assumption that Islamist terrorism now operates, more often than not, in a transnational fashion. Neither is accurate. This will become evident in Chapters 3 and 4 which focus on Islamist movements, other than al Qaeda, that employ terrorist tactics while remaining firmly embedded in their respective domestic contexts.[1] Furthermore, although other Islamist terrorist entities do operate transnationally,[2] Islamist terrorism is not epitomized

---

[1] The definition of 'transnational' terrorism was discussed in the Introduction. But although al Qaeda can best be understood as a transnational phenomenon, it is not a 'purely stateless force' in the sense that 'it needs and seeks the sanctuary or material assistance of states, whether Sudan, Afghanistan or Somalia'. Patrick Porter, 'Long Wars and Long Telegrams: Containing Al-Qaeda', *International Affairs*, 85 (2) March 2009, p. 287.

[2] See for example the case of al Takfir wal Hijra. Originating within Egypt, al Takfir wal Hijra has also operated transnationally and shared many of al Qaeda's characteristics of mobility and rootlessness which I will discuss later in this chapter. Joshua L. Gleis, 'National Security Implications of Al-Takfir Wal-Hijra', *Al Nakhlah: The Fletcher School Online Journal for Issues Related to Southwest Asia and Islamic Civilization*, Spring 2005, Article 3, http://fletcher.tufts.edu/al_nakhlah/archives/spring2005/gleis. pdf, accessed 11 July 2009. Others find the view that there exists such a transnational organisation extremely problematic. See Thomas Hegghamer, 'Jihadi-Salafis or Revolutionaries? On Religion and Politics in the Study of Militant Islam', Roel Meijer (ed.), *Global Salafism: Islam's New Religious Movement*, London/New York: Hurst/ Columbia University Press, 2009, p. 248.

by any one movement or manner of operation. Al Qaeda's particular type of transnational Islamist terrorism deserves consideration in the context of this study because of its major impact on contemporary world politics, magnified by the US government's decision after 2001 to wage a 'war on terror'.

The inclusion of al Qaeda in a book on the Middle East may seem out of place given that Pakistan and Afghanistan are more closely associated with its emergence and remain its hub at least at the time of writing (2010). The movement's impact has also reached Africa, South Asia, South East Asia and Europe, as well as the North American continent. However, there are two major connections between al Qaeda and the Middle East which justify its inclusion in the present study. First, many of the stated objectives of al Qaeda (such as the protection or 'liberation' of the holy sites of Islam in Mecca and Medina, and the pursuit of Palestinian rights), although of pan-Islamic concern, are geographically situated within the Middle East. Second, although the movement emerged in Pakistan and Afghanistan, its roots can also partly be found in the domestic politics of Middle Eastern states, specifically Saudi Arabia and Egypt.

Are the emergence of al Qaeda and its use of terrorist tactics the product of repression, authoritarianism and the lack of political participation within and outside the Middle East? To address this question, I will trace the growth and development of the movement and then selectively explore the histories of some of its individual members and sub-groups. I will show that the experience of repression and, more importantly, the lack of political participation – the inevitable outcome of a transnational, rootless[3] existence which cuts individuals off from the day-to-day give-and-take of politics – are plausible and relevant explanations of al Qaeda's choice of terrorist tactics. However, they do not provide the whole story nor do they offer the key explanation of al Qaeda's terrorist tactics. The counter-example of the Hizb ut Tahrir (Liberation Party) – discussed in the chapter's last section – demonstrates that a transnational, rootless existence does not necessarily lead to the adoption of violent or terrorist tactics, even though it may be conducive to a radical

---

[3] Transnationalism and 'rootlessness', as I interpret them in this chapter, are not necessarily the same thing. A movement may be transnational without its members having a constantly shifting abode, which is what the term 'rootless' signifies. However, a great number of those affiliated with al Qaeda, which is a transnational movement, do also have a rootless existence, as I show below. So do those affiliated with Hizb ut Tahrir, although less so by comparison to al Qaeda.

or even fundamentalist interpretation of Islam. The chapter will conclude by assessing the strength of political explanations compared to other possible causes of al Qaeda's adoption of terrorist tactics.

Al Qaeda's Evolution as a Terrorist Actor

In this section, I outline how al Qaeda's origins and subsequent development shaped its ideology and strategy and provided the context for its adoption of terrorist tactics. The history of al Qaeda's beginnings is murky and contested, not least because certain groups were given the label 'al Qaeda' only retrospectively. The word or phrase 'al Qaeda' – which can be translated as 'a base, as in a camp or a home, or a foundation, such as what is under a house' – was in use by the mid-1980s among Islamic radicals fighting the Soviet Union in Afghanistan. Its meaning was not clear, however: 'al Qaeda' did not necessarily refer to a concrete organisation but rather to the idea of a 'vanguard' of Islamist radicalism having a 'base' of operations. Alternatively, it referred to a mode of activism or a tactic. As the Soviet withdrawal from Afghanistan approached and finally occurred in February 1989, unity between the *mujahedeen* (the fighters of the *jihad*, in this case against the Soviet Union) disintegrated. To overcome these divisions, and create an 'international army' for the defence of Muslims locally and worldwide, in 1988–9, Osama Bin Laden and a dozen associates set up a militant group in Peshawar, Pakistan's staging post for the Afghan war. However, it is unlikely that at that stage, the group around Bin Laden called itself 'al Qaeda'.[4]

The early phases of the movement which was eventually more consistently called 'al Qaeda' were marked by debates and divisions over objectives and strategy. Important differences arose over the meaning and purpose of *jihad* as a general concept (not with specific reference to tactics, let alone terrorist tactics). Contrasting views were held by Abdallah Azzam, a Palestinian scholar and one of the chief ideologues and organisers of the struggle in Afghanistan in the 1980s, who became Bin Laden's mentor; and Ayman al Zawahiri, a leader of the Egyptian

---

[4] Jason Burke, *Al-Qaeda: Casting a Shadow of Terror*, London: I. B. Tauris, 2003, pp. 7–9. For the meaning of the word 'al Qaeda', Burke is referring to Abdallah Azzam's writings: the source of the quotes is Rohan Gunaratna, *Inside Al-Qaeda*, London: Hurst, 2002, pp. 3, 7–9. The time of al Qaeda's creation is also confirmed by Wright who writes that 'al Qaeda had already been secretly created some months before [August 1988] by a small group of bin Laden insiders'. Lawrence Wright, *The Looming Tower: Al-Qaeda's Road to 9/11*, London: Penguin Books, 2006, p. 133.

Islamic Jihad organisation, who was later to become Bin Laden's deputy chief and most important ideologue within al Qaeda. Azzam advocated a more traditional interpretation of *jihad* against outside encroachment on 'Islam' which meant struggling against non-Muslims while eschewing fighting fellow Muslims or Muslim governments. Zawahiri was a major proponent of *takfirism* which classifies all those Muslims deemed not to practice Islam properly as *kafirs* (infidels)[5] and opens the door to targeting Muslim governments seen as having strayed from the righteous path (the 'enemy within'). Azzam's murder in Peshawar in 1989 precipitated Bin Laden's and al Qaeda's shift in Zawahiri's direction.[6] An important ideological mutation had occurred within the movement which could henceforth turn its sights on non-righteous Muslims. Although not the cause of terrorist tactics per se, the idea of *takfirism*, with its inclusion of Muslims considered 'beyond the pale', justified their use. More broadly it enabled the killing of civilians by de-humanising and depicting them as the proverbial 'other'.

Osama Bin Laden left Pakistan to return to his native Saudi Arabia in 1989. Having alienated the Saudi authorities, whom he condemned for a variety of reasons including their invitation to US forces to defend the kingdom, he moved to Sudan in 1991 or 1992. Bin Laden chose Sudan because Hasan Turabi's National Islamic Front (NIF), in alliance with the army, had taken power there in 1989. The marriage of convenience between NIF and al Qaeda was temporary and problematic. Their leaders were ideologically and culturally poles apart, shaped by their different national and social contexts, educations and personalities. (I caught a glimpse of this when I asked the Sorbonne-educated Hasan Turabi in Khartoum in February 2004 what he thought of Bin Laden as a person – 'well', he responded with a languid, slightly disdainful move of the hand, 'he is a Saudi....'). The al Qaeda 'project' flagged during the Sudan years. Bin Laden was certainly not registering on the radar of US intelligence as a significant terrorist suspect. He was mentioned in the 1995 trial over the 1993 World Trade Centre attack in New York, but only in passing and as one name among thousands.[7]

---

[5] Syed Saleem Shahzad, 'Takfirism: A Messianic Ideology', *Monde Diplomatique*, July 2007, and Stephen Vertigans, *Militant Islam: A Sociology of Characteristics, Causes and Consequences*, London: Routledge, 2009, pp. 104–6.

[6] Marc Sageman, *Understanding Terror Networks*, Philadelphia: University of Pennsylvania Press, 2004, pp. 35–7.

[7] Burke, *Al-Qaeda*, pp. 9–10. Lawrence Wright also suggests that by 1995, al Qaeda 'had come to nothing'. Wright, *The Looming Tower*, p. 199. Marc Sageman paints a somewhat different picture of this period as marked by considerable activity, albeit in a disparate

The attempted assassination of Egyptian President Hosni Mubarak in the Ethiopian capital, Addis Ababa, in June 1995 was attributed by the Egyptian government to the Sudanese security services and Zawahiri in Khartoum (although others, such as the Egyptian Gamaa Islamiya, were also implicated). Under growing international pressure following the attack, the Sudanese government was forced to expel al Qaeda. Bin Laden and approximately 150 followers left Khartoum in May 1996 to return to Afghanistan. From there, in August 1996, having struck an alliance with the recently installed Taliban government led by Mohammed Omar, Bin Laden issued a 'Declaration of War Against the Americans Occupying the Land of the Two Holy Places'. In February 1998, Bin Laden announced the creation of a 'World Islamic Front for Jihad against the Jews and Crusaders' and called for the killing of American civilians and military personnel and their allies. In the same statement, Bin Laden reiterated what was effectively a major innovation in the interpretation of *jihad* – which had traditionally been understood as a collective task which must take place under the proper sanction and banner of an Islamic government – that such killings should be carried out by Muslims pursuing their *individual* religious obligations.[8]

The announcement of a 'World Islamic Front for Jihad against the Jews and Crusaders' symbolised a vital strategic shift in the 1990s within al Qaeda and transnational Islamism generally, from the 'near enemy', impious Muslim regimes nearer to home, to the 'far enemy', namely the United States and its allies. Towards the latter half of the decade, it was clear that the internal Islamist challenges to incumbent regimes in Egypt, Algeria and elsewhere in the Middle East had 'crashed on the rocks of state power and the lack of public support'.[9] A move to other targets therefore became imperative and was followed by a corresponding change of emphasis on Western 'aggression' in Muslim lands. This aggression was epitomised by the stationing of US troops in Saudi Arabia after the 1991 Gulf war, which was presented by the Saudi regime as necessary for the defence of the kingdom but was interpreted

---

fashion, in Sudan, Yemen, the Philippines and Bosnia. Sageman, *Understanding Terror Networks*, pp. 40–5. The prime organiser behind the 1993 World Trade attack was the blind sheikh Omar Abdul Rahman, leader of Egypt's Gamaa Islamiya who at the time lived in Jersey City, United States. Wright, *The Looming Tower*, chapter 9.

[8] For the text of Bin Laden's 1996 declaration, see http://www.pbs.org/newshour/terrorism/international/fatwa_1996.html. For the 1998 announcement, see http://www.fas.org/irp/world/para/docs/980223-fatwa.htm, both accessed 24 November 2009.

[9] Fawaz A. Gerges, *The Far Enemy: Why Jihad Went Global*, New York: Cambridge University Press, 2005 p. 130.

by Bin Laden as 'occupation' of the holy places of Mecca and Medina. The United Nations 1992 intervention in Somalia was also seen as a US operation because of that country's leading role in it and was interpreted as yet another attempt to dominate Muslim lands. The long-standing issue of Israel's occupation of Palestine and other Muslim causes such as Chechnya and Kashmir also figured prominently in the al Qaeda' rhetoric against the 'far enemy'.[10]

Al Qaeda's decision to internationalise its struggle and pursue what it portrayed as a global military *jihad* was the outcome of an assessment by Bin Laden that a direct confrontation with the United States was essential for the struggle to go forward. Bin Laden was eventually able to convince a number of activists in favour of this change of strategy.[11] The most important convert was Zawahiri who until the late 1990s had been a staunch advocate of the view that revolution must first occur at home and rejected calls to internationalise the conflict. He ultimately reconsidered his position and joined Bin Laden's struggle, thus precipitating a split within his own organisation, the Egyptian Islamic Jihad, most of whose members expressed shock at his decision and distanced themselves from it.[12]

---

[10] Porter argues that it remains unclear whether the ultimate objective for Bin Laden was the defence of the *umma* or the offensive waging of an indiscriminate war against infidels rooted in 'existential fury'. Porter, 'Long Wars and Long Telegrams', pp. 295–6. Lawrence's view is that, for Bin Laden, *jihad* was not waged against US imperialism but at 'global unbelief,' and that the war for him was a religious war. Bruce Lawrence, *Messages to the World: The Statements of Osama Bin Laden*, London: Verso, 2005, trans. James Howarth, p. xx. Contrast the discussion in Quintan Wiktorowicz and John Kaltner, 'Killing in the Name of Islam: Al-Qaeda's Justification for September 11', *Middle East Policy*, 10 (2) 2003, pp. 83–5, which emphasises a defensive interpretation of *jihad* by al Qaeda.

[11] International Crisis Group (ICG), *Saudi Arabia Backgrounder: Who Are the Islamists?*, Middle East Report 31, 21 September 2004, pp. 5–6; Gerges, *The Far Enemy*, p. 133.

[12] Overall, the development of al Qaeda ideology can be surmised only in very general terms, by focusing on Bin Laden's and Zawahiri's statements. A number of works have been devoted to this task. See, for example, Peter Bergen, *The Osama Bin Laden I Know*, New York: Free Press, 2006; Lawrence, *Messages to the World*; Gilles Kepel and Jean-Pierre Milelli (eds.), *Al Qaeda in its Own Words*, Cambridge, MA: The Belknap Press of Harvard University Press, 2008, trans. Pascale Ghazaleh. When it comes to more specific and positive goals about the character of the ideal society al Qaeda wanted to promote, the picture is very hazy. True, some of Bin Laden's demands since 1996 have been mundane and specific to Saudi Arabia (such as tax, currency and sanitation reform in the kingdom) – see Burke, *Al-Qaeda*, p. 24. But the grand objectives of resurrecting the Muslim caliphate as a focus for unity and leadership for the Muslim *umma* and creating an Islamic state run on *sharia* law remain unspecified. When Peter Arnett, the CNN

Within this context, al Qaeda's terrorist tactics gradually evolved. The attack on Egypt's interior minister, Hasan al Alfi, in August 1993 was the first use of suicide bombing in the Sunni world. Although this attack is attributed to Islamic Jihad, the suicide bombing tactic eventually became the signature of al Qaeda. In November 1995, Zawahiri's men bombed the Egyptian embassy in Islamabad in revenge for the hounding of the Islamists in Egypt following the attempted assassination of Mubarak in Addis Ababa, mentioned earlier. Again, although this was an Islamic Jihad operation, it became the prototype for later al Qaeda attacks. Following al Qaeda's strategic shift from the 'near' to the 'far enemy', the highly destructive August 1998 attacks on the US embassies in Nairobi and Dar es Salaam took place. These were al Qaeda's first documented terrorist strikes.[13] In October 2000, the USS *Cole* was bombed in Aden. In September 2001, the United States was attacked on its own territory.

Between 1996 and 2001, Osama Bin Laden had provided a focus for disparate radical Islamist elements. A fairly sophisticated organisation had formed around him by the late 1990s.[14] By the time of the September 2001 attacks, he and a dozen or so close associates had been able to attract and maintain the loyalty of around 100 highly motivated individuals from throughout the Islamic world – an al Qaeda 'hardcore'.[15] But al Qaeda's 'success' in attacking the United States on its own territory backfired because it triggered an overpowering US reaction. The United States responded to the 11 September 2001 attacks by intervening in Afghanistan in October 2001 and removing the Taliban regime from power in the space of a few weeks. The overthrow of the Taliban

reporter who interviewed Bin Laden in the caves of Tora Bora in March 1997, asked him what kind of society he hoped to create in Saudi Arabia, his response was the following:

> We are confident, with the permission of God praise and glory be to Him, that Muslims will be victorious in the Arabian Peninsula and that God's religion, praise and glory be to Him, will prevail in this peninsula. It is a great pride and a big hope that the revelation unto Mohammed, peace be upon him, will be resorted to for ruling. When we used to follow Mohammed's revelation, peace be upon him, we were in great happiness and in great dignity, to God belongs the credit and praise.

As Wright succinctly put it, Bin Laden's statement revealed 'the complete absence of any real political plan'. Wright, *The Looming Tower*, p. 246.

[13] Wright, *The Looming Tower*, pp. 185, 217 and 270. Bin Laden also claimed responsibility for the ambush of US forces in Mogadishu, Somalia, in 1993, the attack against the National Guard Training Center in Riyadh in 1995 and the Khobar Towers bombing in 1996, but there is no evidence to substantiate any of these claims (p. 246).

[14] Thomas Hegghammer, 'Global Jihadism After the Iraq War', *Middle East Journal*, 60 (1) Winter 2006, p. 13–14, note 7.

[15] Burke, *Al-Qaeda*, pp. 12–13.

stripped al Qaeda of its protective shell and led to the dismantling of al Qaeda's central command-and-control structures.

This dispersal caused the transfer of terrorist operations to small semi-autonomous local affiliates which were inspired by al Qaeda and carried its ideological banner. Bin Laden built 'tacit understandings and informal alliances' with fringe factions in the Middle East, East Asia and Africa, such as Ansar al Islam and Abu Musab al Zarqawi's al Tawhid wal Jihad in Iraq; Algeria's Salafist Group for Preaching and Combat (GSPC); Jama'a al Islamiya in Indonesia; the Islamic Movement in Uzbekistan; the Libyan Islamic Fighting Group; and the Moroccan Salifiya Jihadi. Some of these groups, such as al Tawhid wal Jihad in Iraq and the GSPC in Algeria, established more formal alliances with al Qaeda and changed their names accordingly. Al Qaeda affiliates acted independently – but no less lethally – with little or no guidance or planning from the 'parent' organisation.[16] Terrorist attacks in Djerba (April 2002); Bali (October 2002); Casablanca (May 2003 and April 2007); Istanbul (November 2003); Madrid (2004); Jakarta (September 2004); Egypt (October 2004, July 2005); London (July 2005) and Amman (November 2005) were linked to al Qaeda, some more convincingly than others. During those years, Al Qaeda seemed to have spread its 'tentacles' from the Maghreb and Somalia in the west and southwest, through the Middle East, to Central, South and Southeast Asia.[17]

---

[16] Gerges, *The Far Enemy*, p. 247. The fact that the attacks were less sophisticated did not make them necessarily less destructive, as the 2004 and 2005 bombings in Madrid and London demonstrated, pp. 217–8.

[17] The debate on how to describe and label post-2001 al Qaeda is heated and ongoing. Rather than a global network of groups 'guided' by Bin Laden, Burke argues that it is more accurate to depict al Qaeda in the post-2001 period as a loose 'network of networks' (Burke, *Al-Qaeda*, p. 16). For Gerges, it can be seen as 'an ideological label, a state of mind, and a mobilisational outreach program to incite attacks worldwide' which, after 2001, became even more decentralised and amorphous (Gerges, *The Far Enemy*, p. 40). For Roula Khalaf and Stephen Fidler, al Qaeda became less of an organisation and more of an 'order', in the sense of an association, in which 'a central base would provide primarily ideological guidance to semi-autonomous cells around the world' (Roula Khalaf and Stephen Fidler, 'From Frontline Attack to Terror by Franchise', *Financial Times*, 5 July 2007). Shaul Mishal and Maoz Rosenthal, argue that al Qaeda after 2001 changed from a network to a de-territorialised 'dune' organisation which constantly appears and disappears rather than having an institutional presence (Shaul Mishal and Maoz Rosenthal, 'Al Qaeda as a Dune Organization: Toward a Typology of Islamic Terrorist Organizations', *Studies in Conflict and Terrorism*, 28 (4) 2005, pp. 279–80). Finally, Thomas Hegghammer prefers not to use the term 'al Qaeda' in the post-2001 period at all, arguing that the term 'global jihadist movement' 'better reflects the decentralised and multipolar nature of the phenomenon' (Hegghammer, 'Global Jihadism after the Iraq War', p. 14). Sageman introduces the idea of 'leaderless jihad'

Rootlessness and Terrorist Violence

The pervasiveness of authoritarianism in the Middle East is linked to al Qaeda's choice of ideology and tactics in multiple and subtle ways. For one, the lack of formal outlets to publically express opinion, grievances and concerns made it easier for Bin Laden to hijack the Arab 'street'.[18] Al Qaeda found a ready pool of recruits among those who became marginalised and disillusioned by the politics of their respective states. However, al Qaeda's ideology and tactics were also influenced by the movement's mode of operation and organisational structures. Not all al Qaeda recruits were alienated citizens of repressive societies, but once they had joined the movement, the rootlessness of their existence, which was a *sine qua non* of al Qaeda's transnational mode of operation, heightened their radicalisation and their predilection towards terrorist tactics.

Such a transnational mode of operation is not conducive to political participation and impedes any incorporation in political processes. Al Qaeda affiliates live a transient and nomadic existence. Consorting with small numbers of equally isolated individuals in secret training camps and caves, rather than within the bustle of social and political interaction, marks their daily lives. They constantly criss-cross state boundaries to spread their message and link up with fellow radicals. Even when moving into major urban centres, they live and operate in a 'bubble', separate from the society and politics around them even if it provides them with safe haven and the opportunity, at least formally, to become involved in public affairs (as in the case of democracies). More often than not, their conversations are conducted in cyberspace rather than face to face. Caught in 'spirals of encapsulation', as described by Donatella Della Porta,[19] they increasingly veer away from the mindset necessary for compromise and negotiation. Terrorist tactics entailing the 'de-humanisation' of the enemy are a comprehensible outcome of this type of existence.

(Marc Sageman, *Leaderless Jihad: Terrorist Networks in the Twenty-First Century*, Philadelphia: University of Pennsylvania Press, 2008; see especially chapter 7) and Burke also gradually moved towards abandoning the label 'al Qaeda', arguing that to do so will help us understand the chaotic nature of the terrorist threat (Jason Burke, 'Al Qaeda – A Meaningless Label', *The Guardian*, 12 January 2003).

[18] Dale F. Eickelman, 'Bin Laden, the Arab "Street", and the Middle East's Democracy Deficit', *Current History*, 101 (651) January 2002, p. 38.

[19] Donatella Della Porta, *Social Movements, Political Violence and the State: A Comparative Analysis of Italy and Germany*, Cambridge: Cambridge University Press, 1995, p. 12.

The personal tale of Ayman al Zawahiri typifies these processes. Zawahiri's political formation occurred at the time of the Muslim Brotherhood's suppression in Nasser's Egypt in the 1960s.[20] Born into a prestigious Cairene family, the young Zawahiri became influenced by the writings of Sayyid Qutb and formed a clandestine group with his brother and three high school friends to oppose Nasser's regime. He remained involved in the Egyptian militant scene over the next two decades, vehemently rejecting the Muslim Brotherhood's adoption of moderate political positions.[21] After a short stint in Peshawar in 1980, he returned home and was caught in the wave of arrests following the assassination of Anwar Sadat by his organisation, Islamic Jihad (a plan known to Zawahiri only a few hours before its execution). He was released in 1984, left Egypt for Jeddah in 1985 and in 1986 returned to Peshawar to continue a clandestine existence.[22]

During a visit to Cairo in April 2005, I had the opportunity to interview Mamdouh Ismail, a former Islamist radical turned political activist and lawyer for Zawahiri's mother and sisters. He had known Zawahiri personally and described him as a noble and pleasant man of high standards and strong convictions. According to Ismail, Zawahiri's thought was a product of the complete oppression he experienced in the late 1960s.[23] He was toughened even more over the following two decades. In the 1980s, he emerged from Egypt's prisons a hardened radical; he had been abused, tortured and forced to betray a fellow conspirator.[24] His prison experience cemented a worldview which had been created while living underground – a life which, according to Kamal al Said Habib, one of his associates and a former leader of Islamic Jihad, is 'not just politically "unhealthy" but it also distorts reality and leads to hasty and reckless decisions.' Fawaz Gerges argues that Zawahiri became divorced from Muslim reality as if he had 'slept through two decades of important developments and debates among his coreligionists', and was leading a movement which ignored reality and rationality and existed 'in its own bubble'.[25]

---

[20] See Montasser al Zayyat, *The Road to al-Qaeda: The Story of Bin Laden's Right Hand Man*, London: Pluto Press, 2004, trans. Sara Nimis.

[21] Gerges, *The Far Enemy*, pp. 111–3.

[22] Sageman, *Understanding Terror Networks*, pp. 26, 32–3 and 34. It appears that Zawahiri joined what became Islamic Jihad in its initial stages, in the 1970s.

[23] Author's interview with Mamdouh Ismail, lawyer and political activist, Cairo, December 2005.

[24] Angelo Rasanayagam, *Afghanistan: A Modern History*, London: I. B. Tauris, 2003, p. 228 and Gerges, *The Far Enemy*, p. 93.

[25] Gerges. *The Far Enemy*, pp. 90, 112 and 207.

The life of Abu Mus'ab al Suri who is described as an 'architect of global *jihad*' by his biographer, Brynjar Lia, is also typical of a particular type of rootless existence which can be convincingly linked to the adoption of terrorist tactics. Al Suri was born in Aleppo, Syria, in a conservative family living in a well-off part of the city and through the 1970s gradually became involved in Islamist politics there. In 1980, at the age of twenty-one, he joined an armed Islamist group, the Combatant Vanguard Organization of the Muslim Brotherhood (which, despite the name, was not subordinate to the Muslim Brotherhood itself but presented a challenge to it). His involvement got him into trouble with the authorities and he was forced to leave Syria for Jordan. He probably never returned to his native land. From that point onwards, al Suri's life was a series of 'exiles'. From Jordan, where he became more active in militaristic activities, he travelled around the Middle East. The crushing of the Muslim Brotherhood by Hafez al Asad's regime in Hama in February 1982 added to his disillusionment with the path of political compromise which that movement represented. He moved to Saudi Arabia and from there to France in 1983 and subsequently to Spain. In 1987, he went to Afghanistan and Pakistan. He was back in Spain in 1991–2 and then in London in 1994. He relocated to Afghanistan in 1997 and became a fugitive in 2001 until his capture in Quetta in 2005.[26]

Al Suri's first steps towards Islamist terrorism and political extremism clearly occurred in his early youth and can arguably be linked to the authoritarianism of the Syrian regime. His biographer does not give details about its causes but implicitly suggests that they were connected to the turmoil in Syria at the time and in particular the repression of the Islamist movement.[27] What is more relevant to my argument, however, is al Suri's subsequent life story. Radicalisation during one's youth is a common enough phenomenon but one often followed by a 'mellowing' in subsequent years, particularly as the demands of work and family force individuals to negotiate with and accept their social environment. As for many others like him, al Suri's nomadic existence in the Middle East, Europe and South Asia mitigated against such a shift.[28]

[26] Brynjar Lia, *Architect of Global Jihad: The Life of al-Qaida Strategist Abu Mus'ab al-Suri*, New York: Columbia University Press, 2008, see especially chapters 3–9.

[27] Ibid., pp. 37–8.

[28] For a number of similar stories of highly mobile individuals who participated in the 11 September 2001 attacks against the United States, see *The 9/11 Commission Report: Final Report of the National Commission on Terrorist Attacks upon the United States*, New York: W. W. Norton & Co, 2004, chapter 5.

The worldview of Ayman al Zawahiri, Abu Mus'ab al Suri and many other members of al Qaeda was shaped by the experience of the Afghan wars against the Soviet Union during the 1980s, the internal wars of Afghanistan in the 1990s and the alliance with the Taliban.[29] Lawrence Wright describes eloquently how, from the 1980s, the many economic and political failures in the Arab world filled the lives of young men with emptiness and frustration and pushed them to seek death in Afghanistan, lured by Abdallah Azzam's paeans to martyrdom. Not all Arab 'Afghans', as they came to be called, were suicidal or apocalyptic thinkers and some of them were not even religious. They included those who simply sought excitement or some meaning to their lives. Mohammed Loay Baizid, a Syrian immigrant to the United States studying engineering in Kansas City, Missouri, who subsequently took the *nom de guerre* Abu Rida al Suri (not to be confused with Abu Mus'ab al Suri), decided to travel to Afghanistan after reading one of Azzam's tracts. He planned to stay for three months, but his experience upon his arrival was transformative, as he himself describes it: 'I went to Afghanistan with a blank mind and a good heart. Everything was totally strange. It was like I was born just now, like I was an infant, and I have to learn everything new. It was not so easy after that to leave and go back to your regular life.'[30]

The mindset of the core al Qaeda fighters was shaped within Afghanistan's Islamist milieu. The foreign volunteer militants who fought alongside the Afghan *mujahedeen* to oust the Soviet Union, and in particular the Arabs amongst them, constituted an important pool for al Qaeda recruitment. The Arabs who came to Afghanistan were not in contact with the society around them but with foreign, mostly Arab volunteers like themselves.[31] A great number of these volunteers came

---

[29] Al Qaeda's alliance with the Taliban which emerged in 1994 in Afghanistan was not coincidental but was based on similar ideas and similar formation. Literally 'children of the *jihad*' who had known nothing but war and who received their basic education in the madrasas of Pakistan's North West Frontier Province and in Baluchistan, the Taliban were rootless and receptive to extreme ideological influences. But the Taliban were also inseparable from the Afghan social fabric, associated with religious schools, mosques, shrines and all kinds of Islamic activities. The young rootless Afghans who were to become the future cadres of the Taliban were taught in the rural areas and the Afghan refugee camps in Pakistan by semi-educated mullahs, whose reading of the *sharia* texts was heavily influenced by the tribal code of the Pashtuns, the Pashtunwali. Rasanayagam, *Afghanistan*, pp. 177, 180.

[30] Wright, *The Looming Tower*, pp. 109–10.

[31] Author's interview with Moheb Mudessir, journalist, BBC World Service, London, July 2007.

from Saudi Arabia and Yemen.[32] The Egyptians also formed an important contingent. This changed in the 1990s when many of the recruits in Afghanistan came from Europe or Algeria. Altogether between 10,000 and 20,000 trainees are said to have passed through the Afghan camps between 1996 and 2001,[33] although it is clearly difficult to verify these figures. During those years, Bin Laden 'reached the apogee of his power'.[34]

The Saudis' role was pivotal to al Qaeda's development. For most of the young Saudis who went 'on *jihad*' to Afghanistan, the trip was little more than a summer holiday. For those who stayed, the experience was profoundly transformative, as they immersed themselves in the romanticised culture of violent resistance that flourished within the Arab contingent of the *mujahedeen*. These militants experienced their initial political awakening outside their own country and developed a highly militaristic worldview which in some cases facilitated their turn to terrorism.[35]

Following the Soviet withdrawal in 1989, a new generation of roaming freelance former *mujahedeen* left Afghanistan and travelled from one front to another in support of their persecuted and oppressed 'Muslim brethren' worldwide. Thousands of veterans of the Afghan wars joined the campaigns in Bosnia-Herzegovina, Chechnya, the Philippines, Kashmir, Eritrea, Somalia, Burma, Tajikistan and elsewhere. Saudis played a pivotal role in these developments as top chiefs, operatives and financiers and fought in Bosnia, Somalia and Chechnya in particular.

In contrast to many other Arabs, Saudis who had fought in Afghanistan were free to return to their home country, but given Saudi Arabia's hermetically sealed, repressive political system, there was no domestic political process into which they could integrate. Instead, the Afghan returnees' violent culture shaped Saudi politics. It spread to many Saudi Islamist circles and fed from the early 2000s into a serious internal challenge to the Saudi regime by the movement that came to be called al Qaeda in the Arabian Peninsula.[36] This challenge took the form

---

[32] Gerges, *The Far Enemy*, pp. 178–9: his source is *The 9/11 Commission Report*, p. 232.

[33] Wright, *The Looming Tower*, pp. 301–2.

[34] Bergen, *The Osama Bin Laden I Know*, p. 161.

[35] In contrast to the Egyptian volunteers who had already been politicised at home, Saudi militants came to Afghanistan with low politicisation and limited or non-existent domestic agendas or ideological bases for opposing the Saudi state. Gerges, *The Far Enemy*, pp. 133–4.

[36] According to an International Crisis Group report of 2004, the Saudi regime's crackdown on radical Islamists in February and March 2003, designed to pre-empt possible

of terrorist incidents within Saudi Arabia in 2003–5. Information about the terrorists involved in these attacks indicates that most had very close connections to Afghanistan, many of them having trained there at a young age.[37]

The dismantling of al Qaeda's central command-and-control structures after 2001, mentioned in the previous section, did not mean that the Afghan-Pakistani border areas ceased to be important as a hub of operations. The al Qaeda leadership is still (2010) presumed to be hiding in the caves of the Tora Bora mountains of Afghanistan and in the tribal areas of Pakistan bordering it.[38] The Taliban were resurgent after 2007 in Pakistan's Waziristan and Baujur regions, adjacent to Afghanistan, and training in weapons and bomb making as well as religious indoctrination is continuing for locals and foreigners, including Chechens, Uzbeks and a small number of Britons.[39] Nevertheless, and as discussed earlier, the bulk of al Qaeda's operations have been transferred to local affiliates. Although this represents a relative return to emphasis on the national level rather than the 'far enemy', and can largely be ascribed to local conditions and concerns, it does not mean that groups affiliated with 'al Qaeda' have been integrated into domestic political processes – far from it.

One example of such a group operating in a gray area between global and local levels is the Algerian GSPC, which renamed itself 'al Qaeda in the Islamic Maghreb' after concluding an alliance of sorts with al Qaeda in late 2006 – early 2007. The GSPC was initially created in September 1998 after splintering from the Groupe Islamique Armé (GIA), one of the main protagonists of the Algerian Islamist insurrection in the 1990s

militant action during the Iraq war, most likely triggered the decision to carry out operations under the name 'al Qaeda on the Arabian Peninsula' (QAP). QAP has a loose structure but militants view themselves as part of an overarching movement, an awareness created by fraternal bonds acquired in Afghanistan or through shared experiences as fugitives and rebels in Saudi Arabia. In all likelihood, lines of communication with Bin Laden and Zawahiri have long been broken, even though QAP considers them supreme guides. The inclusion within QAP of former Saudi rejectionists (Saudi Islamists who had previously focused on private faith and often advocated withdrawal from public affairs) helps to explain why it is openly hostile to the Saudi regime in ways that go beyond Bin Laden's attitude. ICG, *Saudi Arabia Backgrounder*, pp. 12–17.

[37] Roel Meijer, 'Jihadi Opposition in Saudi Arabia', *International Institute for the Study of Islam in the Modern World (ISIM) Review*, 15, Spring 2005, p. 16.

[38] Mark Mazzetti and David Rohde, 'The Doomed Hunt for Al Qaeda's Leaders', *International Herald Tribune*, 30 June 2008.

[39] Farhan Bokhari and Stephen Fidler, 'Rivalries Rife in Lair of Leaders', *Financial Times*, 5 July 2007.

(to be discussed extensively in Chapter 4). By 2005–6, the GSPC had become 'politically isolated, under pressure of the security forces, and lacking basic infrastructure and means (money, weapons, logistics, popular support)'.[40] Hit hard by the Algerian authorities and watching their ranks shrink, its leaders saw a lifeline in al Qaeda in logistical and possibly also in ideological terms. The GSPC's drive to integrate into a global network was influenced by Algerians who had fought in Afghanistan and then returned home.[41] The alliance with al Qaeda gave the GSPC a boost and they became increasingly active. Their terrorist operations within Algeria started to bear al Qaeda's hallmarks, especially in the use of suicide bombings which had been virtually unknown in Algeria before 2007.[42] Their targets also became increasingly 'global', comprising both the United Nations and Western interests.[43]

The terrorist violence perpetrated by al Qaeda in the Islamic Maghreb, like the GSPC before it, 'finds its seedbed more in domestic political and social conditions than in the global ideological ether'.[44] Despite these important local roots, however, the movement continues to operate in geographical and socio-political isolation, mostly confined to the Algerian mountains and other hideouts. It remains an 'outcast in the Algerian arena'[45] and divorced from ongoing developments in Algerian politics. The connection with al Qaeda has doubtless further deepened the gulf which separates al Qaeda in the Islamic Maghreb from the Algerian social and political mainstream. So has the spread of the group's influence to the Sahel, the region of the Sahara comprising parts

---

[40] Sami Zemni, 'From Local Insurgency to Al-Qaida Franchise', *International Institute for the Study of Islam in the Modern World (ISIM) Review*, 21, Spring 2008, p. 16.

[41] Craig Whitlock, 'Al-Qaeda's Far-Reaching New Partner', *Washington Post*, 5 October 2006; Roula Khalaf and Stephen Fidler, 'Why Algerian extremists "rebranded" as al-Qaeda', *Financial Times*, 20 April 2007.

[42] Note, however, that in the view of Jean-Pierre Filiu, there is considerable continuity between the GSPC and al Qaeda in the Islamic Maghreb. Jean-Pierre Filiu, 'The Local and Global Jihad of al Qa'ida in the Islamic Maghreb', *Middle East Journal*, 63 (2) 2009, p. 224.

[43] Cherif Ouazani, 'Algérie: Jusqu'où Ira al-Qaïda?', *Jeune Afrique*, 2449, 16–22 Décembre 2007, pp. 41–4.

[44] James McDougall, 'After the War: Algeria's Transition to Uncertainty', *Middle East Report*, 245, Winter 2007, p. 37. McDougall argues that Islamist terrorist violence in Tunisia in December 2006–January 2007 and in Morocco in March and April 2007 were also home-grown. Mounir Boudjema, Algerian journalist for the newspaper *Libération* and analyst of the Islamist movement in Algeria, pointed out that there is no network as such linking Islamist terrorist activities in Tunisia, Morocco and Algeria. Author's interview, Algiers, March 2007.

[45] Filiu, 'The Local and Global Jihad of al Qa'ida in the Islamic Maghreb', p. 225.

of Mauritania, Mali, Niger and southern Algeria, where they are apparently increasingly active, specialising in tourist kidnappings.[46] Trainees
from these countries, plus Nigeria, Morocco, Tunisia, Libya and Senegal,
congregate in training camps in remote regions of northern Mali[47] where,
again, they live a clandestine, isolated existence.[48]

Al Qaeda in Mesopotamia is another example of how an al Qaeda
affiliate operating in a gray area between global and local levels encourages the use of terrorist tactics. Following the US invasion of 2003, a
Sunni insurgency wreaked havoc against the occupying forces and
fanned the flames of sectarian conflict in Iraq. A key participant in the
insurgency, until he was killed in June 2006, was the Jordanian Abu
Musab al Zarqawi. His group, al Tawhid wal Jihad, declared in October
2004 that it had 'joined' al Qaeda and henceforth referred to itself as
al Qaeda in Mesopotamia (its other names were al Qaeda in Iraq and
al Qaeda in the Land of the Two Rivers). The terrorist violence spearheaded by Zarqawi and his cohorts was exceptionally horrific and
included large-scale killings of civilians by suicide bombings, abductions
and decapitations.[49] Clearly the brutalisation of Iraqi society over three
and a half decades of harsh authoritarianism, wars, sanctions and priva-
tions created a permissive environment for such tactics, but the mode of
existence and operation of the perpetrators of these terrorist acts also
played a role. This was not, as is commonly assumed, because al Qaeda
in Mesopotamia was dominated by foreigners who came into Iraq to
wage their personal war. In the words of one of the Sunni insurgents,
interviewed by the International Crisis Group in April 2007, 'al Qaeda is
very much Iraqi [now]'. The interviewee continued with this very revealing statement: 'The problem is that al Qaeda sees Iraq as a battleground,
whereas others are attached to its unity and fate. The conflict is about
global Islamism versus national Islamism. Our mantra is "at the end of

[46] Christophe Boisbouvier, 'Otages: Business au Sahara', *Jeune Afrique*, 2512, 1–7 Mars
2009, pp. 30–1.

[47] Andrew England and Roula Khalaf, 'Building Bridges to Destruction', *Financial
Times*, 6 July 2007.

[48] The International Crisis Group points out that the GSPC leaders who were active in
the southern Algerian Sahara, at least until 2004, were northerners, 'outsiders with
no representative political standing'. The local resentment they aroused meant that 'it
is doubtful that they represent any significant current of local opinion in the southern
Sahara regions where they have been operating'. International Crisis Group, *Islamism,
Violence and Reform in Algeria: Turning the Page*, Middle East Report 29, 30 July
2004, p. 16; see also note 124 in the same document.

[49] International Crisis Group, *Iraq after the Surge I: The New Sunni Landscape*, Middle
East Report 74, 30 April 2008.

the rifle comes the pen" – meaning resistance ultimately has to give way to politics – whereas al Qaeda's mantra is "at the end of the rifle comes the cannon", meaning the fight against the unbelievers and apostates can only go crescendo'.[50] In other words, al Qaeda in Mesopotamia's pursuit of 'global' goals meant their complete disregard of local conditions and their refusal to take social and political local balances into account – arguably leading to a high level of viciousness in the terrorist methods used. These methods ultimately created internal friction within the insurgency, making it easier to suppress for the US-assisted 'tribal awakening' councils from early 2007.

Thousands of miles separate the killing fields of Iraq and the training camps in the Sahara or Waziristan from the urban centres of Europe, where many of the conspiracies linked to al Qaeda since the late 1990s have been hatched by 'sleepers' formerly trained in Afghanistan. Even though the conditions and lifestyles of the two may seem poles apart, al Qaeda operatives in Europe also led a clandestine and isolated existence, albeit in different ways. Many of them were either immigrants to Europe or non-Europeans who were transient in it. For example, the majority of the perpetrators of the March 2004 bombings in Madrid were recent immigrants to Spain from the Middle East and North Africa. The main perpetrator of the Djerba attacks in Tunisia in April 2002 had lived in France and Canada and was assisted by a German national who had converted to Islam.[51]

The numbers of Muslims living in the West who have turned to terrorism are small, especially when contrasted to the vast majority of their co-religionists who have not. Why did the existence of democracy not inoculate those few from terrorist proclivities? A variety of responses to this question are possible, some of which were already highlighted in Chapter 1. Western Europe offered asylum to exiled radicals fleeing persecution from Egypt, Jordan, Syria, Algeria and other repressive states in the Middle East and elsewhere. They, in turn, used the democratic safe havens in which they found themselves 'to prey upon deracinated Arab youth, cut off from their families, feeling the sting of discrimination, and looking for some colourful purpose to orient their drifting lives'.[52]

[50] International Crisis Group interview, spokesman for the Jihad and Reform Front, April 2007, *Iraq after the Surge I*, pp. 16–17. I have removed the Arabic translation of the terms from the quote.
[51] Samy Ghorbal, 'Attentat de Djerba: Les Liens du Sang', *Jeune Afrique*, 2507, Janvier 2009, pp. 25–31.
[52] Stephen Holmes, 'Al-Qaeda, September 11, 2001', Diego Gambetta (ed.), *Making Sense of Suicide Missions*, New York: Oxford University Press, 2005, p. 167.

The Islamist radicals were often 'a mix of educated middle-class leaders and working-class dropouts', a pattern reminiscent of most Western European terrorists of the 1970s and 1980s, such as the Italian Red Brigades and the German Baader-Meinhof gang.[53] For some members of Muslim minorities, the West's mature democracies must have appeared as 'blocked societies' impervious to peaceful attempts for change and limiting rather than expanding social and political 'choice'.[54]

Olivier Roy offers us an excellent interpretive framework for understanding the phenomenon of the radicalised Muslim in the West who may in certain circumstances turn to terrorism. His concept of 'global Muslims' describes 'either Muslims who settled permanently in non-Muslim countries (mainly in the West), or Muslims who try to distance themselves from a given Muslim culture and to stress their belonging to a universal *umma*, whether in a purely quietist way or through political action'. Islamism, in the sense of building an Islamic state, has little appeal to many who are uprooted migrants and/or living in a minority which experiences a 'de-territorialised' Islam. Their religious revivalism follows other paths, including 'neo-fundamentalism', a closed, scripturalist and conservative view of Islam which has gained ground amongst rootless Muslim youth, particularly amongst second- and third-generation migrants in the West who do not identify with any nation-state. For Roy, feeling that you are part of a minority is not an issue of demography but of alienation from a dominant culture. Many practicing Muslims consider Islam to have been 'minoritised' in their own countries too, for example, in Turkey where the dominant political structures are secular (although this may have been changing in recent years). The experience of de-territorialised Islam can therefore occur even without physically departing from one's own country.[55]

According to Roy, 'global Muslims' *occasionally* (my emphasis) turn to internationalist militancy directed against the West.[56] The shift is facilitated, in terms of ideas, by the re-conceptualisation of *jihad* from a collective to an individual duty, as discussed earlier in the chapter. For Roy, 'far from being a collective answer from the "Muslim community" to Western encroachment, the new *jihad* is an individual and personal

[53] Olivier Roy, *Globalised Islam: The Search for a New Ummah*, London: Hurst and Company, 2004, p. 48.
[54] Luigi Bonanate, 'Some Unanticipated Consequences of Terrorism', *Journal of Peace Research*, 3 (16) 1979, p. 205.
[55] Roy, *Globalised Islam*, pp. 2, 19 and 36.
[56] Ibid., p. 2.

decision. [As we shall see,] most radical militants are engaged in action as individuals, cutting links with their "natural" community (family, ethnic group and nation) to fight beyond the sphere of any real collective identity. This overemphasis on personal *jihad* complements the lonely situation of the militants who do not follow their natural community, but join an imagined one'.[57]

In addition to the fifteen who were Saudis, the other three hijackers on 11 September 2001 were social and cultural outcasts who became born-again Muslims in Europe. Stephen Holmes describes some of the personal stories of these men in graphic detail and his descriptions deserve to be quoted at some length. Mohamed Atta was a thirty-three-year-old Egyptian who went to Germany in 1992 to study city planning. With Marwan al Shehhi from the United Arab Emirates and Ziad Jarrah from Lebanon, they were radicalised while living as expatriates there. The three young men 'operated in the lengthy run-up to the attacks as a criminal conspiracy, isolated from older relatives and with minimal solidarity from a wider national community'.[58] Their sequestration from mainstream life in Hamburg insulated them from any pressures to assimilate. They lived like hunted animals for years. Because they were surrounded solely by people who thought like themselves, they lacked the contact with reality which is provided by belonging to a heterogeneous community. Holmes's analysis implies that the ripest recruits for suicide missions 'would be half-way men, stuck in transit between the Middle East and the West, whose frustration is mingled with a feeling of being *tainted* by a society that seduces them'.[59]

Marc Sageman's work reinforces this picture with statistical data. His sample focused exclusively on those Islamist terrorists who engaged in a globally oriented struggle with the aspiration of creating an Islamist

---

[57] Ibid., pp. 41–2.
[58] Holmes, 'Al-Qaeda', p. 143.
[59] Ibid., p. 153. The life of Mahmud Abouhalima, who was convicted of the 1993 attack of the World Trade Centre in New York and is described in some detail by Mark Juergensmeyer, also has many similarities to the stories of the perpetrators of the 11 September 2001 attacks. Of Egyptian origin, Abouhalima migrated to Germany and then to the United States, where he became active in New Jersey's Muslim community and established links with Sheikh Omar Abdul Rahman. Juergensmeyer argues that the volunteers for the 11 September 2001 attacks, like the men around Sheikh Omar Abdul Rahman, were participants in 'semisecret male societies', clandestine groups which 'had at best an uneasy relationship with the immigrant Muslim communities to which they were connected'. Mark Juergensmeyer, *Terror in the Mind of God: The Global Rise of Religious Violence*, 3rd edition, Berkeley: University of California Press, 2003, pp. 62–70 and 223.

state, and primarily targeted the 'far enemy' rather than their own governments. Out of 165 *mujahedeen*, 115 joined the struggle in a country where they had not grown up and where they were expatriates – students, workers, refugees or fighters. Another fourteen were second generation in Europe and the United States. Overall, an exceptionally high number, 78 percent, had severed their links with their cultural and social origins and from their families and friends. After becoming part of a socially disembedded network which lacked any anchor to society, they were 'free to follow abstract and apocalyptic notions of a global war between good and evil'.[60]

Rootlessness and the Absence of Terrorism: The Case of Hizb ut Tahrir

I have argued that al Qaeda's choice of terrorist tactics can be demonstrably linked to the movement's lack of integration in domestic political processes. A number of individuals joined al Qaeda in the first place because of repression and political exclusion at home. Other al Qaeda members operated in democratic societies but in fact remained cut off from them, for a variety of reasons. For almost all, the rootlessness of their existence once they joined the movement reinforced their unwillingness to compromise and pushed them to extremes.

However, although relevant to explaining al Qaeda's course of action, rootlessness and the absence of political participation which can be the outcome of a transnational mode of operation do not *necessarily* lead to the adoption of terrorist tactics.[61] Other Islamist movements, beyond al Qaeda, also have a fluid presence across boundaries in pursuit of their objectives but, although conservative and even fundamentalist, show no propensity for terrorism or violence in general. For example, the missionary Tablighi Jamaat movement, active throughout the Asian subcontinent and the Middle East since its establishment in India in 1926, is puritanical and hard-line in its interpretation of Islam but has never been

---

[60] Sageman, *Understanding Terror Networks*, pp. 92 and 151. Sageman's sample excluded those, like Palestinian groups, whom he considered to be waging a 'traditional' *jihad*, that is, one aimed at the recovery of territory or the resistance to an invader, as well as those activists who had rejected violence. For the criteria of the sample selection, see pp. 61–4.

[61] Similar scepticism is implied by Holmes, who argues that the connections between the uprootedness of the 9/11 hijackers, their envy of the United States, their blind obedience to their superiors and their willingness to die remain unproven. Holmes, 'Al-Qaeda', p. 154.

associated with terrorist or violent acts and has, moreover, remained staunchly apolitical. Although it clearly seeks to influence public morals and reform society, it does not try to do so through capturing political power and rejects political action such as party competition and elections.[62]

Hizb ut Tahrir provides even more solid evidence for the counter-argument I develop in this section. The many similarities between Hizb ut Tahrir and al Qaeda in terms of ideology and, more crucially, in their mode of operation have not led to the use of similar tactics. Founded in 1953 by a Palestinian, Taqiudding al Nabhani al Falastani (1909–77), Hizb ut Tahrir's first recruits originated from the Palestinian section of the Muslim Brotherhood. The organisation developed an increasingly international profile and is presently headed by Abd al Kadim Zallum, also a Palestinian, who took over in 1977. Since its founding, its membership expanded from the Middle East to countries with migrant Muslim populations all around the world. In recent years, it has set up offices in several European countries, including Germany and the United Kingdom. Hizb ut-Tahrir has experienced remarkable growth in Central Asia despite being officially banned there.[63] Its members claim that, beyond Europe, the Middle East and Central Asia, it has spread to other parts of Asia and Africa.

Hizb ut Tahrir advocates that an Islamic party must spearhead change to create an Islamic state and re-resurrect the caliphate. Its methods are top-down. In contrast and in reaction to Islamist organisations which argued for a gradual, bottom-up Islamisation of society (such as the Muslim Brotherhood to be discussed in later chapters), Hizb ut Tahrir 'insisted that no such order could be created without first establishing the Islamic state' – hence the imperative to elaborate a detailed constitution for it, which Hizb ut Tahrir has done.[64] Al Nabhani called for drastic change and denounced the trend towards democratisation in the Muslim world as a Western ploy. His organisation refused to take part

---

[62] International Crisis Group, *Understanding Islamism*, Middle East/North Africa Report 37, 2 March 2005, p. 8.

[63] Alisher Khamidov, *Countering the Call: The U.S., Hizb-ut-Tahrir, and Religious Extremism in Central Asia*, The Saban Centrer for Middle East Policy at the Brookings Institution, Analysis Paper 4, July 2003, pp. 1–2.

[64] Suha Taji-Farouki, *A Fundamental Quest: Hizb al-Tahrir and the Search for the Islamist Caliphate*, London: Grey Seal, 1996, p. 189. For Hizb ut Tahrir's methods, see chapter 3. For the text of the Constitution, see Taqiuddin an-Nabhani, 'A Draft Constitution of the Islamic State', *The Islamic State*, New Delhi: Milli Publications, 2001, pp. 240–76.

in the politics of organised opposition and pressure, setting itself apart from Islamist groups which involved themselves in local political processes.[65] Al Nabhani believed that an avant-garde transnational elite, such as Hizb ut Tahrir, could drive an Islamic global revival.[66]

The parallels between the ideas propagated by al Qaeda and Hizb ut Tahrir are remarkable and have frequently been commented on. Both are puritanical and fundamentalist in their interpretation of Islam; both seek an Islamic state through militant means; both reject the West and its influences; and both hope to re-establish the caliphate. The conditions under which al Qaeda and Hizb ut Tahrir operate are also quite similar. Except for a number of Western states, both are illegal in all the countries they operate in and have mostly functioned in conditions of repression. From its important London hub – the organisation's largest, most energetic branch – Hizb ut Tahrir has been 'exported' to Denmark. London has also dispatched hundreds of activists to Pakistan and Bangladesh, deemed 'ripe' for revolution, and has established branches in Indonesia and Malaysia.[67]

Although not necessarily as mobile as al Qaeda affiliates, Hizb ut Tahrir activists live and operate in a 'bubble', sustained by intra-network links and fuelled by an ideology which makes little reference to the issues of public concern in the society surrounding them, even though they recruit from it. Their existence is 'rootless' in that sense.[68] The personal stories of Hizb ut Tahrir activists conform to Olivier Roy's depiction of a 'de-territorialised', global Islam described in the previous section. I had direct experience of this during my visit to the West Bank in October 2007. I met activists of all persuasions, Islamist and non-Islamist, with whom I discussed some of the major issues of the day, such as terrorism and the response to it and Islam's relations to the West. As might be expected, however, most of my conversations were taken up by the Israeli-Palestinian conflict and the divisions among the Palestinians themselves, specifically between Fatah and Hamas, which had flared up only a few months before my visit and had been followed by Hamas's

---

[65] Ibid., pp. 190–1. However, the author's statement appears to contradict her claim (on p. 188) that 'the party participated actively in the institutionalised politics of opposition and pressure, contesting elections and criticising government policies'.

[66] Jean-Pierre Filiu, 'Hizb ut-Tahrir and the Fantasy of the Caliphate', *Monde Diplomatique*, June 2008.

[67] Author's interview with Ghaffar Hussain, Quilliam Foundation, former activist within Hizb ut Tahrir, London, January 2009.

[68] See note 3 to this chapter.

takeover of the Gaza Strip the previous June. One interviewee, whom I met in Beitin, a village near Ramallah (and who will remain anonymous), was introduced by my contact as a member of Hizb ut Tahrir, which is illegal in the Occupied Palestinian Territories. He was a sullen and aggressive man, a local businessman who did not openly acknowledge his Hizb ut Tahrir affiliation for obvious reasons. He spoke in generalities: about Islam overwhelming the world and overcoming US oppression, unity among Muslims, how the caliphate will be established once people adhere to proper religious ways. He hardly commented on local issues, and when I asked him about the conflict, he argued that 'the Israeli occupation is a secondary issue', as the Prophet Muhammad said that Muslims must first spread the word and then everything else will follow.[69]

Nevertheless, for all their physical or ideological isolation, clandestine mode of existence and operation and their hard-line interpretation of Islam, members of Hizb ut Tahrir have not turned to terrorism or violence. In fact, the group has consistently advocated non-violent methods in achieving its objectives.[70] In my conversation with him in London in January 2009, former Hizb ut Tahrir activist Ghaffar Hussain argued that the organisation does not reject violence in principle but for the pragmatic reason that it is ineffective and that, what is more, its hard-line views indirectly but surely encourage violence. For these two reasons, according to Hussain, it is inaccurate to describe them as a non-violent organisation.[71] This view cannot be dismissed lightly because there is often no clear line separating overt from covert violence. However, the fact remains that Hizb ut Tahrir – on a formal but significant level – have consistently claimed they are a non-violent organisation, and it has never been proven that they have used terrorist violence in the pursuit of their objectives.[72]

Conclusion

Repression and the lack of political participation due to a rootless existence which was linked to a transnational mode of operation are

---

[69] Author's interview with Hizb ut Tahrir activist (anonymous), West Bank, October 2007.

[70] Khamidov, *Countering the Call*, p. iv.

[71] Hussain interview.

[72] See, for example, their official website, http://www.hizb.org.uk/hizb/who-is-ht/our-method/our-method.html, accessed 13 July 2009.

important explanations of al Qaeda's adoption of terrorist tactics. In the case of Hizb ut Tahrir, analogous conditions do not produce the same result. To understand the reasons behind transnational Islamist terrorism as exemplified by al Qaeda, we have to move away from an exclusive or primary emphasis on political explanations. I argued in Chapter 1 that although ideas, and in particular a hard-line interpretation of Islam, may justify Islamist terrorism, they are not *in themselves* the cause of it, and that focusing on structural factors – socio-economic, political and strategic/instrumental – is analytically more rewarding. If, out of these three, political explanations are not the key to understanding transnational Islamist terrorism as exemplified by al Qaeda, how do we assess the relevance of socio-economic and strategic/instrumental factors?

Socio-economic explanations of transnational Islamist terrorism and in particular of the al Qaeda phenomenon, such as poverty, absolute and relative deprivation and social alienation, are extremely popular and widely espoused, both in academia and in public debate.[73] According to this line of argument, the impasse and desperation created by the many failures of development in the Middle East are fertile ground for al Qaeda's message to take root. They have driven particular individuals, especially the young, to join al Qaeda and resort to terrorist acts. There are numerous instances of such analysis. In typical language, one of the suicide bombers of the al Qaeda in the Islamic Maghreb attack on the UN building in Algiers in 2007, Larbi Charef, originally from a poor neighbourhood of Algiers and a former convict, was described as a 'textbook example of a militant Islamist in a volatile region', where 'poverty is the soil, and prison the fertilizer' for terrorist acts.[74]

But Charef's case is the exception. As a rule, socio-economic background is not causally linked to the adoption of terrorism by al Qaeda in any consistent manner. Economic trends are poor indicators of the extremist interpretations of Islam which provide the necessary if not sufficient conditions for Islamist terrorism. Wealth does not inoculate against such extremist interpretations and, conversely, poverty, or a declining economy, do not generate them.[75] It can be readily observed – not just in the

[73] Ivan Manokha, 'Al-Qaeda Terrorism and Global Poverty: New Social Banditry, *Journal of Global Ethics*, 4 (2) 2008, pp. 95–105; Alan Richards, *Socio-Economic Roots of Radicalism?: Towards Explaining the Appeal of Islamic Radicals*, Carlisle, PA: Strategic Studies Institute, Army War College, 2003.

[74] Katrin Bennhold, 'Poverty in the Streets of Algiers, Breeding Ground for Terrorism', *International Herald Tribune*, 13 November 2007.

[75] Daniel Pipes, 'God and Mammon: Does Poverty Cause Militant Islam?', *The National Interest*, 66, Winter 2001/02.

attacks of 11 September 2001 but other terrorist incidents as well – that Islamist terrorists are often university-educated individuals of middle-class backgrounds. The stories of individuals affiliated with al Qaeda, told in this chapter, such as Osama Bin Laden, Ayman al Zawahiri, Abu Mus'ab al Suri and Mohamed Atta, confirm this. The majority of al Qaeda operatives cannot be classified as poor or downtrodden and, when they are, they tend to be the 'foot soldiers' in operations guided by those in higher echelons.[76] The profile of the al Qaeda terrorist is 'skewed more towards that of educated young men exposed to the West than towards that of impoverished, uneducated youth living in the Middle East'.[77] Rather than appealing to the working-class poor, Osama Bin Laden's audience is the middle class and in particular the middle class of Saudi Arabia – who since the 1980s increasingly feel aggrieved for not getting a good deal from the Saudi state.[78] Transnational Islamist terrorism appeals to the intelligentsia, professionals and university students.[79] Far from being an antidote to transnational terrorism of the al Qaeda type, a certain level of education, sophistication and income are, more often than not, positively associated with it.

Are strategic/instrumental explanations more convincing? Is al Qaeda's adoption of terrorist tactics the result of a rational calculation about their effectiveness? I would argue that the evidence supporting this view is stronger. We can glean from the analysis of al Qaeda in this chapter that its leadership has made a calculation that terrorism 'works'. Like all terrorist actors, al Qaeda crucially depends on the high visibility of its acts to get its message across – what Bakunin, in a different context, called the 'propaganda of the deed'.[80] For Robert Pape, al Qaeda's

[76] See for example the story of Khalfan Khamis Mohamed, a native of Tanzania, who was involved in the Dar es Salaam bombing. Of modest and deprived background, with little formal education, Mohamed was one of many 'dispensable young men' recruited to act only in the implementation phase of an attack'. Jessica Stern, *Terror in the Name of God: Why Religious Militants Kill*, New York: HarperCollins, 2003, p. 248.

[77] Karen J. Greenberg (ed.), *Al Qaeda Now: Understanding Today's Terrorists*, Cambridge: Cambridge University Press, 2005, p. xii.

[78] Denis McAuley, 'The Ideology of Osama Bin Laden: Nation, Tribe and World Economy', *Journal of Political Ideologies*, 10 (3) October 2005, pp. 281–2.

[79] Gerges, *The Far Enemy*, p. 219. One of the conclusions of a study of foreign fighters in Iraq conducted by Hewitt and Kelley-Moore is that 'nations with higher rates of literacy, longer life expectancies, and a higher standard of living have higher rates of jihadism'. Christopher Hewitt and Jessica Kelley-Moore, 'Foreign Fighters in Iraq: A Cross-National Analysis of Jihadism', *Terrorism and Political Violence*, 21 (2) 2009, p. 218.

[80] 'All of us must now embark on stormy revolutionary seas and from this very moment we must spread our principles, not with words *but with deeds for this is the most*

suicide terrorism follows a pattern similar to other suicide terrorist campaigns in the period 1980–2001 which were driven primarily by nationalist objectives (in this case the liberation of Mecca and Medina, and other Muslim lands, from Western occupation).[81] Similarly to those other cases, for example in Sri Lanka, Chechnya and Kashmir, al Qaeda's terrorist campaigns have targeted democratic governments, in the expectation that their publics will pressure them to succumb to the terrorists' demands. Other analysts share this approach to al Qaeda's 'strategy'.[82] Al Qaeda has failed to achieve unity among Muslims, install the caliphate or liberate subjugated fellow Muslims. It received a massive blow in operational terms after 11 September 2001. The cost of its actions to the Muslim world has been high and may be even higher in the long term. However, Bin Laden's many spectacular successes – removing US forces from Saudi Arabia, provoking an American response of massive proportions in Afghanistan and Iraq, exaggerating the 'terrorism' threat and becoming a household name across the globe – lend credence to the view that he has opted for the cruellest tactics in the expectation that they would deliver superlative results.

---

popular, the most potent, and the most irresistible form of propaganda.' Michael Bakunin, 'Letters to a Frenchman on the Present Crisis', Sam Dolgoff (ed. and trans.), *Bakunin on Anarchism*, Montreal: Black Rose Books, 1980, pp. 195–6.

[81] Robert A. Pape, 'The Strategic Logic of Suicide Terrorism', *American Political Science Review*, 97 (3) August 2003. A similar approach to suicide bombing more generally is taken by Ehud Sprinzak, 'Rational Fanatics', *Foreign Policy*, 120, September–October 2000. For Michael Mann, Bin Laden's ideology is 'deeply anti-imperialist'. Michael Mann, *Incoherent Empire*, London: Verso, 2003, p. 114.

[82] See, for example, Audrey Kurth Cronin, *Ending Terrorism: Lessons for Defeating al-Qaeda*, Adelphi Paper 394, Abingdon, Oxon: Routledge for the International Institute for Strategic Studies, 2008; and Brynjar Lia and Thomas Hegghammer, 'Jihadi Strategic Studies: The Alleged al Qaida Policy Study Preceding the Madrid Bombings', *Studies in Conflict and Terrorism*, 27 (5) September–October 2004.

3

Islamist Terrorism and National Liberation: Hamas and Hizbullah

Associating Islamism and Islamist terrorism with national liberation, as I do in this chapter, is controversial. The rejection of nationalism and the nation-state and the positing of the *umma* – the community of believers – as the primary object of identity is one of the great unifying themes of Islamism. If one focuses solely on the anti-nationalist discourse of Islamist movements, describing any of them, including the two case studies in this chapter, Hamas (Harakat al Muqawama al Islamiyya, Islamic Resistance Movement) and Hizbullah (Party of God), as nationalist, will appear contradictory. However, I argue that Islamist movements are political entities and, as such, employ and interpret doctrines and beliefs in a flexible and inventive manner. Islamist ideology is not inherently and necessarily opposed to any set of ideas, including nationalism, but dynamically interacts with them.

Undoubtedly, Hamas's call to *jihad* has been cast in nationalist hues and 'customised' to the specific Palestinian milieu.[1] The organisation has tried to overcome the apparent incompatibility between Islamism and the nation-state by arguing that the territory of Palestine is holy; for instance, Article 11 of the Hamas Charter states that: 'The Islamic Resistance Movement believes that the land of Palestine is an Islamic land entrusted to the Muslim generations until Judgement Day. No one may renounce all or even part of it.' Article 12 further asserts: 'Nationalism from the point of view of the Islamic Resistance Movement is part and parcel of religious

---

[1] Beverley Milton-Edwards, *Islamic Politics in Palestine*, London: I. B. Tauris, 1996, p. 191.

ideology.'[2] The case of Hizbullah is more contentious because its claim to represent the interests of Lebanon's Shia community, within Lebanon's confessional system, is in permanent tension with both Lebanese nationalism and the movement's own pan-Islamist aspirations, particularly as expressed in the movement's Open Letter of 1985.[3] Be that as it may, Hizbullah has also used a conventional nationalist discourse by casting its objective of securing Israel's withdrawal from Southern Lebanon (attained in 2000) in terms of protecting Lebanon's territorial integrity. It has also supported Palestinian nationalism, albeit in the context of pan-Islamic solidarity in a wider struggle against Israel and the West.

Similarly to other such movements across history, Islamists engaged in national liberation struggles aim to galvanise and control 'the people' and achieve political power on the basis of their own ideological blueprint for the ideal society, either in conjunction with winning the war against the outside oppressor or as an aim in itself. Trying to distinguish which of the two aims takes precedence – the struggle against the occupier or winning political power to establish the 'ideal society' – can be a futile exercise. The Hamas case demonstrates this most clearly: Its declared objective is to liberate Palestine and turn it into an Islamic state, but which comes first remains disputed. Hizbullah's ambition of establishing an Islamic state in Lebanon eventually foundered on the country's confessional rifts. Its objective of fighting Israel and the West was pursued concurrently with protecting the interests of Lebanon's Shia community and promoting the movement's political power in the context of the Lebanese state.

[2] The Hamas Charter, Khaled Hroub, *Hamas: Political Thought and Practice*, Washington, DC: Institute for Palestine Studies, 2002, Appendix 2, pp. 273 and 274. Another interesting formulation of the relationship between Islamism and Palestinian nationalism is contained in the 'Memorandum prepared by Hamas Political Bureau in the last 1990s at the request of Western diplomats in the Jordanian capital Amman': 'The Islamic Resistance Movement (Hamas) is a Palestinian national liberation movement that struggles for the liberation of the Palestinian occupied territories and for the recognition of Palestinian legitimate rights.'; quoted in Azzam Tamimi, *Hamas: Unwritten Chapters*, London: Hurst & Co., 2007, Appendix 1, p. 247. See also Andrea Nüsse, 'The Ideology of Hamas: Palestinian Islamic Fundamentalist Thought on the Jews, Israel and Islam', Ronald Nettler (ed.), *Studies in Muslim-Jewish Relations*, Chur: Harwood Academic Publishers, 1993, p. 108.

[3] 'The text of the Open Letter addressed by Hizbullah to the oppressed in Lebanon and the world', Joseph Elie Alagha, *The Shifts in Hizbullah's Ideology: Religious Ideology, Political Ideology, and Political Programme*, Leiden: Amsterdam University Press, International Institute for the Study of Islam in the Modern World, (ISIM) Dissertations, 2006, Appendix B, pp. 223–38.

Islamist movements engaged in national liberation struggles are also typical of the wider phenomenon of national liberation in adopting violence and claiming to be engaged in a *war* against their oppressors. My aim is not to pass judgement on whether Hamas and Hizbullah's claims to be at war with Israel at any given time were legitimate. Nevertheless, some such judgements will become inevitable because, depending on whether a state of war or peace exists, I define the targeting of civilians either as a violation of non-combatant immunity or as terrorism. There is a very fine, arguably even a false, line between the two, but I will attempt to maintain my focus on the latter, terrorism, as it is the subject of this study. Therefore, I will exclude, for instance, consideration of the targeting of civilians by Hizbullah in its confrontation with Israel until 2000 and again in the war of 2006: In both cases, full-scale military action was undertaken by both sides, so the targeting of civilians falls under the category of violating the principle of non-combatant immunity. For similar reasons, I will also exclude consideration of Hamas's exchange of missile fire with Israel from Gaza.

My task in this chapter is to investigate whether repression and political exclusion were causal factors in the adoption of terrorist methods by Hamas and Hizbullah. The chapter explores the two case studies in sequence. It tracks Hamas's history since its inception in 1988 to demonstrate that repression and political exclusion have *not* been the key factors behind Hamas's use of terrorist tactics, although repression may have played a limited role in their escalation at various points. The partial inclusion of Hamas in Palestinian political processes in the 1990s and 2000s, truncated though these may have been, has led to moderation in its social and political ideological positions but not the abandonment of terrorist methods whose threat continues to be latent against the 'outsider', Israel. My argument on Hizbullah is more intricate. Hizbullah was indisputably a terrorist organisation in the first decade of its existence but largely abandoned terrorist (but not other violent) methods after the 1990s. My analysis of Hizbullah's early history will demonstrate that the oppression experienced by the Shia community in Lebanon, in the context of Lebanon's history and civil war, plus intervention by Israel and Western powers, was one element leading to the adoption and use of terrorist tactics. Political participation after 1992 was indirectly linked to the abandonment of terrorism. Given the limited explanatory power of repression and political exclusion, the chapter's conclusion will highlight alternative strategic/instrumental explanations of Hamas and Hizbullah's use of terrorist methods.

Hamas

The Muslim Brotherhood and the Emergence of Hamas in the First Intifada

Despite an attempt to trace Hamas' origins to the radical anti-colonial Islamist Sheikh Izz ad Din al Qassam (1882–1935), the stance of the Muslim Brotherhood, Hamas's precursor which dominated Islamist politics in Palestine until the 1980s, was non-violent and even apolitical. The Egyptian Muslim Brotherhood, which was set up in 1928, sent emissaries in 1945 to establish new branches in the towns of Jerusalem, Nablus, Gaza and Haifa.[4] The incorporation of the West Bank into Jordan between 1948 and 1967 meant that the Muslim Brotherhood was amalgamated with the Jordanian branch of the movement and flourished as a result. In the Gaza Strip, by contrast, the Brotherhood languished alongside the Egyptian branch due to the harsh repression meted out by Nasser in the 1950s and 1960s.

That situation was profoundly transformed by Israel's occupation of the West Bank and Gaza Strip in 1967. Palestinian politics after the 1960s was dominated by the Palestine Liberation Organisation (PLO), an umbrella structure for more than ten nationalist groups whose strategy was one of Palestinian liberation through armed struggle and the support of *fedayeen* (guerrilla) forces. In the years following the 1967 occupation, the Palestinian national movement shifted towards political violence and terrorism,[5] but the Muslim Brotherhood did not go down that path. The West Bank section, despite being now physically separated from the Jordanian Muslim Brotherhood, continued to toe the latter's line and remained staunchly pro-Hashemite, ignoring the 'stirrings of Palestinian nationalism' and relinquishing the role of nationalist 'vanguard' to secular left-wing groups.[6] Jordan did not permit cross-border violence against Israeli targets and so no tradition of armed militancy against Israel formed in the West Bank. Whereas Muslim Brothers in the West Bank continued to look to their

---

[4] Ziad Abu-Amr, *Islamic Fundamentalism in the West Bank and Gaza: Muslim Brotherhood and Islamic Jihad*, Bloomington: Indiana University Press, 1994, p. 3.

[5] Yezid Sayigh, *Armed Struggle and the Search for State: The Palestinian National Movement, 1949–1993*, Oxford: Clarendon Press, 1997, Part II, see esp. pp. 306–12.

[6] Milton-Edwards, *Islamic Politics*, pp. 76 and 93. Milton-Edwards's general argument is that the rise of Islamism in Palestine cannot be dated from the defeat of 1967, as is typically the case for other Islamist movements in the Arab world, but occurred later.

colleagues in Jordan, their Gazan counterparts remained generally independent of outside ties.[7] Even so, Muslim Brothers in Gaza played no part in resisting the Israeli occupation in its first decade and did not join the growing trend towards armed struggle. Instead, they focused on social and cultural activities. By the early 1970s, the leader of the Gaza section, Sheikh Ahmad Yassin, had attracted a small band of followers and in 1973 formed a welfare- and charity-based society called the Mujama (Islamic Congress) which organised a network of welfare and education services. The second decade of occupation (1977–87) saw the expansion of the Mujama's social, educational and cultural activities. It also engaged in the policing of 'morals' – by physically attacking, for instance, cafes, video shops and liquor stores – in the Gaza strip. The Muslim Brotherhood in the West Bank also attracted a new generation of supporters. As in Gaza, the activities of the Brotherhood in the West Bank were facilitated by the Israeli authorities, who acquiesced to their activities to counter-balance the secular Palestinian nationalists.[8]

If the Muslim Brotherhood eschewed politics and the armed struggle in favour of a gradualist, reformist approach primarily through its peaceful social and religious activism, Hamas, by contrast, was created with explicitly political objectives which included, from the start, the possibility of armed struggle (if not, necessarily, the use of terrorism).[9] Hamas's establishment was driven by a younger, more activist generation of leaders who broke with the old elite along ideological and class lines, and challenged the Brotherhood's twin policy of avoiding confrontation with Israel and gradual Islamisation.[10] Hamas's creation in

---

[7] Glen E. Robinson, 'Hamas as Social Movement', Quintan Wiktorowicz (ed.), *Islamic Activism: A Social Movement Theory Approach*, Bloomington: Indiana University Press, 2004, p. 120.

[8] Milton-Edwards, *Islamic Politics*, pp. 100–1 and 103–16. For the early history of the Islamist movement, see also Abu-Amr, *Islamic Fundamentalism in the West Bank and Gaza*, chapters 1 and 2.

[9] There is an ongoing debate on the relationship between the political and military functions of Hamas at the time of its creation and throughout its history. This debate, which is highly ideologically charged, centres on two important questions, first whether Hamas is primarily a political or military organisation and, second, which of the two sections of the movement – the political or military – dominates the other. Matthew Levitt, *Hamas: Politics, Charity, and Terrorism in the Service of Jihad*, New Haven, CT and London: Yale University Press, 2007, argues that the political and military wings are inextricably linked. By contrast, Jeroen Gunning maintains that Hamas is, at its core, a political movement: Jeroen Gunning, 'Peace with Hamas? The Transforming Potential of Political Participation', *International Affairs*, 80 (2) 2004, p. 236.

[10] Robinson, 'Hamas as a Social Movement', pp. 120–5.

February 1988 was precipitated by the outbreak of the first Intifada in the Occupied Palestinian Territories in December of the previous year. Contrary to its own claims, Hamas did not generate the Intifada, but it benefited most from it, especially in terms of gaining popular appeal.

Hamas's rejectionist stance towards negotiating with Israel became apparent when it condemned the PLO's acceptance of UN Security Council resolutions 181, 242 and 338 and attacked its Declaration of Palestinian Independence issued in November 1988. Hamas's targeting of Israeli soldiers increased by the second year of the Intifada and was accompanied by knife attacks on civilians and the burning of forests in Israel proper. Some of these knife attacks had no organisational link to Hamas, even though it presented them as a manifestation of Islamic devotion. By 1989, the Israeli-Hamas relationship took a turn for the worse. Israel declared Hamas a terrorist organisation and outlawed it in June of that year.[11] However, in the first few years of the Intifada, Hamas's use of terrorist methods was very limited. For the most part it targeted soldiers and took part in civil disobedience activities which included demonstrations, stone throwing, strikes, writing slogans and directives on walls and blocking roads. This was despite the severe repression by the Israeli occupation authorities during that time. Hamas's senior leaders were rounded up and detained in September 1988 and many of its members were henceforth arrested and deported. Administrative detention and mass arrests were used more broadly, as were curfews and punitive economic measures.[12]

Terrorism and the Oslo Peace Process

In contrast to its record in the first few years of the Intifada, from 1991, Hamas increasingly began to engage in terrorist activities. Even in the context of an overall rise in the level of violence during that time, Hamas's targeting of both Israeli military and civilians, and its use of firearms, increased and exceeded in volume and frequency similar tactics undertaken by other factions. For this purpose (and also to target Palestinian 'collaborators'), a special unit was created in 1991, the Izz al Din al Qassam Brigades.[13] In December 1992, Israel deported 415 Islamic activists to Lebanon where they learned the technical skills and

---

[11] Shaul Mishal and Avraham Sela, *The Palestinian Hamas: Vision, Violence and Coexistence*, New York: Columbia University Press, 2000, pp. 56–7.

[12] Don Peretz, *Intifada: The Palestinian Uprising*, Boulder, CO: Westview Press, 1990; Mishal and Sela, *The Palestinian Hamas*, pp. 55–64.

[13] Abu-Amr, *Islamic Fundamentalism in the West Bank and Gaza*, p. 67.

efficacy of suicide bombing from Hizbullah. Car and suicide bombs came into use, from 1992 and 1993 respectively, and in April 1993, an al Qassam booby-trapped car exploded between two buses in the Jordan Rift Valley (without causing casualties, however, because the passengers had already disembarked).[14]

Israeli repression, by exacting a mounting toll, may have played a role in the escalation of Hamas's military activity and gradual shift towards terrorism in the post-1991 period. For instance, the creation of the al Qassam Brigades was partly in response to an Israeli crackdown in late 1990 and early 1991. The spectre of peace was also a factor because it threatened the continuation of the armed struggle which Hamas saw as the main source of its political legitimacy. An international peace conference – the first formal public negotiation between Israel and a Palestinian delegation from the West Bank and Gaza Strip – took place in Madrid in late 1991. Hamas's shift towards terrorist violence accelerated when the signing of the Declaration of Principles of September 1993, informally known as the Oslo Accords, superseded the Madrid talks and initiated the Oslo peace process between Israel and the Palestinians.

Oslo changed Hamas's strategic situation. Hamas's military activity against Israel by that time far outweighed that of Fatah and other Palestinian movements, so Oslo presented it with no less than an existential threat.[15] Hamas publicly rejected the Oslo Accords and formed the Palestinian Forces Alliance with those secular and leftist organisations which also opposed it. However, after the Israeli army withdrew from Gaza and the Jericho area in May 1994, an internal debate occurred within Hamas about whether to participate in the emerging Palestinian Authority (PA) structures. The establishment of the PA in June 1994 was a direct outcome of the Accords and was accepted by Hamas.[16] Although Hamas was in competition with the PLO and later the PA over the Accords, it wanted to keep the channels of communication with them open and prevent civil war.[17] It did not turn its weapons against the PA, organise demonstrations or resort to the assassination of its officials.[18] For a while, Hamas tried to strike an uneasy balance between avoiding open confrontation with the PA and continuing the anti-Israeli armed

[14] Mishal and Sela, *Palestinian Hamas*, pp. 65–6.
[15] Ibid., pp. 66–7.
[16] Menachem Klein, 'Hamas in Power', *Middle East Journal*, 61(3) 2007, p. 444.
[17] Klein, 'Competing Brothers: The Web of Hamas-PLO Relations', *Terrorism and Political Violence*, 8 (2) 1996, pp. 115–23.
[18] Hroub, *Hamas: Political Thought and Practice*, pp. 62–3.

struggle, but by the time of Oslo, most Palestinians in the occupied territories supported negotiations with Israel. Hamas thus increasingly found
itself in a minority position.

In the first few months after the signing of Oslo, Hamas escalated
attacks against Israeli soldiers and civilians alike. Attacks were carried
out against civilian buses in Hadera and Afula (both in April 1994), Tel
Aviv (October 1994), attacks against soldiers in Jerusalem (December
1994) and the Beit Lid junction (January 1995).[19] In my conversation with
him in Jerusalem in October 2007, Israeli analyst Hillel Cohen described
how individuals within Hamas, whom he knew personally and who
had hitherto opposed terrorist methods, gradually changed their minds
about them.[20] The shift in Hamas's tactics was precipitated by Baruch
Goldstein's massacre of twenty-nine Palestinian worshippers at the cave
of the Patriarchs, in Hebron, in February 1994. Goldstein's actions were
not seen as the work of an individual acting alone but rather as directed
by Israeli agents. (In my visit to the cave, some thirteen odd years after
the event, a local Palestinian 'guide' reinforced the point that this was
not the isolated act of a disturbed individual; he hovered around me,
constantly repeating the phrase 'Goldstein doctor, not crazy'). Hamas
perpetrated an average of three terrorist attacks per year until the terrorist violence declined at the end of the 1990s.

Hamas activists argued that the use of terrorism was a direct response
to Israeli repression. For instance, Khaled Dwaib, a long-standing member of Hamas whom I interviewed in Bethlehem during the same visit
to the West Bank (October 2007), claimed that killing civilians was not
a preferred Hamas strategy but that it was undertaken in response to
Israel's targeting of civilians and tremendous loss of Palestinian lives.[21]
There is some evidence that Hamas responded to repression by employing terrorist methods. For example, the attack in Afula and subsequent
attacks led to Israel's closure of the Occupied Palestinian Territories.
Israel's assassination of al Qassam Brigades bomb-maker Yahya Ayyash
in January 1996 triggered a spate of suicide bombings in Israel proper.
Collaborating with Israeli intelligence services, the PA also subjected
Hamas to repressive measures. Under Israeli pressure, following the Beit
Lid attack in January 1995, Yassir Arafat, Chairman of the PLO, President

---

[19] Mishal and Sela, *Palestinian Hamas*, p. 67; Klein, 'Competing Brothers', p. 124.
[20] Author's interview with Hillel Cohen, author and expert on Islamist movements, Hebrew University of Jerusalem, Jerusalem, October 2007.
[21] Author's interview with Khaled Dwaib, Hamas activist and Palestinian Legislative Council member, Bethlehem, West Bank, October 2007.

of the Palestinian National Authority and Chairman of Fatah, moved against Hamas and after April 1995 intensified his efforts against it.[22] Intermittently, during the mid- to late-1990s, hundreds of al Qassam Brigades and Hamas supporters were arrested by the PA; many were tortured or otherwise ill-treated and imprisoned after unfair trials or held for prolonged periods without charge or trial.[23] Such repression may have caused an *escalation* in Hamas's use of terrorism but it was not the main cause behind the movement's shift in that direction.

Nor did political exclusion during the Oslo years push Hamas to adopt terrorist tactics, despite appearances to the contrary. The Palestinian legislative elections of January 1996 were an important outcome of the Oslo Accords and were seen as a means of cementing and advancing peace between Israel and the Palestinians. Hamas did not participate in the electoral process and *increased* terrorist attacks in the two subsequent months carrying out four terrorist attacks between 25 February and 4 March 1996, and killing seventy people.[24] However, as I will show, there is no 'cause and effect' – political exclusion followed by terrorism – in this instance.

In our discussion during my visit to the West Bank in October 2007, a former member of Islamic Jihad, who will remain anonymous, reiterated the point that Hamas hailed from the Muslim Brotherhood, whose strategy of gradual reform sometimes entailed participating in electoral processes within their respective societies.[25] Such gradualism was apparent in Hamas's participation in various electoral processes within the Palestinian context in the years leading up to Oslo. Starting from the year 1976, Hamas had participated in professional, labour and student union elections, the main arena of electoral contestation in the Occupied Palestinian Territories.[26] Hamas had embraced coalition politics in

---

[22] Klein, 'Competing Brothers', pp. 125–6.

[23] Amnesty International, *Occupied Palestinian Territories Torn apart by Factional Strife*, MDE 21/02/2007, 24 October 2007, http://www.amnesty.org/en/library/asset/MDE21/020/2007/en/642b5fe4-d363-11dd-a329-2f46302a8cc6/mde210202007en.pdf, accessed 15 December 2009. The campaign was led by Muhammad Dahlan, head of the notorious Preventive Security Service in Gaza, where detainees were routinely tortured and some died as a result (note 46). By the summer of 1999, Arafat had neutralised the al Qassam Brigades as an effective military force. Mia Bloom, *Dying to Kill: The Allure of Suicide Terror*, New York: Columbia University Press, 2005, p. 25.

[24] Klein, 'Competing Brothers', p. 129.

[25] Author's interview with anonymous former Islamic Jihad activist, West Bank, October 2007.

[26] Jeroen Gunning, *Hamas in Politics: Democracy, Religion, Violence*, London: Hurst, 2007, p. 144.

numerous professional and student bodies. It collaborated with its ideological rivals. Tentative cooperation between some Islamist women and
leftist feminist groups was established.[27] Hamas formed alliances with
the Palestinian left, for example, the Palestinian Front for the Liberation
of Palestine (PFLP) and the Democratic Front for the Liberation of
Palestine (DFLP), against Fatah.[28]

In the period leading up to the legislative elections of January 1996,
Hamas was clearly divided over the question of participation, with its
leader, Ahmed Yassin, appearing initially in favour under certain conditions. This internal debate settled against participation by November
1995, and Hamas announced it would boycott any forthcoming presidential and legislative elections. Even after that, there was some ambivalence. There had been an ongoing debate within Hamas since 1992 about
the benefits of establishing a political party, part and parcel of the wider
question of participating in elections. The National Islamic Salvation
Party was created in November 1995 and officially launched in March
1996. Although its leadership was connected to Hamas on an individual
basis, the party never had official links to Hamas.[29] Some Hamas members put themselves forward as independent candidates in the election
but their decision was presented as an individual one, not sanctioned by
the organisation. Despite the Hamas boycott, a great number of its own
supporters voted in the elections.[30]

Far from excluding Hamas from the elections, Israel and the United
States wanted it to participate. The PA urgently pressed Hamas to do so
in addition to giving up armed operations.[31] Reportedly, Arafat came
close to securing Hamas's participation in late 1995.[32] An informal
ceasefire was in place at the time between the PA and Hamas and it
permitted negotiations on Hamas's eventual participation in the polls.
Hamas suggested it was prepared to contest legislative elections if the
electoral system was changed from district constituencies to national

---

[27] Gunning, 'Peace with Hamas?', p. 247.
[28] Milton-Edwards, *Islamic Politics*, p. 197.
[29] Mishal and Sela, *The Palestinian Hamas*, pp. 140–6. The party did not come to much,
politically, after that point in time. On the National Islamic Salvation Party and internal
debates in Hamas, see Menachem Klein, 'Against the Consensus: Oppositionist Voices
in Hamas', *Middle Eastern Studies*, 45 (6) November 2009.
[30] Klein, 'Competing Brothers', p. 129.
[31] Hroub, *Hamas*, p. 228. On the internal debates on the elections during this phase, see
pp. 215–29.
[32] Alain Gresh and Dominique Vidal, *The New A-Z of the Middle East*, London: I. B.
Tauris, 2004, p. 109.

proportional representation. Arafat refused and the negotiations broke down. How serious Hamas was in these discussions is unclear. Hamas itself has since maintained that it was never prepared to contest elections under Oslo.

Hamas's limited participation, and the influence of a political environment marked by greater stability and competitiveness in the years prior to 1996, contributed towards ideological moderation and encouraged it to drop some of its absolutist demands regarding an Islamic state.[33] Very different issues were at stake in 1996. In contrast to the earlier student, professional association and municipal elections in which Hamas had participated, it decided not to take part in the 1996 general elections because they were seen as the legitimisation of the Oslo Accords and continuing Israeli occupation. Ultimately, Hamas was not excluded from the Palestinian political process but chose not to participate. This was not an inescapable choice: Other opponents of Oslo had opted to participate in the legislative elections.[34] It cannot therefore be said that political exclusion caused the movement's adoption and continuing use of terrorist methods.

The al Aqsa Intifada and the 2006 Legislative Elections

Popular support for Hamas in the post-Oslo era declined.[35] In response, Hamas reduced its calls for political or military action against the occupation and shifted its attention to social work and religious activities. However, support for Hamas started to climb, albeit incrementally, after the failure of the Camp David negotiations in July 2000[36] and the outbreak of the al Aqsa Intifada in September of the same year (named after Ariel Sharon's visit to the Haram al Sharif and the al Aqsa Mosque, which sparked the uprising). The al Aqsa Intifada involved a variety of methods, some similar to the first Intifada; it also included both strikes against Israeli soldiers and terrorist attacks against civilians by Hamas

---

[33] Gunning, 'Peace with Hamas?', pp. 246–7.

[34] For example, Haidar Abdel Shafi, a prominent Palestinian figure in Gaza, sought and won election to the Palestinian Legislative Council in 1996 despite his opposition to the Oslo Accords. Cherif Ouazani, 'Mort d'un juste', *Jeune Afrique*, 2438, 30 Septembre–6 Octobre 2007.

[35] Milton-Edwards, *Islamic Politics*, p. 177, and Hroub, *Hamas*, p. 250. In an attempt to deflate international criticism following its suicide operations in February and March 1996, Hamas expressed 'regret' for the 'death of some innocent people' and described these fatalities as a common outcome in war: Hroub, *Hamas*, p. 246.

[36] Sara Roy, 'Hamas and the Transformation(s) of Political Islam in Palestine', *Current History*, 102 (660) January 2003, pp. 14–17.

as well as by other groups – mainly the al Aqsa Martyrs' Brigades, local clusters of armed activists most of whom were apparently affiliated with Fatah, but also Islamic Jihad and the Popular Front for the Liberation of Palestine (PFLP).[37] Initially, Hamas mounted only a few attacks inside Israel proper. This changed after Ariel Sharon took office in February 2001, vowing to bring security to his people 'within 100 days', and Hamas began a campaign of suicide bombings targeting civilians in Israel which became the uprising's signature and most lethal weapon.[38] Hamas's strategy increased its support among the Palestinian population, a two-thirds majority of whom came to believe 'that violence paid, and that it was contributing to achieving national rights in ways that negotiations could not'.[39] A culture of 'martyrdom' developed in which suicide bombing was seen as a legitimate act of personal sacrifice for a higher cause.[40]

As in the Oslo years, there is a link between repression and Hamas's use of terrorist methods during the al Aqsa Intifada – but it is tenuous and mostly explains their escalation, not their initial causation. Immediately after the confrontation started in September 2000, Israel applied excessive force, 'generating a cycle of violence that has been escalated at each stage'. Sharon's tough measures caused the mounting of terrorist acts, and Israel responded to these with massive retaliation, the 'targeted' assassination of militant leaders and building demolitions.[41] Its assault on Hamas after 2003 was unprecedented.[42] These repressive measures appeared to result, at least temporarily, in the *abandonment* of terrorism (though not necessarily the wider application of violence) and,

---

[37] Human Rights Watch, *Erased in a Moment: Suicide Bombing Attacks against Israeli Civilians*, New York: Human Rights Watch, October 2002, p. 77.

[38] Graham Usher, 'The New Hamas: Between Resistance and Participation', *Middle East Report Online*, 21 August 2005, http://www.merip.org/mero/mero082105.html, accessed 19 September 2005.

[39] Palestinian Center for Policy and Survey Research (PSR) polls 2001–4 quoted in Khalil Shikaki, *With Hamas in Power: Impact of Palestinian Domestic Developments on Options for the Peace Process*, Working Paper 1, February 2007, Brandeis University: Crown Center for Middle East Studies, p. 4.

[40] Author's interview with Mahdi F. Abdul Hadi, Chairman of the Palestinian Academic Society for the Study of International Affairs, Jerusalem, October 2007.

[41] Bloom, *Dying to Kill*, pp. 23 and 34. Yassin was assassinated in March 2004. Note, however, that many of Hamas's leaders operated from outside the Occupied Palestinian Territories. The leader of Hamas's Political Bureau, Khaled Mishal, moved to Damascus after his attempted assassination by Mossad agents in Amman in 1997. The intricacies of Hamas authority structures are interesting in themselves but not directly relevant to my argument.

[42] The military assault was coupled with political and financial sanctions by the PA. Usher, 'The New Hamas', pp. 3–4.

alongside the Israeli decision to withdraw from Gaza, were an important reason why in March 2005, Hamas agreed to a *tahdiya* (calm,
effectively a ceasefire).

Jeroen Gunning argues that an additional reason, for the *tahdiya* was
Fatah and the PA offering Hamas a political future through electoral
participation.[43] In the presidential election that took place in January
2005, following Arafat's death in November of the previous year, Hamas
refused to field candidates and called for their own members to boycott
the process.[44] However, Hamas participated and registered victories in
the first two rounds of municipal elections in December 2004 and May
2005. As Khaled Dwaib pointed out, Oslo was dead by that time, so
participating in elections was not seen as its legitimisation.[45] In response
to these successes, al Aqsa Martyrs' Brigades attacks disrupted the third
and fourth round in late 2005. The fifth and sixth rounds of municipal
elections never took place due to the increase in armed clashes between
Hamas and Fatah, following the former's success in the legislative elections.[46] Building on its successes in municipal elections and hoping to
take advantage of it growing popularity, but also as an insurance policy
against possible repression from the PA, Hamas decided to participate
in the legislative elections which had been postponed from July 2005 to
January 2006.[47] It won an unexpected and resounding victory in what
was widely acknowledged as a fair contest.

In the period leading up to the January 2006 elections, Hamas took
strides towards greater ideological moderation and pragmatism[48] (in
political if not always social issues[49]). Its local councillors, voted into

---

[43] Gunning, *Hamas in Politics*, pp. 232–3.

[44] The Palestinian Islamic Jihad (PIJ), and the leftist Democratic Front for the Liberation
of Palestine (DFLP) also announced a boycott. Note, however, that the three organisations called on their own members not to vote rather than a general boycott of the
election. International Crisis Group (ICG), *After Arafat? Challenges and Prospects*,
Middle East Briefing, 23 December 2004, p. 5, see also note 5.

[45] Interview with Dwaib.

[46] Amnesty International, *Occupied Palestinian Territories: Torn apart by Factional
Strife*, note 44.

[47] Klein, 'Hamas in Power', p. 446.

[48] Palestinian politics remains authoritarian in many ways and is clearly severely
constrained by Israeli occupation. But compared to most, if not all, of its Arab counterparts, the Palestinian political process is more vibrant and tolerant of political
diversity and free speech. Legislative and judicial authorities are relatively strong. This
has also influenced Hamas. ICG, *After Arafat?* p. 3; Nathan J. Brown, *Evaluating
Palestinian Reform*, Carnegie Paper 59, Carnegie Endowment for International Peace,
June 2005, pp. 3–5.

[49] Hamas's messages on social issues have been mixed. When vigilantes or self-styled
morality police surfaced, the movement was quick to characterise them as isolated

office in the 2004–5 municipal elections, appeared ideologically sub-
dued and very similar to their predecessors.[50] After attaining office in
January 2006, Hamas pledged to respect the Palestinian constitutional
and legal framework and appeared to subordinate its religious agenda
to the immediate tasks of establishing 'clean' government and ending
the chaos in the streets. Far from seeking the Islamisation of Palestinian
laws, Palestine's new leaders were hard pressed to identify any specific
legislative agenda, let alone an Islamic one.[51] This was partly due to the
fact that a Fatah and international boycott blocked Hamas from carrying out any effective legislative programme.[52] It may also have been due
to an underlying decision by Hamas to leave the contentious issue of an
Islamic state aside while the Israeli occupation continued.[53]

Did ideological moderation, however, affect Hamas's attitude to
terrorism? On the one hand, it is plausible that Hamas's ideological
transformation influenced its attitude to Israel and the occupation. Once
opposed to the peace process, Hamas publicly accepted – at least during
the period of political participation, 2004–5 – that it would negotiate
with the Jewish state.[54] Hamas seemed at least prepared to tolerate a
negotiated two-state solution to the Israeli-Palestinian conflict, albeit

and unauthorised aberrations. But women employed in Hamas municipalities were
uniformly veiled, though it is not clear if this was the result of an official directive
or informal pressure. International Crisis Group, *Enter Hamas: The Challenges of
Political Integration*, Middle East Report 49, 18 January 2006, pp. 13–14. In July
2005, the Hamas-controlled municipality in the West Bank town of Qalqilya, in coor-
dination with local religious leaders, cancelled a music festival because it offended con-
servative social mores – in the words of a Hamas member of the Palestinian Legislative
Council, Ayman Daraghmeh, such festivals 'contradict the purpose of our society'.
Author's interview with Ayman Daraghmeh, member of the Palestinian Legislative
Council, Ramallah, October 2007. On social and other ideological issues, see also
Khaled Hroub, 'A "New Hamas" through Its New Documents', *Journal of Palestine
Studies*, 35 (4) Summer 2006.

[50] ICG, *Enter Hamas*, pp. 10–13.
[51] Nathan J. Brown, *Living with Palestinian Democracy*, Carnegie Endowment for
International Peace, Policy Brief 46, June 2006, p. 4.
[52] Author's interview with Miriam Saleh, former Minister for Women's Affairs,
Ramallah, October 2007.
[53] According to Ahmad Hamad, Editor in Chief of al Risala, a weekly Hamas newspaper,
'the liberation of the Palestinian land from Israeli occupation is the most urgent and
important objective, taking priority over the contentious question of the "Islamic
state"'. Ghazi Ahmad Hamad, 'The Challenge for HAMAS-Establishing Transparency
and Accountability', unpublished document, courtesy of the Geneva Centre for the
Democratic Control of Armed Forces, Ramallah, West Bank, 2006, www.dcaf.ch/pub-
lications/kms/details.cfm?ord279=title&q279=hamas&lng=en&id=21665&nav1=4
p. 4, accessed 9 December 2009.
[54] Usher, 'The New Hamas'.

with more stringent conditions than the ones enunciated by the PLO.[55] In effect, it retained its revolutionary goals but put them on hold until the distant future.[56]

On the other hand, the presumed connections between political participation, ideological moderation and the renunciation of terrorism are much weaker than they appear at face value. Although it may have taken some pragmatic steps in that direction, Hamas has not renounced terrorism in principle or distinguished between terrorism and armed resistance. During the al Aqsa Intifada, there was no differentiation between those who died in legitimate armed struggle and those who died while indiscriminately killing civilians.[57] In the campaign leading up to the legislative elections of January 2006, Hamas, like most other parties, 'glorified the intifada and resistance (however vaguely defined)'.[58] Claiming that it had 'forced' Israel out of Gaza in August 2005, Hamas's record of violence, indistinguishable from terrorism, was central to its election campaign and – combined with Fatah's corruption – instrumental in its victory.[59] After the electoral victory, it refused to renounce terrorism, one of the preconditions for recognition by the international 'Quartet' (the United States, the European Union, Russia and the United Nations).[60] More recently – specifically in the context of Hamas's response to the

---

[55] ICG, *Enter Hamas*, p. 21.

[56] Klein, 'Hamas in Power', pp. 443–4.

[57] Human Rights Watch, *Erased in a Moment*, pp. 36–7.

[58] Nathan J. Brown, *Aftermath of the Hamas Tsunami*, Carnegie Endowment for International Peace, Web Commentary, 2 February 2006, http://www.carnegieendowment.org/publications/index.cfm?fa=view&id=17975&prog=zgp&proj=zdrl,zme&zoom_highlight=brown+hamas+tsunami, accessed 11 December 2009.

[59] Gunning, *Hamas in Politics*, pp. 175–6. Elections or not, Hamas declared that 'the struggle goes on'. In the words of the ICG, 'it is a safe assumption that for most Islamists integration [into the political process] is meant to complement armed struggle rather than replace it'. Indeed, around the time of the election, Hamas did not eschew attacking Israeli targets either by shooting missiles from Gaza into Israel or by perpetrating a number of attacks in the West Bank. Hamas argued that these acts are responses to Israeli attacks upon Palestinian population centres and particularly its cadres. But, seen from this perspective, it is equally noteworthy that a number of Israeli attacks, including assassinations, passed without a direct (or at least immediate) response. ICG, *Enter Hamas*, p. 6.

[60] In June 2007, a split occurred between Gaza and the West Bank, with Hamas and Fatah, respectively, assuming control in the two territories. Throughout these developments, the levels of violence remained high as persecution and 'punishment' was meted out between the two rivals who sought to suppress opposition in each territory. During my visit to the West Bank, I met a number of Hamas activists or sympathisers who claimed they lost their jobs or were prevented from finding employment. They also alleged that they were persecuted, imprisoned and tortured.

United Nations Report ('Goldstone Report') into Israel's incursion into Gaza in December 2008–January 2009 – Hamas appears to have taken some steps towards acknowledging that targeting civilians is wrong but this development still remains too contingent on Israel's response to constitute a formal renunciation.[61] In sum, although political participation around 2006 appears to have increased ideological moderation, this did not cause a clear break with terrorist tactics.

Hizbullah

Hizbullah Terrorism in the 1980s

Hizbullah emerged as a specifically Shia movement in the context of Lebanon's inter-confessional civil war (1975–90). The movement's inception can be dated to around 1982 or even before, but it was over the next three years that the various groups which eventually became Hizbullah coalesced into a coherent organisation.[62] The publication of Hizbullah's Open Letter marked the formal arrival of the movement in 1985.

Hizbullah was born out of a combination of factors internal and external to Lebanon. Its domestic roots were in the gradual politicisation of the Shia community in Lebanon from the 1950s onwards. This politicisation occurred in tandem with growing Shia migration from South Lebanon and the Bekaa valley to Beirut, accelerated by the impact of the Lebanese civil war. The war broke out in 1975 when the dysfunctional nature of the Lebanese political system, which remained unable to accommodate demographic change, subtly and perniciously combined with the influence of regional and global actors who used Lebanon to pursue their rival interests. The war brutalised all segments of Lebanese society, but the Shia were particularly affected because of their already weak political and social position. In this context of conflict and deprivation, Shia

---

[61] *Human Rights in Palestine and Other Occupied Arab Territories: Report of the United Nations Fact Finding Mission on the Gaza Conflict*, headed by Richard Goldstone, 23 September 2009, http://www2.ohchr.org/english/bodies/hrcouncil/docs/12session/A-HRC-12-48_ADVANCE1.pdf, accessed 16 August 2010. On Hamas's response to the report, which includes an acknowledgement that targeting civilians is wrong, see, for example, http://www.shalomlife.com/eng/4906/Special:%20Excerpts%20from%20Hamas'%20Official%20Response%20to%20Goldstone%20Report, accessed 16 August 2010.

[62] Magnus Ranstorp gives 1982 as the year of Hizbullah's creation, whereas Augustus Richard Norton dates it at 1985. Magnus Ranstorp, *Hizb'Allah in Lebanon: The Politics of the Western Hostage Crisis*, Basingstoke, Hampshire and London: Macmillan Press, 1997, pp. 25–6; Augustus Richard Norton, *Hezbollah: A Short History*, Princeton, NJ: Princeton University Press, 2007, p. 34.

political and social frustrations initially found a focal point in the person of Musa al Sadr who established the Amal militia in 1975. After al Sadr's 'disappearance' in mysterious circumstances in 1978 during a trip to Libya, Amal came under the leadership of Nabih Berri and became increasingly dominated by a Beirut-centred, secular, middle-class elite. Deeming that the original organisation had deviated excessively from al Sadr's populist line, Hussayn al Musawi split off to found Islamic Amal in 1982.[63] A key figure in the early years of Hizbullah's formation was Sheikh Muhammad Husayn Fadlallah.[64]

These internal Lebanese Shia developments combined with external influences in producing Hizbullah. The religious and cultural links between the Lebanese Shia and Iran have been long-standing, but the emergence of Hizbullah can be traced to the post-Iranian Revolution phase of this relationship. The Iranians played a direct military, political, religious and financial role in the birth of Hizbullah by providing the radical ideological message plus material and practical support, including military training. An Iranian hand was already behind al Musawi's schism.[65] Following the Israeli invasion of Lebanon in 1982 (which precipitated the split of Islamic Amal from Amal when Berri chose to participate in the National Salvation Committee established by President Elias Sarkis), Iranian intervention became much more direct, under the guidance of Iranian ambassador to Syria, Ali Akbar Mohtashemi. The Iranians were intent on helping the radical Shia to remake Lebanon in their own revolutionary image[66] and sent Revolutionary Guards to the Bekaa Valley to train Islamic cadres. Iran's role was crucial, therefore, in the creation of Hizbullah, not least in enabling a number of disparate groups, including Islamic Amal, to coalesce into an umbrella organisation which, in turn, merged into a single institutional framework by 1985.

In sum, when the Israeli invasion of Lebanon occurred in 1982, the circumstances were already propitious for the emergence of Hizbullah.

---

[63] International Crisis Group, *Old Games, New Rules: Conflict on the Israel-Lebanon Border*, Middle East Report 7, 18 November 2002, p. 3.

[64] Despite Fadlallah's important role in Hizbullah in its first years, he became increasingly dissociated from the movement after the death of Khomeini in 1989. Author's interview with Ahmed Beydoun, journalist, Beirut, September 2009.

[65] Author's interviews with Hazem Saghieh, journalist, Beirut, September 2009, and Wadah Charara, journalist and author on Hizbullah, Beirut, September 2009.

[66] H. E. Chehabi and Hassan I. Mneimneh, 'Five Centuries of Lebanese-Iranian Encounters', H. E. Chehabi (ed.), *Distant Relations: Five Centuries of Lebanese-Iranian Ties*, London: Centre for Lebanese Studies in Association with I. B. Tauris, 2005, pp. 35–6.

As with the previous Israeli intervention in 1978, the invasion had multiple causes but it was also partly a response to the growing Palestinian
presence in Lebanon following the Six Day War of 1967 and the PLO's
expulsion from Jordan in 1970. The Palestinians' abrasive and arrogant
attitude increasingly offended local sensibilities (one of my interviewees
in Beirut remembered, as a child, the PLO official who changed his car's
punctured tyre in the middle of the highway, stopping the traffic and
creating a long queue behind him). Palestinian-Lebanese relations were
becoming particularly fraught in South Lebanon to the extent that, when
the Israelis invaded in the summer of 1982, the local people welcomed
them, as the local expression goes, 'with rice and roses'. It soon became
clear, however, that the Israelis had not come as liberators, but as occupiers, and the feelings of the local population began to change. From
1982–3, a movement towards resisting the Israeli occupation emerged in
South Lebanon, although not, as yet, centrally directed. This movement
acquired greater momentum in October 1983, when the Israeli army's
violent disruption of the celebration of Ashura in Nabatiyeh provoked a
strong reaction by local people.[67]

In 1982–5, a wide range of groups, including leftists, comprised the
resistance to Israeli occupation. During those years, South Lebanon was
still dominated by Amal which was also clashing with the Palestinian
groups for control. Hizbullah was initially strongest in the Bekaa and only
arrived in the South in late 1983 (not, at first, to a warm welcome).[68] After
wrestling with Amal for control of the villages in the South – and because
of Amal's gradual loss of power and legitimacy due to internal weak-
nesses – Hizbullah emerged as the more powerful movement. Hizbullah
was able to use local leaders who were already resisting the Israelis as a
shortcut to establishing its own insurgent networks. By the late 1980s, it
dominated the resistance (which had not necessarily been created by it)
after sidelining Amal and the leftists. Hizbullah also moved to Beirut by
the late 1980s.[69] In this period, many members of Amal – though not those
at the very top who benefited from their proximity to Berri – moved to
Hizbullah, attracted by its pro-resistance, incorruptible image.[70]

[67] Hala Jaber, *Hezbollah: Born with a Vengeance*, New York: Columbia University
   Press, 1997, p. 18.
[68] Author's interview with Timur Göksel, former spokesperson for United Nations
   Interim Force In Lebanon (UNIFIL) and political analyst, Beirut, September 2009.
[69] Jaber, *Hezbollah*, p. 27. In battles between Hizbullah and Amal, parts of Beirut
   changed hands a few times. Interview with Beydoun.
[70] Author's interview with Oussama Safa, General Director, Lebanese Centre for Policy
   Studies, Beirut, September 2009.

In the second half of the 1980s, the conflict between Amal and Hizbullah developed into a proxy war between Syria and Iran. Despite an otherwise close relationship between Iran and Syria, Assad 'was not prepared to let his ally [Amal] lose ground to the new, Iranian-backed movement of Hezbollah'. Furthermore, a fundamental incongruity existed between Iran's keenness to establish an Islamic order in Lebanon and Syria's traditional divide-and-rule policy (plus, possibly, the Syrian Baath regime's secular orientation). In 1985–6, Amal – with Syrian blessing – attacked Palestinian camps to prevent the Palestinian forces from regaining control of them, and Hizbullah came to the Palestinians' aid.[71] Matters came to a head with the attempted assassination of Syria's strongman in Lebanon, Ghazi Kanaan in 1987. Kanaan, suspecting Hizbullah complicity, sent his soldiers to break up a Hizbullah meeting and had nineteen unarmed Hizbullahis lined up against the wall and shot.[72] Syria thus established a clear 'red line'. A new balance of power took shape out of these confrontations which demonstrated to Iran and Hizbullah that the only conduit in Lebanon for Hizbullah's success would be through Syria.

One can glean many hard-line elements in Hizbullah's worldview in the early 1980s. Depicting the Lebanese system and government as 'rotten' and corrupt to the core, the Open Letter of 1985 stated Hizbullah's aim to replace it with an Islamic state based on *sharia* law.[73] Uncompromising rhetoric was matched by intolerance of political and ideological rivals, especially among non-affiliated Shia who were 'retired', exiled and even killed.[74] Between 1985 and 1991, under Subhi al Tufayli's leadership, Hizbullah carried out an assertive process of Islamisation in the areas it controlled within Lebanon, though with varying levels of intensity and mixed success.[75]

---

[71] Jaber, *Hezbollah*, pp. 31–2.

[72] Interviews with Safa and Charara.

[73] 'The text of the Open Letter addressed by Hizbullah to the oppressed in Lebanon and the world', Alagha, *The Shifts in Hizbullah's Ideology*, Appendix B, pp. 229–30.

[74] Author's interview with Hani Fahs, Shia leader and commentator, Beirut, September 2009. See also Norton, *Hezbollah*, pp. 35–41. Others emphasise different aspects of Hizbullah's behaviour. Harik argues that, in the 1980s, it was 'never involved in meting out "punishment" to the Christian militias and had never kidnapped, car bombed or sniped at Lebanese civilians as most other militias had at one time or another': Judith Palmer Harik, *Hezbollah: The Changing Face of Terrorism*, London: I. B. Tauris, 2004, p. 67.

[75] International Crisis Group, *Hezbollah and the Lebanese Crisis*, Middle East Report 69, 10 October 2007, p. 18, note 155, and Harik, *Hezbollah*, p. 84. In South Lebanon, alcohol and parties, dancing and loud music were banned and coffee shops closed down. Generally, a strict code of social behaviour was imposed. On the other hand,

During its early history, Hizbullah (or what eventually became the organisation of that name) also became associated with a series of terrorist acts. In September 1981, the French ambassador to Beirut was killed and in March 1982, the French embassy in Beirut was bombed. In April and October 1983, respectively, the US embassy and French and US peacekeepers fell victim to suicide bombings with huge loss of life. In June 1985, TWA flight 847 to Beirut was hijacked. Finally, between 1982 and 1992, Hizbullah became linked to the holding of Western hostages in Lebanon.

Responsibility for all and any of these acts is still very much disputed. Some analysts question whether the 1983 attacks against the US and French peacekeepers can be called terrorist at all, arguing that they were a military act because these forces had begun to take sides in the Lebanese civil war.[76] Others dispute that any evidence directly links Hizbullah to these terrorist acts.[77] Some see Lebanon's Islamic Jihad – a separate movement, it is claimed, which was never part of Hizbullah's organisational structure – as responsible for several of these violent acts, including the 1983 bombings.[78] More plausibly, Islamic Jihad was a phantom organisation, a cover name for Hizbullah and a deliberate attempt to muddy the waters.[79] Hizbullah itself denies it was behind the 1983 attacks (although they applauded them) or the taking of Western hostages. It is often impossible to separate Hizbullah's responsibility from the role of Iran and Syria. For instance, Shia extremists, possibly belonging to the al Dawa group and sponsored by the Revolutionary Guards, were suspected of the 1981 and 1982 attacks. Iran and Syria were most probably also involved in the 1983 attacks against the US and French peacekeepers. They also played important roles in the taking of hostages (for which a total of seventeen different 'phantom' organisations claimed responsibility[80]). Whichever way responsibility is shared, the bottom line is that all the aforementioned terrorist acts in the 1980s can be linked to Hizbullah in some way or another. The link can be

---

Ahmed Beydoun argued that although there was a period Hizbullah tried to be strict with social mores in the Saida-Tyre area in the South, they did not fully succeed in imposing them. In Beirut, women were never really forbidden to go out uncovered, though social pressures ensured they did. Interview with Beydoun.

[76] This point was raised by Nicholas Blanford. Author's interview with Nicholas Blanford, journalist, Beirut, September 2009.
[77] Author's interview with Omayma Abdel Latif, journalist, Beirut, September 2009.
[78] ICG, *Old Games, New Rules*, p. 3.
[79] Ranstorp, *Hizb'Allah in Lebanon*, pp. 62–5.
[80] Jaber, *Hezbollah*, pp. 113.

established largely through the person of Imad Mughniyeh who headed the organisation's military apparatus. When I travelled to Lebanon in September 2009, two years after Mughniyeh's killing in Damascus by unknown assassins, his portrait was pasted all over South Lebanon and Beirut next to portraits of Hizbullah leaders – clearly this is a man with whom Hizbullah retains a proud association.

Can we attribute Hizbullah's use of terrorist methods in the 1980s to the repression and the political exclusion of the Shia community? In the years leading up to the outbreak of the Lebanese civil war, the Shia community within the Maronite-dominated Lebanese political system was undoubtedly politically marginalised, but the response to this marginalisation was Musa Sadr's Amal movement. Hizbullah emerged as Amal became co-opted by the Lebanese system of confessional horse-trading and patronage. It reasserted the rights of those Shia who felt excluded by Berri's secularised, Beirut-based elite. By that time, the Lebanese civil war was in full swing and its impact should not be underestimated: We can no longer speak of political exclusion by the Shia given that the entire political process was suspended. However, the clandestine and secretive mode of operation by Hizbullah during those years was arguably an important factor in their adoption of terrorist methods. Eminent Lebanese journalist and specialist on Hizbullah, Wadah Charara, maintained that the groups associated with Hizbullah were formed under anonymity, without social roots or reference points. For Charara, terrorism was the outcome of confusion, and confusion was inextricably linked to the lack of due democratic process.[81] According to former United Nations Interim Force In Lebanon (UNIFIL) spokesperson Timur Göksel: 'Until 1988, they [Hizbullah] were paranoid, very unkind to foreigners, too suspicious and secretive, impossible to talk to and communicate with and extremely, unrealistically fundamentalist.'[82]

The Trajectory of Terrorism and Violence in the 1990s and Beyond

The end of the Lebanese civil war in 1990, following the Taif Agreement, restored a modicum of peace to Lebanon, albeit under Syrian occupation. Firmly allied to Syria by that time, Hizbullah was, exceptionally among Lebanese militias, allowed to retain its arms, but during the 1990s, Hizbullah ceased being 'an Iranian-influenced conspiratorial terrorist

---

[81] Interview with Charara. He highlighted the role of outside powers, especially Syria, in stoking this confusion.

[82] Quoted in Jaber, *Hezbollah*, p. 30.

group'.[83] With the exception of the (disputed) attacks against Jewish targets in Argentina in 1992 and 1994, Hizbullah increasingly avoided actions that would allow it to be branded a terrorist organisation.[84] The organisation's discourse also reflected this shift in tactics: For instance, it condemned the murderous activities of the Groupe Islamique Armé (GIA) in Algeria in the 1990s and the killing of Western civilians by the Gamaa Islamiyya in Luxor in 1997.[85]

Not everyone accepts that Hizbullah has moved away from terrorism since the 1990s. It is on the US and Israeli government lists of terrorist organisations, and at the time of writing (2010), the UK government described its military wing as terrorist. The European Parliament passed a non-binding resolution in 2005 also describing it as a terrorist movement. A key reason for categorising Hizbullah as a terrorist organisation is its support for Palestinian Islamic Jihad[86] and Hamas, an organisation which has employed terrorist tactics as we saw from the earlier discussion. Hizbullah argues that the cause of Palestinian national liberation justifies the use of all available means by Hamas.[87] For Hizbullah's leader, Hassan Nasrallah, 'there are no citizens [*madaniyin*] in the Zionist entity [as] all of them are aggressors and participants in the onslaught against the [Palestinian] people'.[88] The outbreak of the al Aqsa Intifada in September 2000 gave Hizbullah a renewed purpose, following Israel's withdrawal from Southern Lebanon. Hizbullah provided both propaganda and, possibly, material support to Hamas and there was increasing evidence of Hizbullah supporting Palestinian operations in Israel and the Palestinian territories.[89] However, pro-Palestinian rhetoric and covert support for

---

[83] Norton, *Hezbollah*, p. 6.

[84] ICG, *Old Games, New Rules*, p. 20. Note that Hizbullah denied being behind the 1992 and 1994 attacks.

[85] Amal Saad-Ghorayeb, *Hizbu'llah: Politics and Religion*, London: Pluto Press, 2002, p. 101.

[86] On Hizbullah's links with Palestinian Islamic Jihad, see information provided by The Graduate Institute, Geneva, Transnational and Non-State Armed Groups, http://www.armed-groups.org/6/section.aspx/ViewGroup?id=69, accessed 16 August 2010.

[87] Saad-Ghorayeb, *Hizbu'llah*, p. 146: 'Hizbu'llah's conception of terrorism hinges on the essential goodness or badness of a cause'.

[88] ICG, *Old Games, New Rules*, pp. 14–15, Nasrallah cited in As-Safir, 15 December 2001. As we saw earlier in the chapter, in December 1992, Israel deported 415 Islamic activists to Lebanon where they learned the technical skills and efficacy of suicide bombing from Hizbullah.

[89] Hizbullah put its television station, *al Manar*, at the service of the Intifada and was alleged to have been involved in attempts to smuggle arms to the Palestinians on board the vessel *Karine A* from Jordan in January 2002. Eyal Zisser, 'The Return of Hizbullah', *Middle East Quarterly*, 9 (4) Fall 2002, http://www.meforum.org/499/the-return-of-hizbullah, accessed 20 July 2009.

Hamas has not been matched by overt action because direct military intervention by Hizbullah on the Palestinian front would have exposed it to severe Israeli retaliation.[90] Hassan Nasrallah carefully stressed that the job of liberating Palestine belongs to the Palestinians.[91] Hizbullah's support for Hamas does not in itself render it a terrorist organisation, although its refusal to differentiate between terrorism and legitimate violent methods of resistance is indicative that it is skirting the issue.

Over and beyond its support for Hamas, critics allege that Hizbullah is behind many other terrorist operations in Lebanon and across the globe, and that its violence, both at home and abroad, is no less effective and 'real' for being latent and indirect. The attacks in Argentina in 1992 and 1994 were mentioned already. More recently, it has been alleged that Mugniyeh played a role in the chaos of post-2003 Iraq and even that Hizbullah has meddled in the Gulf, for example in the Huthi rebellion in Yemen which has flared up intermittently since 2004. In the case of support for the Huthi rebellion (a rebellion which cannot simply be categorised as 'terrorist' in any case), a clearer line of responsibility can be traced to Tehran, though this is also questionable. Very few of these allegations are plausible. More seriously, however, Hizbullah may be implicated in the assassination of Rafiq Hariri in 2005 – although admittedly the responsibility of Hizbullah can be difficult to disentangle from that of Syria.[92]

In sum, Hizbullah's shift away from terrorism in the 1990s and beyond was substantial though not total. During this time, the focus of its activities was Israel's occupation of its self-proclaimed 'security zone' in the Lebanese south. In a telling passage, one of Hizbullah's leaders, Naim Qassem, explains why national liberation of the disputed land eventually came to be seen at odds with the use of terrorist tactics:

The Resistance considered it futile to target Israelis around the world. Confrontation within the circumference of occupied lands is not only righteous but also fruitful, convincing, and could draw tremendous support for the movement. Land liberation is an objective and substantiated aim, and may the direct occupiers bear the consequences of their actions. Despite the fact that external support can foster a widespread confrontation, increasing the scope in this manner was thought to be controversial and a waste of effort.[93]

[90] ICG, *Old Games, New Rules*, pp. 14–15; International Crisis Group, *Hizbollah: Rebel without a Cause?*, ICG Middle East Briefing, Amman/Brussels, 30 July 2003, p. 9.

[91] Norton, *Hezbollah*, p. 93.

[92] At the time of writing (2010) the UN Special Tribunal for Lebanon, charged with investigating the murder of Hariri, was investigating the role of Hizbullah in the assassination. http://www.stl-tsl.org/sid/195, accessed 16 August 2010.

[93] Naim Qassem, *Hizbullah: The Story from Within*, trans. Dalia Khalil, London: Saqi, 2005, p. 74.

On the basis of this pragmatic logic, Hizbullah during the 1990s changed from a clandestine insurgency into a more conventional military force, which entailed greater discipline overall.[94] During the struggle against Israel in South Lebanon, it also made 'a determined effort to stay clear of all terrorist activities'.[95] This did not preclude its use of suicide bombings. In fact, early on (for the stated reason of equalising the power imbalance between Hizbullah and the Israelis[96]), the organisation started to use 'human bombs' – young Shia fighters who volunteered to drive vehicles laden with explosives into Israeli targets.[97] Suicide bombing is not enough to characterise an act as 'terrorism', however, given that the targets were military ones. Furthermore, Hizbullah also restrained itself, more often than not, from targeting civilians during that war. Overall practical 'rules of the game' were worked out between Israel and Hizbullah to limit attacks against civilians on both sides.[98] Deservedly or not, Hizbullah acquired a reputation of treating civilians well. In 2000, Hizbullah's objective was achieved with Israel's withdrawal from South Lebanon. Skirmishes continued, although on a much lower level, mostly around the disputed Shebaa Farms.[99] The conflict escalated again into a full-blown conflagration between the two sides in summer 2006, and the targeting of civilians by Hizbullah during that war was criticised by international human rights organisations.[100] Be that as it may, Hizbullah

---

[94] Author's interview with Nadim Houry, Human Rights Watch, Beirut, September 2009.

[95] Harik, *Hezbollah*, p. 194.

[96] Qassem, *Hizbullah*, p. 74.

[97] Jaber, *Hezbollah*, p. 22.

[98] Norton, *Hezbollah*, pp. 83–8. See also 'Hizballah: Through the Fog of the Lebanon War: An Interview with Augustus Richard Norton', *Journal of Palestine Studies*, 36 (1) Autumn 2006, p. 67, and Adir Waldman, *Arbitrating Armed Conflict: Decisions of the Israel-Lebanon Monitoring Group*, Huntington, NY: Juris Publishing, 2003.

[99] The Shebaa Farms is a 25-square-kilometre area which Hizbullah, on flimsy evidence, claims belongs to Lebanon (not Syria) and therefore that Israel's 2000 withdrawal from Lebanon was not total. See ICG, *Old Games, New Rules*, Appendix B, p. 33.

[100] Hizbullah was criticised by Amnesty International for violating the principle of combatant immunity by targeting Israeli civilians in 2006. Hassan Nasrallah justified the attacks as a reprisal against Israeli actions and a means to stop Israel from continuing such attacks. Both justifications are inadequate under international law, of course, but the way Nasrallah handled the issue showed that he recognised the principle of non-combatant immunity. Amnesty International, *Under Fire: Hizbullah's Attacks on Northern Israel*, http://www.amnesty.org/en/library/asset/MDE02/025/2006/en/864c5de8-d3f6-11dd-8743-d305bea2b2c7/mde020252006en.html, accessed 20 July 2009. Human Rights Watch made the same criticism of Hizbullah, although it also pointed out that for the most part, Hizbullah did not use civilians as human shields. Human Rights Watch, *Why They Died: Civilian Casualties in Lebanon during the 2006 War*, 19, 5 (E), September 2007, http://hrw.org/reports/2007/lebanon0907/3.htm, accessed 21 December 2007, and interview with Houry.

in this instance must be criticised for violating non-combatant immunity, not for being a terrorist organisation.

Hizbullah's shift away from terrorism and the overt targeting of civilians was partly a result of its incorporation within the Lebanese political process from the 1990s, its 'Lebanonisation'. Conversely, the partial and problematic nature of this inclusion explains why there was no clean break with terrorism. During the 1980s, the idea of taking part in Lebanese elections had been rejected outright by the movement, which saw the Lebanese confessional system as illegitimate. As the guns finally fell silent in Lebanon in 1990, Hizbullah became amenable to the idea of political participation, partly because the political process itself became more inclusive. The ground was prepared in 1989, when an internal organisational restructuring of Hizbullah led to greater openness and transparency. An acrimonious internal debate about electoral participation followed. On one side stood Fadlallah, and others such as Ibrahim Amin al Sayyed and Hassan Nasrallah, who argued that non-participation would deny the armed struggle against Israel the support from Lebanon which it required. On the opposite side, Hizbullah's secretary-general, Tufayli, maintained that political accommodation would subject the struggle against Israel to political considerations and manoeuvrings. A split occurred, with Tufayli leaving the movement and being replaced as secretary-general by the more flexible Abbas al Musawi (who was, however, assassinated by Israel in February 1992).[101]

Hizbullah contested the 1992 elections and entered Parliament as the largest single political party with 12 out of 128 deputies. Thereafter, it regularly participated in national and municipal elections as well as continuing to provide welfare and social services for Lebanon's Shia community. Hizbullah adapted to the non-ideological nature of the Lebanese political game and often made deals with its rivals before and during elections. Its electoral machine became the most effective in the country.[102] In contrast to the Amal movement, which had evolved into a patronage network, Hizbullah constituted a 'fully institutionalized political party'. In municipal elections, Hizbullah was able to negotiate pragmatically with secular opposition groups with whom they had fought viciously in the 1980s.[103] In parliament, Hizbullah behaved in a responsible

---

[101] Harik, *Hezbollah*, pp. 54, 56–7, 59 and 69; see generally chapters 4 and 5.

[102] Ibid., chapters 6 and 7; A. Nizar Hamzeh, 'Lebanon's Hezbollah: From Islamic Revolution to Parliamentary Accommodation', *Third World Quarterly*, 14 (2) 1993, p. 333.

[103] Augustus Richard Norton, 'Why *Hizbullah* is Winning', *Middle East Journal*, 61 (1) Winter 2007, p. 148; Norton, *Hezbollah*, pp. 98–105.

and constructive manner.[104] Hizbullah's wide network of institutions, embedded in Lebanese society, meant that the party became receptive and susceptible to the views of its constituents.[105] With the indefinite postponement, if not yet formal abandonment, of the goal of an Islamic state, much of Hizbullah's political thought focused on the religious and moral bases for political accommodation in non-Islamic states.[106]

In many ways, Hizbullah's worldview remained intolerant and exclusivist towards secularists and non-Muslims. In certain, though certainly not all, Shia areas under its control, it continued to enforce strict social mores such as coercing women into wearing headscarves, segregating the sexes and forbidding cultural events it sees as opposed to Islam.[107] The movement has moved a great distance from the puritanical practices of the 1980s, however. A greater involvement in politics did indeed lead to moderation and compromise. In a revealing remark in my interview with him, Sheikh Hani Fahs, a member of the Shia religious hierarchy in Lebanon and critic of Hizbullah, said that it no longer so much paid attention to whether its supporters covered their hair or consumed alcohol, so long as they pledged allegiance to its political ideas.[108] Having said that, the demand for political allegiance meant that, within the Shia community, those critical of Hizbullah often found their way to office or influence blocked.

Hizbullah's gradual abandonment of terrorism was linked to its participation in the Lebanese political process, its 'Lebanonisation', but only in a roundabout, indirect manner. Political inclusion was the *sine qua non* for it to be allowed to continue its fight against Israel in South Lebanon after Taif. To do so, Hizbullah needed to persuade Lebanese society, including its large Christian population and many secularised groups, that it was no longer a radical Islamic militia which would try to set up an Islamic state in Lebanon at the first opportunity.[109] Alongside the abandonment – or at least postponement – of the aspiration for an Islamic Republic in Lebanon, Hizbullah had to forego subversive activities against the Lebanese state. It had to reassure the Lebanese public that it was a responsible actor, and bombings and kidnappings were

---

[104] Saad-Ghorayeb, *Hizbu'llah*, p. 30.
[105] ICG, *Hizbollah: Rebel without a Cause?*, p. 2.
[106] Saad-Ghorayeb, *Hizbu'llah*, chapter 1.
[107] ICG, *Hizbollah and the Lebanese Crisis*, p. 18. The report stresses that such policies vary from place to place and that there is no clear evidence whether there is central direction on these issues.
[108] Interview with Fahs.
[109] Harik, *Hezbollah*, p. 3.

incongruent with this picture. The image of a legitimate resistance movement that it cultivated in the 1990s did not tally with the use of terrorism. Hizbullah's 1992 electoral participation was meant to protect its weapons and keep the Lebanese government out of its way so that it could continue its struggle against Israel and the West.[110] For insertion into the Lebanese political process, abandoning terrorism (but not violence against Israel which was increasingly legitimised by Hizbullah to the wider Lebanese society as a nationalist struggle[111]) was a prerequisite, along with the postponement of the objective of the Islamic state. This insertion, and Hizbullah's 'Lebanonisation', was, in turn, necessary for it to carry on with the pursuit of the struggle against Israel and the West.

If Hizbullah's incorporation into the Lebanese political process was only indirectly linked to its abandonment of terrorism, the inclusion itself remained limited and partial, which may help to explain why there has been no clean break with terrorism. Hizbullah continued to focus on its anti-Israeli struggle which, since the Israeli withdrawal from South Lebanon in 2000, centred on the Palestinian issue. Undoubtedly, Hizbullah pursues domestic Lebanese goals such as improving the position of the Shia community and augmenting its own power relative to other confessional movements. The relationship between Hizbullah's internal and external goals is complex,[112] but however we assess this relationship and the relative weight of its goals, there is no doubt that the focus on Israel enables Hizbullah to do the bidding of its external sponsors, Syria and Iran. Following the withdrawal of Israel from South Lebanon in 2000 at the same time as the Iranian focus on Israel increased, Hizbullah's regional agenda was strengthened.[113] Hizbullah's concentration on confronting Israel has continued even in the face of rising scepticism within Lebanon (and even among Shia) that the Shebaa Farms constitute sufficient reason for the movement to remain on a war footing, a scepticism that was reinforced by the destructiveness of the 2006 war. Hizbullah wants to be unencumbered within Lebanon so as to

---

[110] ICG, *Hizbollah and the Lebanese Crisis*, p. 15; Harik, *Hezbollah*, p. 47.

[111] Saad-Ghorayeb, *Hizbu'llah*, pp. 82–3.

[112] The interpretations of the exact relationship between Hizbullah's internal and external goals vary extensively among Hizbullah observers. For some, the two sets of goals simply coexist and sometimes are in conflict: interview with Blanford. For others, Hizbullah is 'obsessed' with Palestine: interview with Göksel. Yet a third view is that Hizbullah uses the anti-Israeli struggle in an instrumental fashion and that, far from being the primary issue, the struggle with Israel is combined with other goals, such as enlarging the share of Shia power in Lebanon: interview with Saghieh.

[113] Interview with Safa.

concentrate on Israel and, for one commentator at least, the movement, far from being part of Lebanese politics, can more fully be understood as part of the Iranian political process.[114] The words of Wadah Charara aptly summarise the issue: Hizbullah's exogenous goals are inherently 'opposed to the dossier of democracy' in Lebanon.[115]

Conclusion

There is no single explanation why Hamas and Hizbullah resorted to terrorist tactics. To concentrate on a particular explanation, as I have done in this chapter, may appear artificial. However, I have done so for the purposes of analysis and to demonstrate that, in these two cases, repression and political exclusion were linked to the adoption of terrorist methods only in very tenuous and indirect ways. The inevitable question that follows is: What were the other possible significant causes for the use of terrorist tactics by Hamas and Hizbullah?

A brief examination of socio-economic factors, specifically poverty and relative or absolute deprivation, shows that their explanatory power is also quite limited. Admittedly, such factors may have played a certain role in the rise of the two movements. For instance, Hamas emerged and is stronger, to this day, in the Gaza Strip which has always been poorer and more deprived than the West Bank. The poverty and economic deprivation of the Shia community in Lebanon combined with political exclusion and marginalisation in an explosive mix in the 1980s. Nevertheless, when we get down to specific timings of the decisions to use terrorist tactics, socio-economic explanations are revealed to be rather blunt instruments. In the Palestinian context, suicide bombers (either of Hamas or other groups) are of middle- or upper-class background and have comparatively high levels of education. Fragile or disturbed personalities are not, as a matter of course, selected for suicide operations.[116] I argued earlier in this chapter that the response to the political marginalisation of the Lebanese Shia was the rise of the Amal movement, not Hizbullah. Similarly, Amal, not Hizbullah, can be seen as the response to Shia economic deprivation. A detailed study by Alan Krueger and Jitka Maleckova of Hizbullah members who died in military action

[114] Author's interview with Paul Salem, Carnegie Endowment for International Peace, Beirut, September 2009.
[115] Interview with Charara.
[116] Luca Ricolfi, 'Palestinians, 1981–2003', Diego Gambetta (ed.), *Making Sense of Suicide Missions*, Oxford: Oxford University Press, 2005, pp. 105–14.

(including terrorist attacks) between 1982 and 1994 shows that a standard of living above the poverty line or a secondary-school education or higher is *positively associated* with participation in Hizbullah.[117]

As in the case of al Qaeda, strategic/instrumental analyses of why terrorist methods were chosen by Hamas and Hizbullah are more convincing. Terrorist methods were selected by Hamas's leadership from a wide menu of violent and non-violent options because they were deemed the best means of achieving Hamas's two-fold objective of pursuing political power (by winning the allegiance of the Palestinian people) and defeating Israel, whatever that may have meant at different times. Hamas has always adjusted its positions and shown flexibility depending on its reading of the Palestinian consensus. The challenge to the Muslim Brotherhood coming from the establishment of the revolutionary and hard-line Islamic Jihad in the early 1980s was a key factor in spearheading Hamas's creation. Following the Oslo agreement, the spiralling competition between the two movements also contributed to the escalation of terrorism.[118] Hamas terrorism becomes even more intelligible in the context of its competitive relationship with Fatah and the PLO. By 1992, Hamas had judged that its increasingly successful attacks against Israeli soldiers and settlers gained it popular Palestinian support. After Oslo, Hamas used terrorist methods to undermine the peace process but also to enhance its prestige among the Palestinians and compel Arafat to come to terms with it as a legitimate opposition.[119] Conversely, Hamas carried out very few attacks between 1998 and November 2000 when it had become apparent that the popular appeal of terrorism had fallen. During the al Aqsa Intifada, intra-Palestinian rivalry, and

[117] Alan B. Krueger and Jitka Maleckova, 'Education, Poverty, Political Violence and Terrorism: Is There a Causal Connection?', *Journal of Economic Perspectives* 17 (4) 2003, pp. 129–35.

[118] Islamic Jihad was a small, tightly knit movement, in many ways the antithesis of the Mujama. It was established by a younger Islamist generation – some of whom were Muslim Brothers, others PLO members – which criticised the Muslim Brotherhood's position towards the Israeli occupation. They were influenced by extremist groups in Egypt and the Iranian Revolution. Islamic Jihad rejected the Muslim Brotherhood view that society should be Islamised before resistance could take place. Most of its followers came from modest social origins and lived in poor neighbourhoods and refugee camps and its operations included attacks against Israeli soldiers and police but also some attacks on civilian targets. Abu-Amr, *Islamic Fundamentalism*, chapter 4; Milton-Edwards, *Islamic Politics*, pp. 116–23 and 139–40; Human Rights Watch, *Erased in a Moment*, pp. 73–4.

[119] Mishal and Sela, *Palestinian Hamas*, p. 73.

in particular the clash between the al Aqsa Martyrs' Brigades and al Qassam Brigades, were also primary factors in the escalation of terrorist attacks.[120]

Hamas also made the calculation that terrorism would be the best method to get the Israelis to do what it wanted in a situation of power asymmetry. In the final years of the first Intifada, Hamas became convinced that Hizbullah's methods, which included terrorism, had driven Western forces and Israel out of Lebanon and should therefore be emulated. In the Oslo and the al Aqsa Intifada periods, Hamas portrayed its use of terrorism either as a desperate act of last resort, after all other tactics had failed to produce results in the struggle for Palestinian freedom, or as retaliation to Israel's targeting of Palestinian civilians (although the timing of the attacks does not support the latter view [121]). The implicit assumption of these rationalisations, particularly the first one, is that terrorism 'works' in achieving results where all else has failed.

Hizbullah's embrace – and subsequent partial discarding – of terrorist methods was also the outcome of strategic calculations. Clearly the chaos and violence of the 1980s civil war in Lebanon, which constituted a suspension of the political process for all Lebanese, particularly the marginalised and weak Shia community, contributed to the emergence of terrorism, if only indirectly. However, there were also instrumental considerations at play. The 1983 bombings were effective in getting US and French peacekeepers out of Lebanon and this was a lesson immediately learnt by Hizbullah. It also became quickly evident that Western hostages were a valuable commodity, especially when the Reagan administration appeared willing to trade them for arms. These calculations can be more fully understood when the changing influence of Hizbullah's Iranian sponsors is taken into account.[122] The 1980s was not only a time of chaos and violence in Lebanon but was also, as I will show in Chapter 6, the radical period of the Islamic Republic which did not hesitate to use terrorism abroad to defend and export the Revolution. After Khomeini's death in 1989, a relatively pragmatic Iranian leadership under Rafsanjani came to the fore. It judged that Hizbullah would be more useful for their foreign policy objectives if it accommodated itself within Lebanon's

---

[120] Sara Roy, 'Hamas and the Transformation(s) of Political Islam in Palestine', pp. 13–20; Ricolfi, 'Palestinians 1981–2003', pp. 95–6; Amnesty International, *Occupied Palestinian Territories: Torn apart by Factional Strife*, p. 10.
[121] Ricolfi, 'Palestinians 1981–2003', pp. 98–9.
[122] This is the argument by A. Nizar Hamzeh, 'Lebanon's Hezbollah', p. 323.

new, post-Taif political reality which was emerging under Syrian stewardship. Terrorism still had its uses: For instance, the 1992 Argentina attack was a signal to Israel that it had crossed a red line by assassinating Hizbullah secretary-general Abbas al Musawi. The overall judgement on which Hizbullah and Tehran operated in the 1990s, however, was that terrorism's uses had considerably diminished.

4

Islamist Terrorism in Domestic Conflicts:
The Armed Islamic Group in Algeria
and the Gamaa Islamiya in Egypt

Terrorism is often employed alongside other violent methods in the context of domestic insurgencies against incumbent regimes, heightened domestic conflict and civil war. The boundaries between terrorism and these other forms of conflict are rarely clearly demarcated, and as we have already seen from the previous chapters, Islamist terrorism is no exception to this pattern. Two further groups in the Middle East which used terrorist tactics as part of a wider violent insurrection are the Armed Islamic Group (Groupe Islamique Armé, GIA) in Algeria and the Islamic Group (Gamaa Islamiya) in Egypt during the 1990s. The similarities between the two cases are numerous, although the *scale* of the two conflicts was very different. The total number of deaths for Egypt has been given as approximately 1,300 whereas for Algeria it was estimated to be between 150,000 and more than 200,000.[1] The high death toll in Algeria and the type of conflagration which caused it has led analysts to describe this conflict as a 'civil war'. Others reject this description.[2] Although I recognise the difficulties of defining the

---

[1] In both cases, the numbers are estimates and remain disputed. For a discussion of the Algerian figures, see Omar Ashour, 'Islamist De-Radicalization in Algeria: Successes and Failures', *Middle East Institute Brief*, 21, November 2008, p. 6. For the Egyptian figures, see Omar Ashour, 'Lions Tamed? An Enquiry into the Causes of The De-Radicalization of Armed Islamist Movements: The Case of the Egyptian Islamic Group', *Middle East Journal*, 61 (4) 2007, p. 612.

[2] Luis Martinez describes the conflict as 'civil war' but does not define the term. Luis Martinez, *The Algerian Civil War 1990–1998*, trans. Jonathan Derrick, London: Hurst & Co, 2003. Hugh Roberts rejects the application of the term. His argument, *contra* Martinez, is that during the conflict of the 1990s, there did not develop a stable territorial frontier between the opposing sides or a deep ideological division within

term 'civil war',[3] I have opted not to apply it to the Algerian context (or indeed the Egyptian one). I therefore place the indiscriminate targeting of civilians in both the Algerian and Egyptian cases under the label of 'terrorism' rather than a violation of non-combatant immunity. This is in full awareness of the problems associated with these terms as discussed at some length in the Introduction.

What differentiates this type of Islamist terrorism from the cases of al Qaeda, Hamas and Hizbullah studied in the previous chapters – where 'outsiders' were the primary, if not exclusive, targets – is that terrorist tactics were used against fellow citizens as well as the structures and symbols of the state. In patterns typical of a polarised situation due to ideological and socio-political domestic conflict, the GIA and the Gamaa Islamiya attacked not just their own governments, but those ordinary Algerians and Egyptians whom they saw as opposing them and/or being supportive of the state's structures and institutions. In the case of the GIA, the widening of targets to include the civilian population led to such cruelty that it was condemned for its 'savagery' by other Islamist groups such as Hizbullah, as we have already seen in Chapter 3.

This chapter continues the investigation into whether repression and exclusion from political processes are primary causes of the adoption of terrorist tactics. In the case of the GIA, I argue that the military coup which pre-empted the impending electoral victory of the Islamic Salvation Front (Front Islamique du Salut, FIS) in January 1992 contributed to the radicalisation of some of its supporters and, eventually, their turn to terrorism. Thereafter, the relentless campaign against Islamist forces by the so-called eradicator elements of the Algerian army – who refused to negotiate with the Islamists and aimed to destroy them – led to the further escalation and perpetuation of violence and the use of increasingly

---

Algerian society (which mostly refused to get involved in the conflict unless forced to). Hugh Roberts, *The Battlefield Algeria, 1988–2002: Studies in a Broken Polity*, London: Verso, 2003, pp. 254–9. John Ruedy argues that the conflict can be more accurately described as an insurgency than a civil war because, 'in spite of its toll, only a small minority of Algerians supported the Islamists' resort to war and the number of their combatants peaked at no more than 25,000'. John Ruedy, *Modern Algeria: The Origins and Development of a Nation*, 2nd edition, Bloomington: Indiana University Press, 2005, p. 257.

[3] The Correlates of War (COW) definition of civil wars is "wars that are fought within state borders between a (sic) government and non-government forces" (http://correlatesofwar.org/, accessed 25 August 2010). For a discussion of the COW's data coding and more general definition of civil war, see Nicholas Sambanis 'What Is Civil War?: Conceptual and Empirical Complexities of an Operational Definition', *Journal of Conflict Resolution*, 48 (6) 2004, pp. 814–58.

brutal terrorist methods by some insurgents. However, political exclusion and repression were only some of the factors accounting for terrorist violence in Algeria during the 'dark decade' of the 1990s. The core membership of the GIA, the protagonists of terrorist violence in Algeria, had been radicalised *before* the interruption of the electoral process. The polarisation of the 1990s temporarily increased the GIA's appeal and support among the population, leading to a broad insurrection of catastrophic proportions, but did not cause their initial proclivity to terrorist methods. Egypt followed a similar pattern. Although, on one level, the challenge to the regime posed by the Gamaa Islamiya in the 1990s can be seen as the outcome of political exclusion and repression, appearances can be deceptive. A closer look at the evidence shows that the Gamaa had not been interested in political inclusion anyway, and had been critical of other Islamists – namely the Muslim Brotherhood – which had decided to take part in elections and integrate into Egypt's political process, beginning in the 1970s. As well as responding to government repression, the Gamaa was often the initiator of terrorist violence. The chapter's concluding part discusses socio-economic and strategic/instrumental explanations and argues that they account more fully than political explanations for Algerian and Egyptian terrorism in the 1990s.

The Armed Islamic Group (GIA)

The Background of Islamist Politics in Algeria[4]
The roots of Islamist politics in Algeria can be located in the period leading up to the Algerian war of independence against France (1954–62) and the events of the war itself. The National Liberation Front (Front de Libération Nationale, FLN) led the independence struggle by creating a broad nationalist coalition and co-opting nearly all political tendencies, including the Islamic one. It asserted aims which were inclusive enough for any nationalist, broadly defined, to cooperate with, encapsulated in the phrase that that the FLN aimed 'to restore a sovereign, democratic and social Algerian state within the framework of Islamic principles'.[5] Islamists did not therefore form a rival organisation to the FLN. The Islamic Reform Movement, which had emerged in the 1920s, did not

[4] Note that in some cases the order of Algerian names – first name and surname – is reversed.
[5] FLN Declaration of 1 November 1954, http://www.milestonedocuments.com/documents/view/proclamation-of-the-algerian-national-liberation-front/, accessed 21 April 2010.

enjoy a large following despite offering a clear alternative articulation of Algerian identity.[6] This changed to some degree with the creation of Sheikh Abdelhamid Ben Badis's Association of Algerian Muslim Ulama (Association des Oulemas Musulmans Algériens, AOMA) in 1931, which was a highly organised movement. Still, the AOMA endorsed the FLN's war aims in 1956 and was represented in the FLN leadership. The FLN and the newly independent Algerian state, in turn, endorsed AOMA's key ideas, such as promotion of a reformed, scripturalist and puritanical Islam as well as Arabisation.[7] 'Islam as the essential component of Algerian culture was ascribed the task of national integration, but it was not to count as the defining feature of Algerian citizenship.'[8] In a nutshell, Islam was subordinated to the FLN's nationalist project.

Once Algeria gained independence in 1962, the dominant ideological conflict was between socialism and liberalism, not Islamism, with the former emerging triumphant under the presidency of Ahmed Ben Bella (1962–5) who used it to consolidate his power. Socialism – or what could more precisely be described as state capitalism – was also dominant under the military regime of Houari Boumediene (1965–78). The regime declared that Islam was consistent with socialism and, soon after independence, announced that 'Arabisation' in education and state institutions was an important objective.[9] This did not diminish the fact that until the late 1970s, Algerian politics, although conservative, authoritarian and dominated by the army, was predominantly defined in secular terms.

With the ascent of Chadli Bendjedid to the presidency in 1979, socialism was gradually abandoned. To counter the influence of former regime loyalists, Chadli turned increasingly to the cultural agenda of the Arabists – much to the dismay of Algeria's Kabyle (Berber) minority which became more restive from 1980 onwards. He also began to court the Islamists who asserted their presence on university campuses and became more vocal in their demands. As this occurred, and in a pattern familiar throughout the Middle East region, the government then tried to outflank the Islamists by funding religious education at all levels

[6] Ruedy, *Modern Algeria*, pp. 133–6.

[7] International Crisis Group (ICG), *Islamism, Violence and Reform in Algeria: Turning the Page*, Middle East Report 29, 30 July 2004, p. 1. The exception to co-optation was the die-hard supporters of Messali Hadj, who formed the *Mouvement National Algérien* and whom the FLN eliminated physically. See note 6, p. 1.

[8] Reinhard Schulze, *A Modern History of the Islamic World*, trans. Azizeh Azodi, London: I. B. Tauris, 2000, p. 163.

[9] Ruedy, *Modern Algeria*, pp. 195–201 and 224–8.

and initiating reforms such as the conservative family code in 1984.[10] Hundreds and eventually thousands of new 'free' mosques – outside state control – were established during this period.

The Islamist movement at the time exhibited three main tendencies: the Salafi, which comprised leaders of establishment ulama and dissident AOMA veterans (the latter predominated in the 'free mosques'); the Muslim Brotherhood variant, which included an 'international' and a 'local' tendency of Mahfoud Nahnah and Abdallah Djaballah, respectively; and a specifically 'Algerian' current which became known by the late 1980s as the 'Algerianists'. The Muslim Brotherhood had been initially an offshoot of the Salafi movement but had opted for political engagement towards which the Salafis continued to be ambivalent. The 'Algerianists' were modernists and more accepting of the idea of Algerian nationalism. One must clarify that although Islamism was clearly resurgent during the 1980s, it was not associated with terrorism or political violence. The exception was the Armed Islamic Movement (Mouvement Islamique Armé, MIA), headed by Mustafa Bouyali, which between 1982 and 1987 led an armed revolt in the hinterland of Algiers. This small guerrilla group has been described as an offshoot of the FLN and a populist movement which expressed itself in Islamist terms.[11] However, support for Bouyali's movement was limited and it was shunned by the broader Islamist movement in Algeria.[12]

The Rise and Fall of the Islamic Salvation Front (FIS)

Islamism's popularity increased as the Algerian economy deteriorated during the 1980s, a result of a combination of the familiar woes of state capitalism with a dramatic drop, after 1985, of crude oil prices, on which the country depended for much of its revenue. Two years later, the International Monetary Fund stepped in with a neo-liberal package of reforms. However, although social tensions increased and finally erupted in the riots of October 1988, this did not translate into uniform support for Islamism, which constituted only one strand among many in civil society's reawakening in the late 1980s. As late as 1986–7, the Islamists still did not hold the political initiative and their role in the

---

[10] Martin Evans and John Phillips, *Algeria: Anger of the Dispossessed*, New Haven, CT and London: Yale University Press, 2007, pp. 124–8.

[11] ICG, *Islamism, Violence and Reform in Algeria*, pp. 2–3.

[12] Mohammed M. Hafez, 'From Marginalization to Massacres: A Political Process Explanation of GIA Violence in Algeria' in Quintan Wiktorowicz, *Islamic Activism: A Social Movement Theory Approach*, Bloomington: Indiana University Press, 2004, p. 44.

1988 riots was marginal.[13] Islamism had not become a serious threat to the regime even by the time the FIS was established as a political party in March 1989. Despite its fundamentalist positions and the evident fact that no alternative political group would be able to contain it, it is plausible that Chadli legalised the FIS in September of the same year in the hope he could use it for his own political purposes.[14] In March 2007, I interviewed veteran journalist Mohamed Arezki Himeur in the tiny flat in Algiers where he had hidden from Islamist terrorists for most of the 1990s. He was categorical that Chadli's regime was complicit in the emergence of the FIS.[15]

The FIS contained an array of Islamist elements. Its core was formed by the coming together of dissident Salafis, who overcame their scepticism towards political participation and the grassroots of the Muslim Brotherhood (but not including leaders, Djaballah and Nahnah). The 'Algerianist' tendency led by Mohamed Said had initially opposed the FIS's formation but joined in late 1990.[16] The ideology of the FIS comprised a variety of conflicting positions, reflecting its nature as a 'front'. Its two founding fathers and most important leaders, Ali Benhadj and Abassi Madani, were very different in their style and ideas: The former 'denounced democracy, the state, and opponents in vitriolic terms', whereas the latter sought to reassure the public of the party's essentially moderate message.[17] The FIS declared its intention to replace popular sovereignty with God's, advocated an Islamic state and condemned democracy as 'infidel'.[18] Nevertheless, its ideology remained largely undefined, a fact that possibly explained the 'pluralistic nature of the FIS as a political party'.[19] For Fouad Delici and Mohamed Hamided, two

---

[13] Hugh Roberts, 'From Radical Mission to Equivocal Ambition: The Expansion and Manipulation of Algerian Islamism, 1979–1992', Martin E. Marty and R. Scott Appleby (eds.), *Accounting for Fundamentalisms: The Dynamic Character of Movements*, The Fundamentalism Project, Vol. 4, Chicago and London: University of Chicago Press, 1994, pp. 430–1.

[14] ICG, *Islamism, Violence and Reform in Algeria*, p. 5. ICG claims that there was not even strong popular pressure to legalise the FIS; the Islamists themselves were divided on whether they wanted to form a political party.

[15] Author's interview with Mohamed Arezki Himeur, journalist, Algiers, March 2007.

[16] ICG, *Islamism, Violence and Reform in Algeria*, pp. 3 and 7 (note 55).

[17] Mohammed M. Hafez, *Why Muslims Rebel: Repression and Resistance in the Islamic World*, Boulder, CO: Lynne Rienner Publishers, 2003, p. 37.

[18] Hafez notes that many individuals who opposed the electoral option 'did take part in FIS's demonstrations and rallies, but they often participated with their own slogans and banners'. Mohammed M. Hafez, 'Armed Islamist Movements and Political Violence in Algeria', *Middle East Journal*, 54 (4) 2000, p. 573–4.

[19] Barbara Smith, 'Algeria: The Horror', *New York Review of Books*, XLV (7) 1998, pp. 27–30; John P. Entelis, 'Civil Society and the Authoritarian Temptation in Algerian

former FIS activists whom I talked to during the same visit to Algiers, the primary demands of the FIS were neither for democracy (seen by many as a Western discourse) nor for theocracy, but for social justice, above all provision for the poor.[20]

The FIS was in many ways the product of a populist political culture that had originated in the nationalist movement and had been instrumentalised by the state and the FLN since independence.[21] The FIS's ideological message, which contained radical elements, explained its appeal in popular, poorer areas and newly urbanised quarters. (I caught a glimpse of this appeal when I visited the al Sunnah mosque in Bab el Oued, where Ali Benhadj had preached. Situated in one of the poorest areas of Algiers, the mosque was strikingly unassuming and sparse in its interior.) The FIS sought to represent those who, since independence, had not been offered a stake in the Algerian system and were therefore ready to challenge it.[22] The majority of FIS supporters may not even have been of firm Islamist ideological persuasion, but they were certainly bitter at what they saw as the state's betrayal of the values of the independence struggle.

Why did the FIS opt for an electoral strategy, instead of a violent confrontation, at that point in time? In one interpretation, the FIS's gradualist approach was the outcome of the Algerian regime's relatively permissive attitude towards the Islamists, particularly the fact that they never suffered the kind of harsh repression Nasser meted out to the Egyptian Muslim Brotherhood in the 1950s and 1960s.[23] As the FIS's appeal expanded rapidly on the back of its inclusivist political strategy after 1990, the regime took fright.[24] A spiralling confrontation and

Politics: Islamic Democracy vs. the Centralized State', Augustus Richard Norton (ed.), *Civil Society in the Middle East*, Leiden: E. J. Brill, 1996, Vol. 2, p. 67.

[20] Author's interview with Fouad Delici and Mohamed Hamided, former FIS activists, Algiers, March 2007.

[21] Hugh Roberts states that Abassi Madani, who essentially held the FIS together, was a product of the FLN. Author's interview with Hugh Roberts, Islamist movement and Algeria expert, London, August 2009.

[22] Algerian journalist and political analyst Yassine Temlali pointed out that the FIS's precursors had *not* been active in universities in the 1980s. This is unusual among Islamist movements in the Middle East which, more often that not, have their roots in university activism. Author's interview with Yassine Temlali, journalist and political analyst, Algiers, March 2007.

[23] ICG, *Islamism, Violence and Reform in Algeria*, p. 6, note 41.

[24] Hafez, 'From Marginalization to Massacres', p. 45. In an interesting suggestion, Lahouari Addi maintains that the regime would have been frightened of *any* party challenging its monopoly of power, not just an Islamist party. His implication, as I understand it, is that the Algerian regime was not averse to Islamism in particular but

mutual escalation ensued. In a landmark demonstration in April 1990 the FIS brought together 600,000–800,000 people to march in silence. It swept the board in the June 1990 local elections, winning 850 out of 1,500 municipal councils and 32 out of 48 *wilayas* (provinces).[25] In January 1991, it organised, with others, a 400,000-strong demonstration against the then unfolding Gulf War. Increasingly alarmed, the Chadli government passed an electoral law in April 1991 to counter the FIS by gerrymandering, specifically favouring the rural constituencies where the FLN was stronger. This contributed to the breakdown of relations between Chadli and the FIS and spurred the latter to call a 'general and unlimited strike' in May and June 1991. During the strike, demonstrators denounced democracy and called for an Islamic state. Many citizens were forcibly prevented from working, and the strike developed into a number of rallies and occupations of public squares in Algiers.[26] Finally, this led to harsh suppression by riot police and the deaths of at least twenty people on 4 June.

The FIS's militant action during the strike had frightened many but it did not mean that the FIS had entirely abandoned their accommodationist stance. When it had secured control of municipalities the year before, the FIS had acted moderately and its candidates successfully made the transition from political activists to responsible public servants dealing with mundane issues, although they did show an intolerant attitude in social issues (for example, they closed some cinemas and in some instances coerced women into wearing the headscarf).[27] This relatively measured approach continued even after the strike of May and June 1991, when the FIS leadership exhorted their supporters to refrain from violence and did not break communication links with the government. It was even reported that initially, the FIS did not object too strenuously when the police detained radical elements at the forefront of the clashes.[28] Evidently, although the FIS was using militant tactics in a bid to increase its popularity, it did not want to completely burn its bridges with the Algerian regime.

However, the regime provoked the FIS by suppressing its activities and arresting a large number of its mainstream activists. Abassi Madani

simply sought to guard its power. Lahouari Addi, 'Algeria's Army, Algeria's Agony', *Foreign Affairs*, 78 (4) 1998, p. 50.

[25] Ruedy, *Modern Algeria*, pp. 252–3.

[26] Hafez, *Why Muslims Rebel*, pp. 38–9.

[27] Entelis, 'Civil Society and the Authoritarian Temptation in Algerian Politics', pp. 68–9 and 71; interview with Temlali.

[28] Hafez, *Why Muslims Rebel*, pp. 39–40.

and Ali Benhadj, among others, were taken into custody on 30 June 1991. Even then the FIS did not opt for confrontation. The leadership which emerged in their stead in July 1991 was dominated by pragmatic, cautious elements drawn from the 'Algerianists' and activists from eastern Algeria, under a new interim leader, Abdelkader Hachani.[29] Two rival factions – both to be discussed more extensively later in this chapter – were sidelined by Hachani's ascent. A Salafi group led by Said Guechi, reverting to that trend's apolitical stance, held that the FIS should abandon political action and revert to a social reformist strategy. A second, radical group, some members of which can be described as 'Afghans' because they had fought in Afghanistan in the 1980s, led by Said Mekhloufi and Qameredin Kharban, wanted to boycott the impending parliamentary elections and mobilise the masses against the regime. They all left the movement; Guechi resigned and Mekhloufi and other radicals had their memberships frozen. Hachani was therefore able to moderate the overall tone of the FIS's discourse and issue a communiqué signalling to the regime that it would not tolerate those who advocated violence. The FIS ultimately opted for participation in the parliamentary elections of December 1991, but the gamble did not pay off. Its imminent victory was annulled by a military coup on 11 January 1992.[30]

Immediately after the coup, and despite Hachani and others calling upon their supporters to avoid violence, the military began widespread arrests. This increased the intensity of the protests. The FIS was subjected to severe and indiscriminate repression which included torture, disappearances and extrajudicial killings. Thousands of Islamist activists, including hundreds of FIS mayors and councillors, were detained between January and March 1992. No distinction was made between those who had been ready to use violence and peaceful supporters of the FIS. Many were held in the five detention centres specially constructed in the Sahara desert for that purpose. In 1992–3, a total of 166 Islamists were sentenced to death, mostly in absentia. The communal and departmental councils which were dominated by the FIS were dissolved and thousands lost their jobs.[31] Repression was complemented

---

[29] ICG, *Islamism, Violence and Reform in Algeria*, p. 7, note 55.

[30] Hafez, *Why Muslims Rebel*, pp. 40–1. Hafez, and other analysts describe Mekhloufi as an 'Afghan', but Hugh Roberts states that he had never been in Afghanistan (in contrast to Kharban who had fought there): interview with Roberts. ICG describes Mekhloufi as a prominent Salafi within the FIS. See ICG, *Islamism, Violence and Reform in Algeria*, p. 6, note 45.

[31] Hafez, *Why Muslims Rebel*, pp. 77–82. An estimated 20,000 were held in concentration camps in the southern Sahara. François Burgat, *Face to Face with Political Islam*, London: I. B. Tauris, 2003, p. 105.

by political exclusion when the FIS was banned as a political party in March 1992. In subsequent months and years, the ascendant 'eradicator' section of the Algerian army refused to negotiate with the FIS – even while other elements of the state kept discussions going – pointing to Islamist terrorism as justification for its unyielding policy.[32] Whereas the FIS was excluded from the political process, rival Islamist parties which derived from the Muslim Brotherhood – Hamas, al Islah and Nahda – were allowed to participate as counter-weights, to split the Islamist vote.[33]

As a consequence, the leadership of the FIS was effectively fragmented by 1994. As previously noted, a Salafi element had already broken away in July 1991. The Salafis had initially opposed the formation of a political party but the 'collusion' between the regime and FIS allowed many of them to overcome their reluctance for political activism and join the party, even becoming prominent in its leadership. However, true to their non-confrontational stance, most of the Salafis opposed Abassi's decision to call a general strike and clash with the regime in May–June 1991. After departing from the FIS, some eventually even accepted public office.[34] The rump FIS, which remained in clandestine existence after the interruption of the electoral process, moved towards more moderate ideological positions as it sought, unsuccessfully, a political solution to the crisis. Shortly before being banned, the FIS had formed an alliance with the FLN and the Socialist Forces Front (Front des Forces Socialistes, FFS), a left-wing party with a strong Berber connection which had splintered from the FLN in the 1960s and was also legalised in 1989. In the post-1992 period, the alliance encouraged the movement's greater acceptance of democracy, which, in turn, entailed a revision of the concept of the Islamic state on the basis on a modernist understanding of Islamic

---

[32] During a brief period when the eradicators were somewhat less dominant, there was a possibility of a peace deal in 1995, under the auspices of the Sant' Egidio Community in Rome, but it fell through. Author's interview with Ali Yahia Abdennour, lawyer and human rights activist, Algiers, March 2007. For a full story of the negotiations, see Michael Willis, *The Islamist Challenge in Algeria: A Political History*, Reading, Berkshire: Ithaca Press, 1996, pp. 340–6.

[33] Hamas was renamed 'Movement for the Society of Peace' (MSP) after 1996. Martinez, *The Algerian Civil War*, p. 182. Islah subsequently attracted some of the FIS support and was more popular than Hamas, which was seen as too close to the regime. Author's interview with Zoubir Arous, Centre de Recherche en Economie Appliquée pour le Développement (CREAD), University of Algiers, Algiers, March 2007.

[34] Overall, the Salafi tendency was critical of the established order but did not wish to subvert it. The regime saw them as a constituency they could do business with. Benhadj was a key leader among them. Interview with Roberts.

law. The FIS also acknowledged the legitimacy of the Algerian nation and its constitution, even protesting the latter's violation.[35]

Terrorism and the GIA

What remained of the FIS may have become more appreciative of democracy in the post-1992 period, but repression, political exclusion and regime intransigence had already driven some of its members to terrorism and violent insurgency. During the events of 1990–1, many FIS activists rejected the moderation of their leadership and began clashing with security forces throughout the country, at first spontaneously but eventually in a more organised fashion. The waves of mass arrests, imprisonments and job dismissals described earlier led many FIS supporters to take up arms against the state, although it is important to stress that exact numbers are uncertain.[36] In my interviews in Algiers in March 2007, former FIS activists argued that they were driven to a clandestine existence by fear of arrest and the terrible conditions of their imprisonment.[37] The FIS's reluctance to organise an armed movement in the months and years after the interruption of the electoral process drove a minority of its activists to gravitate towards the several armed movements which were already developing independently of the FIS. This meant that hitherto marginal movements grew in size and gained the initiative in a ferocious confrontation which gradually engulfed large parts of the country. Increasingly from 1993–4, terrorism came to be used alongside other forms of violence, in a situation which harked back to the war of independence in which the large-scale killing of civilians had been carried out by both the French and Algerian sides.[38] The FIS itself refrained from such engagement until the formation of the Islamic Salvation Army (Armé Islamique du Salut, AIS) in 1994 which is discussed later in the chapter.

What was the trajectory of the radical movements which were already forming *before* the military coup interrupted the electoral process? An early meeting of future leaders of the armed movement took place in

---

[35] ICG, *Islamism, Violence and Reform in Algeria*, pp. 7–9.
[36] Luis Martinez points out that, whereas approximately three million Algerians voted for the FIS in December 1991, the insurgency, at its height, did not claim more than 40,000 members. Martinez, *The Algerian Civil War*, p. 202. As we saw from the earlier discussion in the chapter, Ruedy gives the figure of 25,000 (in 1996). Ruedy, *Modern Algeria*, p. 257.
[37] Interview with Delici and Hamided.
[38] For a history of the war, see Alistair Horne, *A Savage War of Peace: Algeria, 1954–1962*, London: Macmillan, 1977.

the mountains south-east of Algiers in July 1991. Abdelkader Chebouti's reconstituted Armed Islamic Movement (Mouvement Islamique Armé, MIA), which mobilised veterans of Bouyali's earlier movement, was one of the rebellion's initiators. A brutal attack on soldiers by a band including a number of Algerian 'Afghans' took place at a frontier post in Guemmar in November 1991. In 1992, a new group which wanted to open up the armed struggle to greater numbers emerged out of internal disagreements with the MIA leadership over its strict recruitment policy. The resulting Movement for an Islamic State (Mouvement pour un État Islamique, MEI) was led by Said Mekhloufi, who had left the FIS in July 1991.[39] These events remain nebulous: For instance, there is disagreement as to whether Chebouti led the MIA or the MEI in 1992–3;[40] more generally, the timing of the various groups' creation and even their names and separate identities continue to be contested. Be that as it may, for all of these entities which were evolving before January 1992, the coup only confirmed the futility of the electoral strategy. In their eyes, the FIS was finished and only armed rebellion would achieve an Islamic state.[41]

Although there is inevitable uncertainty about the exact sequence of events, it appears that the group which eventually became the mainstay of the rebellion, the GIA, emerged from the MIA, in late 1992–early 1993, under the leadership of Abdelhak Layada (the MIA and MEI were severely weakened by 1993–4). With the exception of Djamel Zitouni, the GIA's founding members had never joined the FIS.[42] Its core leadership was made up of the 'Afghans', Algerians who had participated in the Afghan resistance against the Soviet Union in the 1980s, and whose mindset was shaped by that war and who enjoyed close links with al Qaeda.[43] The extremist al Muwahhidun group (which was also called al Takfir wal Hijra in the Algerian press and academic sources) played an important role in the GIA's formation and became its decisive element.[44]

---

[39] Author's interview with Hamida Ayachi, journalist and specialist on the Islamist movement, Algiers, March 2007.

[40] Hafez, 'Armed Islamist Movements', pp. 574–5, see especially note 11.

[41] ICG, *Islamism, Violence and Reform in Algeria*, p. 10. On Chebouti and the MIA, see p. 7; the source of the information is Séverine Labat *Les Islamistes algériens entre les urnes et le maquis*, Paris: Seuil, 1995, pp. 228–9.

[42] Interview with Zoubir.

[43] It is important to note that not all Algerian 'Afghans' followed the same trajectory. Some had returned home, while others had stayed in Afghanistan. Some came back to participate in Algerian politics, while others engaged in political violence. Interview with Roberts.

[44] ICG, *Islamism, Violence and Reform in Algeria*, p. 12, and interview with Roberts. In an interesting passage, Olivier Roy highlights the GIA's Afghan connection: 'the

The GIA expanded in May 1994 when it was joined by two key figures from the former FIS leadership, namely Mohamed Said's 'Algerianist' faction and Said Mekhloufi's MEI. The May 1994 unification of former FIS elements with the GIA was rejected by the FIS leadership in prison and abroad. The FIS finally concluded that a political settlement was impossible without violence and so backed the formation of an armed group, the AIS, to stop its support haemorrhaging and to offer an alternative to the GIA. The FIS set up the AIS when it appeared that the conciliators were coming to the fore within the regime, as against the eradicators; the idea being that the use of violence through the AIS would create pressure on the regime to negotiate with the FIS.[45] Part of the disintegrated MIA became linked to the AIS (the other part had moved the GIA, which had been the MIA's offshoot, as we saw). It was led by ex-FIS militants Mezrag Madani and Ahmed Ben Aicha. The links between the FIS and AIS are disputed; although the AIS is often described as the FIS's armed wing, it may have enjoyed considerable autonomy.[46] Mezrag Madani himself argued, in my meeting with him in March 2007, that the AIS may have been the continuation of the FIS but was not controlled by it. He also claimed that the FIS and AIS were forced to take up violence in self-defence, after the interruption of the democratic process, and that they had wished to keep the possibility of negotiations with the regime open at all times.[47]

The AIS's objective was not to overthrow the state, but to induce it to mend its ways and to support the FIS's attempts to find a negotiated solution to the conflict. Its methods reflected these moderate objectives.

founding leaders of the GIA (Armed Islamic Group), Tayyeb al Afghani (killed in November 1992), Jaffar al Afghani (killed in March 1994) and Sherif Gousmi (killed in September 1994), were all Afghan returnees. They were also to be found in the Islamic Salvation Front (FIS) with figures such as Said Mekhloufi, Kamareddin Kherbane and Abdallah Anas (real name Boudjema Bunnua, who arrived in Afghanistan in 1984 and married Abdallah Azzam's daughter). But in Algeria they figured most prominently in the GIA: Abu Messaab, a Syrian, and Abu Hazma al Misri (Mustafa Kamel) from Egypt are the main ideologists of *Al Ansar*, the GIA newsletter published in London. Both men have lived in Peshawar.' Olivier Roy, 'Hazy Outlines of an Islamist International: Fundamentalists without a Common Cause', *Monde Diplomatique*, October 1998. Note that Roy is one of the authors who claims Mekhloufi fought in Afghanistan, which is disputed by Roberts.

[45] Interviews with Temlali and Roberts.

[46] Interview with Ayachi.

[47] Author's interview with Mezrag Madani, former leader of the AIS, Algiers, March 2007. Mezrag was arrested after the coup of 1991. He described to me in graphic detail his escape from the hospital where he was being detained, which only became possible after he shaved his beard off and changed into western clothes.

The AIS gave an explicitly political content and justification to its violence and kept its military operations within strict limits. It claimed that it wanted to rehabilitate the meaning of *jihad* which had been distorted by the other armed groups. Mezrag argued that the AIS rejected the infidel (*kufr*) discourse which placed all those who did not support it beyond the pale.[48] It only targeted those who were instrumental in aiding the regime in its repression of the Islamists, such as the police, the army and government officials.[49] The AIS did not, for the most part, employ terrorist tactics and cannot be described as a terrorist organisation. In fact, it came into being partly in response to the indiscriminate targeting of civilians; it denounced such measures and attacked its perpetrators and those who collaborated with them.[50]

In contrast to the AIS, terrorism – indiscriminately targeting civilians – alongside other methods of military and political violence, became the mainstay of the GIA, in a gradual but seemingly inexorable process. Judging that there was a deep-seated 'longing for dissidence among the young', the GIA classified all individuals as either 'enemies of Islam' or 'supporters of the *jihad*'. The combination of these ideas became the justification for its indiscriminate assault on the entirety of Algerian society. It refused to differentiate between the Algerian state and those who worked for it, brooking no difference between soldiers and tax collectors, government officials and state gas company workers. In 1993, the GIA expanded its targets from military personnel and government officials to foreigners, intellectuals and journalists.[51] It ordered foreigners to leave the country in 1993 and started killing those who remained in mounting numbers. Gradually, the GIA shifted from targeting certain categories of civilians to mass butchery in villages and hamlets. By 1994, it had declared 'total war' on the regime and also all-out war on the AIS.[52] By 1996, around which time terrorist attacks reached their peak, it was threatening to kill all who failed to pay the *zakat* (Islamic alms) and women who did not wear the *hijab* (headscarf). Between 1995–8, bombings became more frequent than assassinations or armed attacks and targeted markets, cinemas, cafes, restaurants and other public places.[53] GIA terrorism 'featured the most barbaric forms of brutality and execution,

---

[48] Interview with Mezrag.
[49] Hafez, 'Armed Islamist Movements', p. 580.
[50] Ruedy, *Modern Algeria*, p. 264.
[51] Hafez, 'Armed Islamist Movements', p. 578.
[52] Martinez, *The Algerian Civil War*, pp. 116–7 and 207–8.
[53] Hafez, 'Armed Islamist Movements', p. 584.

including throat slitting, decapitation, mutilation, rape, kidnapping, and the slaughter of children, women and the elderly'.[54]

It is clear that repression and political exclusion were important contributory factors in the enlargement of the GIA. As we saw, former members of the FIS, alienated by the repression of the state, joined the GIA and contributed to its expansion. However – and this is the key to my argument – they had not formed its initial kernel. The repression and political exclusion of the FIS played a more direct role in the emergence of the AIS, which – in contrast to the GIA – did not employ terrorist tactics. The policies of the Algerian state and army contributed to the decision by some FIS supporters to take up arms.[55] Some of these radicalised ex-FIS supporters enlarged the ranks of the GIA, although the exact numbers are impossible to pin down. It is feasible that what eventually became the GIA would not have had the opportunity to grow had the coup not happened, although the GIA's core membership was comprised of Algerian 'Afghans' who had always rejected the FIS electoral strategy and claimed that democracy was un-Islamic. In contrast to the FIS, the GIA rarely made reference to the 1992 coup and when it did it was only to deny that its struggle was a response to the coup. It portrayed its struggle as one against apostasy, infidelism and tyrannical rule. Instead of democratic methods, the GIA envisaged the establishment of an Islamic state following the Islamisation of society through coercion and a reign of terror.[56]

The Gamaa Islamiya

Islamist Politics in Egypt and the Emergence of the Gamaa Islamiya

The symbolic beginning of organised Islamist politics in Egypt was the foundation of the Muslim Brotherhood in 1928 under the leadership of Hassan al Banna. The Brotherhood's early history in the 1930s and 1940s was associated, to some limited extent, with terrorism and political violence, as we shall see in Chapter 5, though this was not unique to the Islamist trend but part of a wider phenomenon in Egyptian politics. Two years after the Free Officer coup in 1952, the Muslim

[54] Hafez, 'From Marginalization to Massacres', p. 37.
[55] Martinez, *The Algerian Civil War*, pp. 20 and 48. Martinez points out (p. 111) that FIS sympathisers older than thirty years of age ceased from 1994 to identify with armed groups.
[56] Hafez, 'From Marginalization to Massacres', pp. 47–8 and 50–2.

Brotherhood suffered severe repression by Nasser's regime. Persecution led the bulk of the movement towards moderation, under the leadership of Hasan Hudaybi. But a minority diverged from Hudaybi's centrist direction, drawn to the radical version of Islamism which Sayyid Qutb popularised before his execution by the Egyptian authorities in 1966.[57] In an interview in Cairo, Diaa Rashwan argued that a clear 'jihadist' tendency emerged after 1967–8.[58] Qutb condemned the Egyptian state to the 'Islamic category of *jahiliyya*, or pre-Islamist barbarism, and argued that the restoration of Islam requires a revolution led by a 'vanguard of the *umma*'. Qutb's impact on the ideological evolution of Islamist movements throughout the Middle East, and indeed globally, has been immense. In his native Egypt, 'Qutbism', often loosely interpreted, provided the intellectual thread connecting a number of disparate radical Islamist entities in post-Nasser Egypt, some of which resorted to terrorist tactics.

Nasser's successor to the Egyptian presidency, Anwar Sadat, gradually released the imprisoned Islamists between 1971 and 1975. The Muslim Brotherhood then resumed its social, political and cultural activities. The most important hubs of Islamist politics at the time were Egypt's universities, which witnessed the rise of vibrant and increasingly popular Islamist student associations. The Islamist university associations reached the height of their power in 1976–7, with the tacit blessing of the regime, which sought in them a counter-weight to the leftist and Nasserist tendencies that challenged its legitimacy. The associations did not form a uniform ideological bloc but represented a wide spectrum of ideological positions on Islamism. The Islamist student activists of the 1970s subsequently joined and influenced a variety of Islamist formations, from moderate to the most extreme. Some of them eventually constituted the Muslim Brotherhood's second generation of leaders and are currently among its pragmatists.[59] Others followed a different course. An inter-university club called the Religious Group had been established by the mid-1970s 'to enhance Islamic awareness and promote religio-social as well as religio-political activism on campus'; the leaders of this

[57] Barbara Zollner, 'Prison Talk: The Muslim Brotherhood's Internal Struggle during Gamal Abdel Nasser's Persecution, 1954 to 1971', *International Journal of Middle East Studies*, 39 (3) 2007, pp. 411–33.

[58] Author's interview with Diaa Rashwan, expert on the Islamist movement, al Ahram Centre for Political and Strategic Studies, Cairo, November 2007.

[59] Author's interview with Khalil al Anani, political analyst and specialist on Islamist movements, al Ahram Foundation, Cairo, November 2007.

group in Assyut University, Nagih Ibrahim and Karam Zuhdi, emerged later as co-founders of the Gamaa Islamiya.[60]

The university associations' ideological diversity became apparent in the student leaders' mixed and ambivalent response – comprising both condemnation and unspoken admiration – to the militant groups which emerged in the 1970s. These groups were small but open to using terrorist methods and violence generally to achieve their objectives, and invoked the concept of *jihad* in the defence of Islam. The so-called Military Academy group, led by a Palestinian, Salih Sirriya, attempted to foment an uprising in the military training school in the Cairene suburb of Heliopolis in 1974, but was quickly suppressed. The Society of Muslims (Jama'at al Muslimin), also known as Takfir wal Hijra, led by Shukri Mustafa, had a greater impact.[61] Shukri and his associates had been radicalised in Nasser's prisons in the 1960s. They advocated an extreme interpretation of Qutb's writings but, judging that *jihad* was not possible for the time being, opted for a life of physical 'separation' (flight, withdrawal) from *jahili* (pre-Islamic, ignorant) society. It was turf rivalry with another group that led it into a small amount of violence, but enough to bring it to regime and media attention. It was in this context that it allowed itself to be drawn into a confrontation with the government for which it was really quite unprepared.[62] In July 1977, Takfir wal Hijra kidnapped and killed Muhammad al Dhahabi, a former minister of *waqfs* (religious foundations), which led to the annihilation of the group by the Egyptian authorities. Despite its short history, Takfir wal Hijra left an enduring legacy which was taken up by Islamist radicals in subsequent years and decades.[63]

The crisis around Takfir wal Hijra was quickly overshadowed by the furore among the Islamists caused by Sadat's visit to Jerusalem in November 1977. Sadat's peace overture to Israel, eventually leading to

---

[60] Ashour, 'Lions Tamed?', pp. 605–6. Ashour notes that in 1978 Nagih Ibrahim was elected the *emir* of all Upper Egypt in the Umar Makram mosque in Assyut, an event which marked the beginning of the transition to the creation of the Gamaa as a distinct and centralised movement.

[61] Takfir wal Hijra was not a self-appellation. On this issue, see Thomas Hegghamer, 'Jihadi-Salafis or Revolutionaries? On Religion and Politics in the Study of Militant Islam', Roel Meijer (ed.), *Global Salafism: Islam's New Religious Movement*, London/New York: Hurst/Columbia University Press, 2009.

[62] I owe this clarification to Hugh Roberts, email communication, February 2010.

[63] Rashwan has argued that the Military Academy group was the first real jihadist group in Egypt. However, he also suggests the precise connections between the Takfir wal Hijra group and al Dhahabi's kidnapping remain nebulous. Interview with Rashwan.

the Camp David accords of 1979, ended the tacit alliance between his regime and the Islamists of various hues. The breakdown in relations was followed by government repression which radicalised a section of the Islamists. Under increasing pressure from the regime, the Islamic associations expanded beyond the universities to poorer neighbourhoods and even rural areas. The Islamic Jihad group, led by Abd al Salam Faraj, arose from a coalescence of small radical groups initially in Alexandria, and then killed Sadat in 1981.[64]

A massive crackdown followed Sadat's assassination, and it was in Egypt's prisons that the Gamaa Islamiya and Islamic Jihad acquired distinct identities in 1982–3, on the basis of both ideology and tactics.[65] The reconstituted Islamic Jihad group, now under the leadership of Abboud al Zomor and Ayman al Zawahiri, argued that the ideal Islamic society would be achieved by directly striking the nerve centres of the regime or by a military coup and not by preaching to the people. What had come to be called 'Gamaa Islamiya' by 1984, and led initially by Omar Abdel Rahman, stood for combining the military struggle with reaching out to the people through preaching and other means of persuasion.[66] Incorporating the strategies of mass agitation used by the university activists in the 1970s, the Gamaa Islamiya believed in creating an Islamic mass movement through social reform and direct militant action. It also reflected the group's roots in Upper Egypt, the poorer and more undeveloped southern part of the country, therefore combining regional with class and sectarian elements.[67] Both Islamic Jihad and Gamaa Islamiya prioritised a violent interpretation of *jihad*, but their different approaches and strategies meant that, whereas Islamic Jihad 'remained an extremely secretive armed group with very few members, the Gamaa Islamiya 'widened and increased both its overt and its armed activities to become the largest and most influential of the Islamic religious groups in Egypt'.[68]

---

[64] Members of what later became Gamaa Islamiya were also involved in Sadat's assassination. International Crisis Group, *Islamism in North Africa II: Egypt's Opportunity*, Middle East and North Africa Briefing, 20 April 2004, p. 7. On Islamic Jihad's emergence, see p. 4. On the Islamic university associations generally, see Gilles Kepel, *The Prophet and Pharaoh: Muslim Extremism in Egypt*, trans. Jon Rothschild, London: Al Saqi Books, 1985, chapter 5; on Shukri Mustafa's Takfir wal Hijra group, ibid., chapter 3; on Faraj, Islamic Jihad and the assassination of Sadat, ibid., chapter 7.

[65] Ashour, 'Lions Tamed?', p. 607.

[66] Gilles Kepel, *Jihad: The Trail of Political Islam*, trans. Anthony Roberts, London: I. B. Tauris, 2002, p. 282.

[67] ICG, *Islamism in North Africa II*, p. 7.

[68] Diaa Rashwan, *Transformations among the Islamic Groups in Egypt*, Strategic Papers, Cairo: Al Ahram Center for Political and Strategic Studies, 2000, p. 15. The

Patterns of Terrorism in the Egyptian Conflict of the 1990s

An important shift in the pattern of the Gamaa Islamiya's activities occurred between the 1980s and 1990s. In the 1980s, the movement was not associated with any major terrorist activities,[69] although it did start targeting the Coptic minority in Egypt and showed other violent tendencies. In the autumn of 1988, the security forces had to forcibly retake a quarter at Heliopolis which had been occupied by the Gamaa.[70] At the time, the Gamaa was gradually establishing strongholds in the Upper Egypt provinces of Assyut and Minya and beginning to target the Coptic minority which is established in unusually large concentrations in that part of Egypt.[71] The Gamaa gained momentum and gradually expanded in Upper Egypt and the shantytowns of Cairo. It increasingly controlled mosques and held meetings overtly critical of the state. It imposed strict social mores.[72] However, in a gradual fashion from the turn of the decade, the movement attempted to incite a popular insurgency against the Egyptian state, using a variety of different methods including the indiscriminate targeting of civilians – namely terrorism. The Gamaa penetrated poverty-stricken areas of Cairo such as Embaba, a slum of low-rise, hastily built constructions with unpaved roads and intermittent electricity supply, which was eventually invaded by the security forces in 1992 to expel the group. Following that important setback, and gradually realising that they were failing to mobilise the masses, the Gamaa Islamiya turned to attacking tourists and police, as well as assassinating prominent personalities and continuing to target the Copts. It attacked the state and its 'agents' (politicians, policemen, etc.) and killed a secularist thinker Farag Foda in 1992. Egyptian citizens and other innocent bystanders were caught in the middle and used for political purposes. The confrontation between the Egyptian state and the Gamaa Islamiya, continued relentlessly from 1992 until 1997 when a ceasefire

---

activities of Islamic Jihad focused increasingly on the international sphere, ICG, *Islamism in North Africa II*, p. 5. See also Chapter 2 in this volume.

[69] There were three assassination attempts of prominent personalities in 1987 but they were carried out by a splinter group known as Najiun al Nar ('Survivors from Hell Fire'). Hafez, *Why Muslims Rebel*, p. 52.

[70] Kepel, *Jihad*, pp. 283.

[71] According to François Burgat, in Upper Egypt, 'denominational confrontation often results from the extension of purely local conflicts to confessional ones' – without this meaning, however, that such confrontations can only be explained in this way. Burgat, *Face to Face with Political Islam*, 2003, p. 82.

[72] Mohammed M. Hafez and Quintan Wiktorowicz, 'Violence as Contention in the Egyptian Islamic Movement', Quintan Wiktorowicz (ed.), *Islamic Activism*, pp. 76–7.

gradually took hold following the massacre of foreign tourists in Luxor in November. The ceasefire was officially declared in March 1999.

Did state repression and political exclusion drive the Gamaa Islamiya to terrorism? A number of prominent analysts have forcefully argued that it did. François Burgat firmly places responsibility for the Gamaa's escalation of the terrorist violence at the government's door. According to Burgat, government repression intensified following the appointment of Zaki Badr as minister of the interior in 1986, who oversaw a gradual increase in the arbitrary killings and other targeting of Islamists. In the early 1990s, against the backdrop of the Islamist challenge in Algeria and the crisis posed by the 1991 Gulf War, the government initiated an unprecedented escalation of repression which included mass arrests, collective punishments and arbitrary killings. The Gamaa responded in kind. Burgat also attributes the revival of political violence in the late 1980s to the Egyptian regime's blocking of legal political partici-pation: '[T]he fact that political forces seeking electoral recognition are prevented from becoming legal generates among them a natural tendency to radicalisation'.[73]

Arguing along similar lines, Mohamed Hafez describes Egypt's Muslim rebellion of the 1990s as 'partly a response to the politics of exclusion that served to delegitimize the ruling regime and the accom-modative Islamists who insisted on working through state institutions'.[74] The entrance of the Muslim Brotherhood to Parliament in the 1980s did not give them access to the levers of power, thereby further dele-gitimizing the Brotherhood among the radicals who rejected the path of accommodation. Hafez supports his argument by pointing out that the Gamaa did not launch attacks against the state in the 1980s. He writes that between 1990 and 1995, the Islamist rebellion *coincided* (emphasis is mine) with political de-liberalisation in Egypt,[75] especially the flawed elections of 1990 and 1995 and the political exclusion of the moderate Islamists. Although in the preceding years the state acquiesced to the expansion of the Gamaa, according to Hafez, it was alarmed by the late 1980s or early 1990s by the Islamists' growing appeal and violent meth-ods, setting off a cycle of violence and counter-violence. In August 1990, the regime assassinated Ala Muhyi al Din, an official spokesman of the Gamaa Islamiya, and in revenge, the Gamaa killed Rifat al Mahjoub, a

[73] Burgat, *Face to Face with Political Islam*, p. 93; see generally chapter 7.
[74] Hafez, *Why Muslims Rebel*, p. 48.
[75] Ibid., p. 52.

former speaker of parliament. Massive security sweeps followed, with a full crackdown launched in mid- and late 1992, which included thousands of arrests (comprising also family members of suspects) and the extensive use of torture. The state's repression was reactive (it occurred after mobilisation had started) and indiscriminate. As such, it turned sporadic violence into sustained insurgency.[76]

Former Gamaa Islamiya and Islamic Jihad activists, as well as moderate Islamists, have also argued that the escalation of violence and the use of terrorist tactics was a response to state policies.[77] In a familiar refrain, former Islamic activist Mamdouh Ismail told me in December 2005 that he and other activists were uncomfortable with the use of such tactics but they became an unavoidable response against government crackdowns and its decision to close down all avenues of negotiation.[78] Prominent Islamist Egyptian thinkers Muhammad Imara and Fahmi Huwaidi also describe the extremists as victims of political tyranny and social oppression.[79] It appears that Islamists who 'otherwise desired just to lead a righteous life and practice their faith in a more devout and concrete way' were forced to a militant position by a government campaign of harassment, arrests, torture and humiliation in police custody.[80]

The array of arguments presented here is less impressive than it may first appear, however. The Gamaa Islamiya's resort to terrorism and armed rebellion in the 1990s was *not* a response to political exclusion. The Gamaa Islamiya had always shunned parliamentary participation and vehemently condemned the Brotherhood for involving itself in an illegitimate political system.[81] As the Gamaa Islamiya was forming

---

[76] Ibid., pp. 82–91. This is also the argument in Hafez and Wiktorowicz, 'Violence as Contention in the Egyptian Islamic Movement'.

[77] Maha Azzam, 'Egypt: The Islamists and the State under Mubarak', Abdel Sidahmed and Anoushiravan Ehteshami (eds.), *Islamic Fundamentalism*, Boulder, CO: Westview Press, 1996, p. 114.

[78] Author's interview with Mamdouh Ismail, lawyer and political activist, Cairo, December 2005. He used the term 'violence', not 'terrorism'.

[79] Sagi Polka, 'The Centrist Stream in Egypt and the Public Discourse Surrounding the Shaping of the Country's Cultural Identity', *Middle Eastern Studies*, 39 (3) 2003, p. 47.

[80] James Toth, 'Islamism in Southern Egypt: A Case Study of a Radical Religious Movement', *International Journal of Middle East Studies*, 35 (4) 2003, pp. 562–72. Mustapha Kamel al Sayyid also quotes Gamaa leaders who argued that the security forces, and not aggression by the Gamaa Islamiya, were responsible for the clashes which began in 1987–8 and escalated in 1992–7. Mustapha Kamel al Sayyid, *The Other Face of the Islamist Movement*, Democracy and Rule of Law Project, Global Policy Program, Working Paper 33, January 2003, p. 19.

[81] Author's interview with Mohamed el Sayed Said, specialist on Islamist movement, Center for Political and Strategic Studies, al Ahram Newspaper, Cairo, November 2005.

during the 1980s, the Egyptian government tolerated the activities of the Brotherhood and allowed it to expand its influence in the professions and through Islamic banks and investment funds. The 1984 election was freer than any other had been in a long time. The beginning of the Gamaa Islamiya's shift towards terrorism in the 1980s coincided with the Muslim Brotherhood's most impressive electoral success, in 1987, when fifty-eight candidates of the Islamic Alliance, including thirty-five Muslim Brothers, gained parliamentary seats.[82] In the 1990s, when the regime reversed its policy of differentiating between radicals and moderates, the Gamaa felt vindicated by the Brotherhood's exclusion from the political process.[83]

The relationship between government repression and Gamaa terrorism is less clear-cut because government action and Gamaa reaction became part of a vicious cycle in which it was difficult to separate cause and effect. The Gamaa was preparing for terrorism and violence from the late 1980s. Its armed wing was established in 1987[84] or – according to other analysts – 1988, when some of its leaders travelled to Afghanistan to train. The killing of Ala Muhyi al Din, mentioned earlier in this chapter, took place in reprisal to the attempted assassination of interior minister Zaki Badr by some of the Afghan returnees in the Gamaa military wing in 1989.[85] According to Diaa Rashwan, the government was very 'aggressive', particularly in Upper Egypt, but the Gamaa was responsible for creating the infrastructure for terrorism and violence. Gilles Kepel argues that it was the continued attacks against the Copts and the Gamaa Islamiya's growing strength that triggered repression on the part of the government, which, in turn, led to the uprising. After 1992, several hundred Egyptian 'Afghans' returned home and presumably played a role in the escalation of terrorist tactics. His interpretation of events is that in 1993–7, the regime opted for head-on confrontation *after* the Gamaa had thrown down the gauntlet. Kepel also implies that the government's decision to stop courting the Brotherhood and to exclude the Brothers from political participation had not predated the radical uprising but was a consequence of it.[86] The June 1995 assassination attempt against Egyptian President Hosni Mubarak in Addis Ababa (attributed

---

[82] Al Sayyid, *The Other Face*, p. 14.

[83] Hafez and Wiktorowicz, 'Violence as Contention', p. 75.

[84] 'What Does the Gama'a Islamiyya Want? Tal'at Fu'ad Qasim Interview with Hisham Mubarak', Joel Beinin and Joe Stork (eds.), *Political Islam: Essays from Middle East Report*, London: I. B. Tauris, 1997, p. 316.

[85] Ashour, 'Lions Tamed?', pp. 610–1.

[86] Kepel, *Jihad*, pp. 276 and 283–98.

to Islamic Jihad but also others) led the Egyptian regime to even harsher repression against all Islamists, including the Gamaa Islamiya.[87]

The years of long and indiscriminate repression, especially within Egypt's prisons where most of the Gamaa's leaders suffered serious illnesses, poor hygiene, maltreatment, torture and even death, finally contributed to the *subsiding* of Islamist terrorism (although there were other causes such as selective inducements and social interaction and influences by other political actors).[88] The infamous Luxor massacre of 1997 was a desperate attempt by one faction of the Gamaa's divided leadership to gain the initiative against their rivals who were giving up the fight.[89] There followed a series of 'recantations' of their former actions by Gamaa leaders. The giving up of terrorism, however, may be only partial and incomplete. The lack of in-depth, open debate within the former movement about what had gone wrong and the meaning of violence, represented in its reluctance to disown the iconic figure of Sayyid Qutb, mean that the abandonment of terrorism may be on the basis of a short-lived calculation, not a real conversion. Regime repression defeated Islamist terrorism in Egypt but may have done so only ephemerally.[90]

Conclusion

This chapter on Islamist terrorism in the context of domestic conflicts in Algeria and Egypt demonstrates that political factors related to repression and exclusion from the political process were only partly and sometimes rather tenuously linked to the decision by Islamist groups to use terrorist methods. If political factors cannot offer wholly convincing answers in this case, to what extent are socio-economic and strategic/instrumental explanations more persuasive?

It does appear that socio-economic factors played an important role in the GIA's terrorist violence. There was, first of all, a strong economic

---

[87] Hesham al Awadi, 'Mubarak and the Islamists: Why Did the 'Honeymoon' End?', *Middle East Journal*, 59 (1) 2005, pp. 76–7. Al Awadi states that the attempt was claimed by Islamic Jihad. On the assassination attempt and its aftermath, see also Chapter 2 in this volume.

[88] Ashour, 'Lions Tamed?', pp. 621–2. Ashour suggests several other causes of deradicalisation, apart from repression (pp. 614–25).

[89] Ashour argues that the Luxor operation took place because those active in the Upper Egyptian areas had not heard that the 'historical' leaders, who were incarcerated, had declared a unilateral ceasefire. The attack, therefore, did not have the approval of the Gamaa leaders either in prison or abroad. Ibid., p. 613.

[90] ICG, *Islamism in North Africa II*, pp. 8–9 and 18. On the Gamaa recantations, see also Rashwan, *Transformations*, pp. 49–60.

rationale behind it. Already by 1993–4, the 'emirs', as leaders of the various radical formations around the GIA came to be called, were reliant upon the control of resources for protecting their groups and securing their power. Resource-rich zones became enclaves dominated by particular leaders, and protection rackets turned into a widespread phenomenon. Terrorism was a means of ensuring control of each turf. The social makeup of those who belonged to the GIA also played a part in the kind of violence they employed. In contrast to the MIA and the MEI in 1992–3, which had been dominated by students, workers and professionals, the GIA gathered 'fanatics', adolescents and criminal elements who were mobilised by prospects of gain and revenge.[91] Mezrag Madani described the GIA members as very young, uneducated and marginal.[92] The perpetration of inexplicable acts of terrorism and violence raised the lowly status of such individuals; it became a path to prestige and power, a means of social advancement.

Strategic/instrumental explanations also have some relevance in accounting for GIA violence, but only in so far as they refer to intra- and inter-group dynamics. Algeria expert Camille al Tawil has argued that 'the armed groups in Algeria developed in competition with one another, *more so* [my emphasis] than in response to predatory state repression following the 1992 coup that ended the electoral drive of the FIS'.[93] Since its creation (and in contrast to the FIS), the GIA was an ideologically exclusivist organisation in that it required total adherence to its radical world-view. But this was coupled with lack of centralised organisational control, which meant that the GIA was a conglomeration of armed militias each of which enjoyed considerable autonomy.[94] From 1994, there was a proliferation of armed bands which claimed to be acting in the name of the GIA – with strong economic interests at stake in their respective fiefdoms, as we just saw – although they were in fact distinct from it. The effect was deadly as each band used terrorism

---

[91] Martinez, *The Algerian Civil War*, pp. 100 and 208; see generally chapters 5 and 6. According to Martinez, whose thesis generally centres on economic motivations behind the conflict, the privatisation of the Algerian economy from 1994 provided the regime with resources which could be used to win over former FIS sympathisers. However, privatisation was also used by the guerrillas to their own advantage, with the creation of a 'plunder economy'.

[92] Interview with Mezrag.

[93] Camille al Tawil, *Al Haraka Al Islamiyya Al Musalahafi Al Jazair: Min 'Al Inqadth' ila 'Al Jama'a' (The Armed Islamic Movement in Algeria: From the FIS to the GIA)*, Beirut: Dar al Nihar, 1998; reviewed by Mohammed M. Hafez, *International Journal of Middle East Studies*, 35 (1) 2003, pp. 175–8.

[94] Hafez, *Why Muslims Rebel*, p. 115; Martinez, *The Algerian Civil War*, p. 208.

and violence to jostle for position.[95] Externally, the GIA had already declared war on the AIS in January 1996, when it became clear that the latter was not going to give up its demands to return to the electoral process. The two movements clashed continuously until the AIS's declared ceasefire in 1997. Internally, the massacres of 1997–8 further accelerated the break-up of the GIA which had already started in 1995, and GIA commander Hassan Hattab broke away in September 1998 to form the Salafist Group for Preaching and Combat (GSPC).[96]

Internal and external competition, combined with the GIA's disintegration, fuelled terrorism. The terrorist violence was not senseless; it formed part of a rational attempt to maximise civilian support and deter defections.[97] It appears, however, that it had the opposite effect. The reality was that popular backing for the GIA declined, as sympathisers found themselves unable to endure the cost of the conflict and stopped offering support or even turned against the movement. Others were simply alienated by the grotesque terrorist violence. The growing realisation that there would be no popular uprising on behalf of the movement consolidated the dominance of the extremists and pushed the GIA to more desperate measures and an upsurge of terrorism.

Islamist terrorism in Egypt also had socio-economic causes. The widespread support for the Gamaa Islamiya in Egypt's deprived urban areas and in poorer Upper Egypt (compared to Lower Egypt) demonstrates its roots in socio-economic protest. In her major study of Egyptian Islamism, Carrie Rosefsky Wickham, while emphasising the lack of precise evidence, argues that by the early 1990s, the militant groups had begun to recruit from further down the socio-economic scale, including younger,

---

[95] Internal divisions also led to bloodletting. In the autumn of 1994, following their merger with the GIA, which had occurred the previous May, the FIS elements led by Muhammad Said and his followers tried to take over or at least moderate the GIA. In 1995, FIS leaders Abdelrazak Rejjam, Yousuf Boubras and Anwar Haddam, who had defected to the GIA the previous year, withdrew their support. Hafez, *Why Muslims Rebel*, p. 172. Temlali argued that Mekhloufi joined the GIA in May 1994 with the objective to politicise it and push it to negotiate. (Interview with Temlali.) The attempt failed when the extremist al Muwahhidun wing reasserted itself and elevated to the leadership Djamel Zitouni, who purged his opponents. Said was executed in November 1995.

[96] ICG, *Islamism, Violence and Reform in Algeria*, pp. 11–14, 16. The rivalry between the AIS and the GIA, and the profound way it formed the two movements, is also a central theme in Hafez, 'Armed Islamist Movements'.

[97] Stathis Kalyvas, 'Wanton and Senseless? The Logic of Massacres in Algeria', *Rationality and Society*, 11 (3) 1999, pp. 243–85. Kalyvas refers to a 'strategy' on the part of the Islamist rebels, but I think the term is not quite accurate given the divisions and competition within them.

poorer, more rural, less educated men than in the 1970s and 1980s.[98] Socio-economic trends in the Muslim Brotherhood played an indirect role in this development. We will see in greater detail in Chapter 5 that the Brotherhood's political strategy had social underpinnings. Indeed, under the leadership of Umar al Tilmisani in the 1970s, it became gradually co-opted by the upper stratum of a merchant class which preferred passive social Islamisation and amiable ties with the regime to the risks of directly challenging it. The moderate Islamist middle classes lost touch with the radical militants among the students and young urban poor.[99] This pushed the Gamaa to increasingly desperate measures, including terrorism.

Strategic/instrumental explanations in the initiation and continuation of terrorist violence by the Gamaa did play a role, but less so than in the cases of al Qaeda, Hamas and Hizbullah. The Gamaa made a strategic error in failing to cultivate a base of support among the Egyptian population and relying on shock tactics to 'jolt' the Egyptian public out of its political slumber. However, terrorism – the random killing of civilians, including the targeting of tourists on whom the livelihood of so many Egyptians depended – had the opposite result and alienated the Egyptian public. As in the case of the GIA, terrorism appears to have been used as a means to 'persuade' the Egyptian population to rally to the cause of the Gamaa, but in Egypt, as in Algeria, the goal of ensuring popular support became ever more distant as terrorism escalated.

---

[98] Carrie Rosefsky Wickham, *Mobilizing Islam: Religion, Activism, and Political Change in Egypt*, New York: Columbia University Press, 2002, p. 115. She quotes Ibn Khaldun Centre studies, particularly Ibrahim, 'The Changing Face of Islamic Activism', *Civil Society*, 4, 1995. It is interesting to compare the social makeup of militant/terrorist groups in the 1990s with the previous decade of the 1980s. In a study of the militants who killed Sadat, Ansari concludes that the phenomenon could be associated with rapid urbanisation and rural migration into the cities, which entailed the break-up of traditional solidarities. Hamied N. Ansari, 'The Islamic Militants in Egyptian Politics', *International Journal of Middle East Studies*, 16 (1) March 1984, pp. 123–44. Saad Eddin Ibrahim's study of the Military Academy and Takfir wal Hijra groups, although based on a limited sample of thirty-four respondents, concluded that its members were far from alienated, marginal, anomic or abnormal: 'The typical social profile of members of militant Islamic groups could be summarized as being young (early twenties), of rural or small-town background, from middle or lower middle class, with high achievement motivation, upwardly mobile, with science or engineering education, and from a normally cohesive family.' Saad Eddin Ibrahim, 'Egypt's Islamic Militants', *Merip Reports*, 103, February 1982, p. 7. Nearly 70 per cent of Islamic Jihad's members in the 1980s were either students or professionals, mostly between twenty and thirty years old. Glenn E. Robinson, 'Hamas as Social Movement', Wiktorowicz (ed.), *Islamic Activism*, p. 118.

[99] Kepel, *Jihad*, p. 86.

5

Moderation and Islamist Movements in Opposition: The Jordanian Muslim Brotherhood/Islamic Action Front, the Egyptian Muslim Brotherhood and the Tunisian Nahda

Although the link between some Islamist movements and terrorism is real and deserves extensive analysis, the fact remains that the great majority of Islamist groups in the Middle East (and in the wider Islamic world) are non-violent and integrated in their respective political systems. Whereas Islamist terrorists grab the headlines, it is the moderate Islamist groups that affect the lives of tens of millions of ordinary Muslims more directly. These are complex social and political movements, with multiple roles, functions and objectives. Each has unique characteristics stemming from their particular contextual formation and development.

In the Introduction, I defined as 'moderate' those Islamist movements which eschew violent methods and have accepted, at least to a degree and on a formal level, democratic and pluralist values. (An equivalent shift towards more liberal and tolerant social ideas is not part of my criteria of moderation and is not, strictly speaking, my concern in this discussion. However, in the next two chapters, I will on occasion refer to Islamists' social views because they present an interesting contrast to their political ideas.) The concept of 'moderation', similarly to the notion of the political 'centre', is a relative one according to geographical and historical context – the same group and its ideas may appear moderate in one society or historical period, but extreme in another. Islamist moderates are *not* liberals – that variant of Islamism remains, at present, a rarity in the Middle East. Nevertheless, moderates have chosen to insert themselves into the social and political systems of their respective countries in the hope of changing them from within. Although they vie for political power, these movements, with very few exceptions to be discussed in the next chapter, continue to operate in opposition to existing regimes. They have acquired a stake in the political system but also remain antagonistic to it in important ways.

Does political inclusion, albeit in a relationship of constant political tension with dominant political forces, lead to greater moderation on the part of Islamist movements? Each of the case studies in this chapter suggests a discrete answer to the question. Jordan's Islamic Action Front, a political party established from within the Muslim Brotherhood, is an example of how inclusion in the political process since the 1950s has ensured the loyalty of the movement to the monarchical regime, the renunciation of terrorism and violence, and centrist positions on political issues. The case of the Muslim Brotherhood in Egypt is ambiguous. From the late 1960s onwards, the decision of the movement to distance itself from terrorism and violence and thereafter participate in the Egyptian political process appears to have contributed to moderation. However, the decision to participate, and moderation more generally, did follow a period of *repression* by Nasser's regime. Furthermore, since the 1970s, the Brotherhood has been subjected to persecution as well as inclusion by the Egyptian government – in a constant alteration of 'carrot' and 'stick' – without this leading to extremism or a return to violence. The third case, of the Nahda movement in Tunisia, is the clearest counter-example of the argument that inclusion leads to moderation. The Tunisian regime has politically excluded, severely repressed and indeed attempted to annihilate Nahda without the latter renouncing its moderate ideological positions or resorting to terrorism.

The Jordanian Muslim Brotherhood/Islamic Action Front

Islamist Politics in Jordan

From the time of its establishment in Jordan in the 1940s, the Muslim Brotherhood followed a non-confrontational approach towards the country's preponderant political institution – the monarchy – and enjoyed a close relationship with the Hashemite dynasty, especially its longest-serving head, King Hussein (1952–99). The Brotherhood incorporated itself in political processes, such as they were, in various stages of Jordanian history. Jordan's formal experience of electoral politics goes back to the 1920s. The 1950s were marked by a 'significant liberalisation', with opposition groups winning twenty-six out of forty seats in the council of deputies (the national parliamentary assembly) in 1951. The Muslim Brotherhood was legalised as a charitable organisation in 1945 and won 'broader legal status and a quasi-political role as a "general and comprehensive committee" in 1953.'[1] It fielded candidates as independents in the parliamentary elections of 1951 and 1954 and under its own distinct banner in 1956.[2]

An internal Brotherhood debate in this early period, on whether participation would bring sufficient gains to justify the symbolic and material costs of working through formal political channels, and the distraction from wider goals this would entail, was resolved in favour of inclusion. Following a period of intense domestic turmoil, all political parties were outlawed in Jordan in 1957, but the Brotherhood continued to operate legally, albeit as a social, charitable organisation.[3] Between 1957 and 1989, when party and then parliamentary politics were, to all intents and purposes, suspended, the Brotherhood carved out its political space close to the ruling regime, supporting King Hussein against the nationalist and leftist groups that were his greatest challengers. He rewarded the Brotherhood handsomely for its role as a 'loyal opposition' by allowing it to spread its influence through Jordanian society. Brotherhood members became influential in various economic, financial and cultural institutions, especially the Ministry of Education.[4]

These troubled decades in Jordanian history were punctuated by crises, first of all the Six Day War of 1967, which cost Jordan the West Bank and Jerusalem (and formally severed the Jordanian Muslim Brotherhood from the West Bank Brotherhood, as discussed in Chapter 3). Jordan was not to renounce its claim to the West Bank until 1988. In 1970, the Palestinian Liberation Organisation (PLO) was evicted from Jordan in a bloody sequence of events which came to be known as 'Black September'. Internally, deteriorating economic conditions in the early 1980s led to a slight easing of restrictions on political activities, to take the steam off discontent, although political parties remained banned and civil liberties circumscribed. In 1984, King Hussein recalled the council of deputies, which had been suspended in 1967 and then dissolved in 1974.[5] Developments were further precipitated by economic

[1] Jennifer Noyon, *Islam, Politics and Pluralism: Theory and Practice in Turkey, Jordan, Tunisia and Algeria*, London: Royal Institute of International Affairs, 2003, p. 84.

[2] Jillian Schwedler, *Faith in Moderation: Islamist Parties in Jordan and Yemen*, New York: Cambridge University Press, 2006, p. 155. On Jordan's electoral politics, see pp. 40–2.

[3] Ibid., pp. 42–3, 86 and 156–7.

[4] Ishaq Farhan, later the first leader of the Islamic Action Front, was minister of education in 1970. On the relationship between the Muslim Brotherhood and the regime generally, see Quintan Wiktorowicz, 'Islamists, The State, and Cooperation in Jordan', *Arab Studies Quarterly*, 21, Fall 1999.

[5] Schwedler, *Faith in Moderation*, pp. 46–7.

crisis and the introduction of a structural adjustment programme by the International Monetary Fund (IMF) in 1989, which led to widespread popular rioting in April of that year. Hussein announced the restoration of parliamentary processes as an attempt 'to re-establish some sort of control over events'.[6] The first competitive elections after a lacuna of thirty-three years followed in November 1989.

Electoral participation once again became a bone of contention within the Brotherhood in the 1980s, initially around the by-elections which immediately followed the recall of parliament in 1984. The decision to participate in the 1989 elections was justified using the Islamic concept of *shura* (consultation).[7] According to Jennifer Noyon:

The Muslim Brotherhood's move into the political arena was a new departure in its history. Despite some members' interest in specific political issues, the focus of the movement as a whole was on social and religious activities rather than on politics. Older, more traditional members in particular were accustomed to their roles as charitable volunteers and local notables, and were uncomfortable with the rough-and-tumble of opposition politics.[8]

The outcome of the dispute went in favour of overt politicisation, and in the November 1989 elections, the Brotherhood won twenty-two out of eighty assembly seats, which – together with twelve independent Islamists – meant that they formed the largest parliamentary bloc (although they had collectively won only 20 per cent of the popular vote). With the legalisation of political parties in 1992, the Islamic Action Front (IAF) was formed as a distinct political party, but was obviously dominated by the Brotherhood.[9] In 2001, a number of IAF members broke away to form the more centrist Wasat party, which occupies a middle position between the more traditional Islamist and the secular, reform-minded parties, but has remained marginal in Jordanian politics.[10]

[6] Philip Robins, *A History of Jordan*, Cambridge: Cambridge University Press, 2004, pp. 166–70; quote on p. 170.

[7] Schwedler, *Faith in Moderation*, p. 157.

[8] Noyon, *Islam, Politics and Pluralism*, p. 87.

[9] The relationship between the Brotherhood and the IAF is complex but not our subject here.

[10] On the Wasat party, see Mona Yacoubian, 'Engaging Islamists and Promoting Democracy: A Preliminary Assessment', United States Institute of Peace, Special Report 190, August 2007, http://www.usip.org/files/resources/sr190.pdf, pp. 8–9, accessed 15 March 2010. Adnan Abu Odeh argued that Wasat tried to 'nibble' at the Muslim Brotherhood. Interview with Adnan Abu Odeh, sociologist and political analyst, Amman, May 2007.

The IAF took part in the 1993 parliamentary election and then again in 2003 and 2007. In 1997, together with other opposition parties, it boycotted the electoral contest complaining of bias in the electoral system and limitations on press freedoms. It is indeed the case that the 'democratic opening' in Jordan since the 1990s has been extremely limited and punctuated by constant reversals. Far from signalling a genuine democratisation and the true relinquishing of control, political reforms were attempts by the regime to remove pressure from itself by facilitating a series of limited openings for the airing of popular grievances.[11] Civil liberties, especially the freedoms of expression and association, continued to be curtailed and the security services have worked assiduously to ensure the population's allegiance to the regime. Instead of agents of pluralist political contestation, political parties became vehicles for delivering patronage (*wasta*) and were seen by voters as such.[12] It is within this deeply flawed, semi-authoritarian system that the Muslim Brotherhood/ Islamic Action Front has operated.

Participation as a Cause of Moderation

What has been the impact of the Muslim Brotherhood's long-standing incorporation in Jordan's political processes, democratic or otherwise? As we saw, the closeness between the monarchy and the Brotherhood in the post-1950s period earned it the description of a 'loyal opposition'. The adoption of a more overtly political role after 1989, however, and particularly with the creation of the IAF in 1992, came at the cost of friction with the palace. The Muslim Brotherhood/IAF became more vocal in their criticism of royal policies, and in response, the palace tried to circumscribe their power. The biggest bone of contention was the 1994 peace treaty with Israel which the Brotherhood considered, in the words of Jordanian journalist Musa Keilani, 'a betrayal of a forty-year old alliance by the monarchy'.[13] The movement's increasingly Palestinian character created tensions with a regime which derives the bulk of its support from the so-called East Jordanian population.[14] Nevertheless,

---

[11] This is the overall argument in Daniel Brumberg, 'The Trap of Liberalized Autocracy', *Journal of Democracy*, 13 (4) 2002, pp. 56–68.

[12] Ellen Lust-Okar, 'Elections under Authoritarianism: Preliminary Lessons from Jordan', Frederic Volpi and Francesco Cavatorta (eds.), *Democratization in the Muslim World: Changing Patterns of Power and Authority*, London: Routledge, 2007.

[13] Author's interview with Musa Keilani, journalist, Amman, October 2007.

[14] Glenn E. Robinson, 'Can Islamists Be Democrats? The Case of Jordan', *Middle East Journal*, 51 (3) 1997, pp. 373–87.

despite occasionally profound differences, relations have never broken down completely.

In general ideological terms, the Muslim Brotherhood/IAF has moved towards greater moderation over the last few decades, albeit in a meandering and uncertain fashion which partly reflects internal divisions and disagreements.[15] On social issues, the Brotherhood/IAF remains very conservative, advocating, for example, segregated class-rooms, mandatory head coverings for women and a ban on nightclubs and alcohol. Despite advocating formal equality between men and women, the latter's position is clearly a subordinate one.[16] On politi-cal issues, however, there has been greater movement towards pragma-tism and openness, even though the espousal of democratic principles appears at times more formulaic than substantial. In its 1989 election programme, the Brotherhood declared a commitment to democracy and pluralism. Signing on to the National Charter of 1991, which codified political practices and citizens' freedoms, placed the Islamists (who had the largest bloc in Parliament at the time) alongside secular opposition members, including leftists, nationalists, and liberals, as well as tribal leaders. Since then, the Muslim Brotherhood, and later IAF deputies, learnt how to cooperate with groups which they had hitherto shunned.[17] In my conversation with him in Amman, Jordan, in October 2007, Abd al Latif al Arabiyat, one of the leaders of the IAF, prided himself on the movement's cooperation with other opposition parties from the 1990s ('for the first time in the Arab world', in his own words) and on the internal rotation of responsibility among the leadership.[18] Parliamentary

---

[15] The IAF is marked by important internal ideological cleavages. The leadership is con-sidered 'hard-line and rigid' and the more doctrinaire faction of the party maintains the upper hand. However, similarly to other Islamist parties, the IAF contains a wide range of views, and some mid-level officials in particular are more moderate and prag-matic. Yacoubian, 'Engaging Islamists and Promoting Democracy' p. 7. Muhammad Abu Rumman commented on the internal divisions between 'hawks' and 'doves'. Author's interview with Muhammad Abu Rumman, journalist and specialist on the Islamist movement in Jordan, Amman, October 2007.

[16] Sabah el Said, *Between Pragmatism and Ideology: The Muslim Brotherhood in Jordan, 1989–94*, Washington, DC: The Washington Institute for Near East Policy, Policy Paper 39, 1995, pp. 29–31. The continuing emphasis on segregation between the sexes and other 'moral' issues was pointed out to me repeatedly by various observers of the Islamist movement in Jordan. Author's interview with Mohammad H. al Momani, Jordan Institute of Diplomacy and Yarmouk University, Amman, October 2007; and with Muhammad Abu Rumman.

[17] Ellen Lust-Okar, 'Divided They Rule: The Management and Manipulation of Political Opposition', *Comparative Politics*, 36 (2) 2004, pp. 171–3.

[18] Author's interview with Abd al Latif al Arabiyat, leader of Islamist Action Front, Amman, October 2007.

participation meant that fundamental Islamist objectives, such as the status of *sharia*, would be open to debate, revision and even the possibility of rejection.[19] The IAF in particular has been flexible with its principles when political convenience necessitated. For example, in the lead up to the November 2007 elections, it moved corruption and good governance issues to the top of its agenda, playing down its conservative social posture, because this would secure it more votes.[20] As the eminent Jordanian sociologist and political analyst Adnan Abu Odeh succinctly put it, 'The new generation [in the Muslim Brotherhood] cares more about power than God.'[21]

Political moderation is combined with a steadfast and long-standing avoidance of any association with terrorism and violence, although not everyone agrees that this is the case. Critics of the Muslim Brotherhood/ IAF claim that despite the severance of formal links with the Palestinian Muslim Brotherhood, *cum* Hamas, the political and ideological connections remain strong, not least because the Jordanian Muslim Brotherhood is dominated by Palestinian Jordanians. The exact nature of these links is very much open to debate and tends to be an ideologically charged issue. IAF secretary general Zaki Bani Irsheid reassured me that there are no organisational links or consultations between the Muslim Brotherhood/IAF and Hamas. However, some observers claim that the Hamas influence on the Jordanian Muslim Brotherhood is inordinate.[22] Despite some hints of support to Hamas's military activities,[23] there is no real proof of the Jordanian Muslim Brotherhood being implicated in Hamas terrorist activities.

Within Jordan, the Muslim Brotherhood/IAF steered clear of any terrorist or other violent activities throughout its history. It remained distinct from the small radical Islamist movements, such as Muhammad's Army and the Armed Vanguard of Islamic Youth, which appeared in

---

[19] Schwedler, *Faith in Moderation*, p. 162.

[20] Yacoubian, 'Engaging Islamists', p. 8.

[21] Quoted in Stephen Glain, 'Mideast: The New Muslim Brotherhood', *Newsweek International*, 30 April 2007, http://www.msnbc.msn.com/id/18246924/site/newsweek/print/1/displaymode/1098/, accessed 8 June 2007.

[22] Author's interviews with Zaki Bany Irsheid, IAF secretary general, and Abdullah Abu Rumman, journalist and member of the office of the Prime Minister, Amman, October 2007. Critics also claim that that the movement's focus is more on Palestinian than domestic Jordanian affairs, which weakens its ability to produce a proper political or economic programme. This constitutes another bone of contention within the movement. Interview with Muhammad Abu Rumman.

[23] David Schenker, *Hamas Weapons in Jordan: Implications for Islamists on the East Bank*, The Washington Institute for Near East Policy, Policy Watch, 1098, 5 May 2006.

the 1990s.[24] The Muslim Brotherhood/IAF non-violent stance was clear and unwavering in the early 2000s, a period marred by Islamist terrorist incidents which culminated in the 2005 bombings of major international hotels in Amman.[25] These activities were linked to the insurgency in neighbouring Iraq, which affected Jordan profoundly. Following the 2003 US invasion of Iraq, there was a steady trickle of Jordanians across the border to join the insurgency against the United States and its allies. This traffic also moved in the other direction, with non-Jordanians using local extremists to perpetrate terrorist attacks in Jordan.[26] In August 2006, two IAF members of parliament were given thirteen-month jail sentences because they paid a condolence visit to the family of Abu Musab al Zarqawi, the infamous Jordanian who led al Qaeda in Mesopotamia prior to his death.[27] However, although individual members' links with the perpetrators can never be ruled out, the Muslim Brotherhood/IAF as a movement has not been implicated in any of these activities and they condemned the 2005 violence.[28]

Egypt's Muslim Brotherhood

The Monarchical and Nasser Eras
The Muslim Brotherhood in Egypt was established by Hassan al Banna in 1928 as a religious group with the purpose of creating the ideal,

---

[24] Beverley Milton-Edwards, 'Climate of Change in Jordan's Islamist Movement', Abdel Salam Sidahmed and Anoushiravan Ehteshami (eds.), *Islamic Fundamentalism*, Boulder, CO: Westview Press, 1996. On the connections between the Salafi movement in Jordan and violent groups in the 1990s, see Quintan Wiktorowicz, 'The Salafi Movement in Jordan', *International Journal of Middle East Studies*, 32 (2) 2000, pp. 222–3.

[25] It appears there is no organised extremist Islamist movement in Jordan as such, but individuals subscribe to an extremist mentality on an individual basis. Salafism, which constitutes a pool for Islamist terrorism, is a 'current', not a well-formed movement. Interviews with al Momani and Keilani.

[26] International Crisis Group (ICG), *Jordan's 9/11: Dealing with Jihadi Islamism*, Middle East Report 47, 23 November 2005, p. 1.

[27] Amr Hamzawy and Dina Bishara, *Islamist Movements in the Arab World and the 2006 Lebanon War*, Carnegie Paper 75, Washington, DC: Carnegie Endowment for International Peace, November 2006, p. 11. The IAF did not disown these members, however. For a discussion of al Zarqawi, see Chapter 2 in this volume.

[28] See http://www.ikhwanweb.com/article.php?id=5623&ref=search.php, accessed 19 March 2010. During the Lebanon war in the summer of 2006, the IAF took a strongly pro-Hizbullah, anti-Israeli and anti-US position, which appeared to be a shift away from their pragmatism of preceding years. Hamzawy and Bishara, *Islamist Movements*, p. 3. This, however, is unrelated to the issue of the IAF and terrorism, particularly in the domestic, Jordanian terrain.

Islamic society. The movement's early history, until the overthrow of the monarchy in 1952, focused on social, cultural and political activism, but the activities of its 'secret apparatus', created in 1942–3, included assassinations and bombings justifiably described as 'terrorism' by the authorities.[29] Such acts were not exceptional within Egypt's wider political context at the time, which was characterised by a high level of contestation and all types of political violence. Those turbulent decades in Egyptian history were shaped by the anti-imperialist struggle against Britain and growing internal strife, eventually leading to the collapse of the 'constitutional experiment' and the monarchy through the Free Officer coup of 1952.[30] Even so, the Brotherhood's resort to violence did not go internally uncontested. It was opposed by important elements within the movement, not least by Hasan Hudaybi, who became Supreme Guide after founder Hassan al Banna's assassination in 1949. Richard Mitchell quotes Hudaybi as having said, in reference to the secret apparatus, that '[t]here is no secrecy in the Message and no terrorism in religion.'[31]

The Brotherhood disseminated a conservative social message on issues such as women and the family, but its primary goal was the establishment of an Islamic order with *sharia* as its cornerstone. However, they were unclear whether this meant the complete reconstitution of society. From the moment of its creation, the Muslim Brotherhood's strategy was reformist, not revolutionary. Rather than being committed to the radical overthrow of the system, it favoured a gradualist building of an Islamic society from the bottom up. This required reforming the individual, through a spiritual awakening, then society at large, finally leading to the crowning achievement of an Islamic order.

The Brotherhood was ambivalent towards democracy, in particular those elements of democratic contestation which coexisted with the dominant monarchical authority structures in Egypt's pre-1952 political system. Under Banna, and later under Hudaybi, it rejected multi-partyism because of its divisiveness. Although the Brotherhood was involved in public affairs since its inception, it did not view itself as

---

[29] Richard P. Mitchell, *The Society of the Muslim Brothers*, London: Oxford University Press, 1969, pp. 66 and 77.

[30] Mitchell, *The Society of Muslim Brothers*, p. xxv. On this period of Egyptian history generally, see Afaf Lutfi Sayyid-Marsot, *Egypt's Liberal Experiment, 1922–1936*, Berkeley: University of California Press, 1977.

[31] Mitchell, *The Society of the Muslim Brothers*, p. 88, Hudaybi was quoted in the Egyptian magazine *Rūz al Yusuf*, 7 December 1953.

political in the *narrow* sense of pursuing particular ('selfish') interests; one of its principles was 'parliament without parties'. There was constant tension between its roles as a religious society and a political organisation, and it held to its traditional view that it would not exercise political power until the nation had been truly 'Islamised'.[32] Nevertheless, the Brotherhood developed links with the liberal nationalist Wafd party and the monarchy. Some of its prominent members, including Banna, even stood for election as independents.[33] Clearly, although not fully in favour of parliamentary democracy, the Brotherhood did not wholly reject it either. An Islamic 'order' rather than a 'state' was the Brotherhood's objective and this indicates that for Banna, Hudaybi and others, 'the existing constitutional parliamentary framework in Egypt, if reformed, would satisfy the political requirements of Islam for a "Muslim state"' – which means they did not seek to overthrow the existing order in the name of a 'theocracy'.[34]

The Free Officer coup of 1952 was followed by a period of political uncertainty for the Brotherhood, finally ending with the complete breakdown of its relations with the new regime's strongman, Gamal Abdul Nasser. A period of severe repression followed the movement's alleged attempt to assassinate Nasser in 1954 and then again in 1965 following the discovery of an alleged Brotherhood plot against the regime. The Brotherhood underwent important internal mutations in Nasser's prisons, leading to the radicalisation of some of its members. Among them, Sayyid Qutb, who was executed by the regime in 1966, produced the intellectual justification for revolutionary Islamist action in Egypt and beyond, as we saw in Chapter 4.[35]

Nevertheless, the greater bulk of the Brotherhood emerged from Nasser's prisons with the conviction that a head-on confrontation with the regime was not only unwinnable, but suicidal. Hasan Hudaybi's 1969 work, *Preachers Not Judges*, was a comprehensive refutation of Qutb's ideas and signalled the Brotherhood's firm, long-term shift towards

[32] Ibid., pp. 103, 132, 218 and 261.

[33] Gudrun Krämer, 'The Integration of the Integrists: A Comparative study of Jordan, Egypt and Tunisia', Ghassan Salamé (ed.), *Democracy Without Democrats?: The Renewal of Politics in the Muslim World*, London: I. B. Tauris, 1994, p. 211.

[34] Mitchell, *The Society of Muslim Brothers*, pp. 234–6.

[35] The relationship between the Brotherhood's early history and Qutbism is a fascinating subject and a very contested one. Ana Belén Soage argues that, in fact, Qutb did not diverge significantly from al Banna's path and that Qutb's thought was the logical continuation of al Banna's. Ana Belén Soage, 'Hasan al-Banna and Sayyid Qutb: Continuity or Rupture?', *The Muslim World*, 99 (2) 2009, pp. 294–311.

moderation.[36] The Brotherhood's subsequent attempts to accommodate itself to the existing political system and its willingness to engage in elections and civil society reflected the fear that they could not withstand a renewal of the attacks such as they had suffered in the 1950s and 1960s.[37]

The Muslim Brotherhood's Ideological Evolution under Sadat and Mubarak

As we have seen, the Muslim Brotherhood's ideological stance during the monarchical and Nasser periods was full of contradictions. Although the movement was radical in rejecting Egypt's social and political system and aiming for its Islamisation, it never wholly rejected existing institutions. We may not be able to describe the movement as 'moderate' during those early decades, but the ideological potential for moderation was there, primarily in its gradual, bottom-up approach to transforming society. A similar ambivalence can be observed in the Brotherhood's use of terrorist methods and political violence in general during the monarchical period. On this matter the ambivalence ended for the bulk of the movement as a result of Nasser's repression. During the presidencies of Anwar Sadat (1970–81) and Hosni Mubarak (1981–), the Muslim Brotherhood took further steps towards moderation by continuing to eschew violent methods and increasingly, if only formally, accepting democratic and pluralist values. The extent of these steps, however, remains profoundly contested and disputed. This section will track the ideological evolution before moving on to discussing its causes.

In a parallel development to its Jordanian counterpart (and indeed many other Islamist movements in the Middle East), the Egyptian Muslim Brotherhood has made the least progress towards moderate positions on social issues. There have been some gestures on the question of women. For example, since the early 1990s, the Brotherhood has declared that women can stand for public office, and there has been an occasional female Brotherhood candidate in national assembly elections. There are no women, however, in the Brotherhood's leadership structures, and as late as 2007, the movement declared that no woman can

[36] Barbara Zollner, 'Prison Talk: The Muslim Brotherhood's Internal Struggle During Gamal Abdel Nasser's Persecution, 1954 to 1971', *International Journal of Middle East Studies*, 39 (3) 2007, pp. 411–33; Barbara H.E. Zollner, *The Muslim Brotherhood: Hasan al-Hydaybi and Ideology*, London: Routledge, 2009.

[37] Maha Azzam, 'Egypt: The Islamists and the State Under Mubarak', Abdel Salam Sidahmed and Anoushiravan Ehteshami (eds.), *Islamic Fundamentalism*, p. 110.

become president of Egypt.[38] The discourse on the position of women in the family and in society remains conservative: Women have certain rights, but in fact enjoy no equal status to men. Makarem el Deiri, the Brotherhood's single female parliamentary candidate in the December 2005 parliamentary elections, whom I met in Cairo's Nasr City, was clear about hierarchy: '[T]he family must be led by the man', she declared, although she continued that 'he must not be a dictator'.[39]

The Brotherhood's approach to Egypt's Christian (Coptic) minority is similar. In 1995, Mustafa Mashour, then Supreme Guide, declared that Copts should not be allowed to join the army because they may betray Egypt, presumably because of their different creed. Such views continued to prevail well into the 2000s and beyond, even under the leadership (from 2004) of the relatively more progressive Muhammad Mahdi Akef. The first draft of the proposed Brotherhood party programme of 2007 created a furore in Egypt because it stated that Copts, similarly to women, should be barred from the presidency.[40]

On freedom of expression, the third major social issue that has occupied Egyptian public opinion over the last few years, the Brotherhood has also put forward restrictive and illiberal views. In Egypt's so-called 'culture wars' of the 1990s and early 2000s, which pitted Islamists against secularists over alleged cases of 'disrespect' towards Islam in literature, academia and the arts, the Brotherhood argued for strict censorship. (Even the allegedly more reformist Muslim Brother Essam el Erian stated, when I interviewed him in November 2005, that a minister cannot spend public funds on books which offend Islam, although he did say they can be published privately.[41]) Human Rights Watch has highlighted the collusion between Islamists and the government in stifling academic debate in Egypt's universities.[42] The Muslim Brotherhood's activities in parliament, and in particular the parliamentary enquiries they have

---

[38] Author's interview with Abu Elela Mady, leader of Wasat Party, Cairo, December 2005.

[39] Author's interview with Makarem el Deiri, electoral candidate for the Egyptian Assembly, Cairo, December 2005. Both el Deiri's father and husband had been Muslim Brother activists.

[40] Nathan J. Brown and Amr Hamzawy, *The Draft Party Platform of the Egyptian Muslim Brotherhood: Foray into Political Integration or Retreat into Old Positions?* Carnegie Endowment for International Peace, Middle East Series, 89, January 2008.

[41] Author's interview with Essam el Erian, Islamic National Conference Coordinator and member of the Muslim Brotherhood, Cairo, November 2005.

[42] Human Rights Watch, 'Egypt: Reading between the "Red Lines": The Repression of Academic Freedom in Egyptian Universities', *Human Rights Watch*, 17 (6) June 2005.

initiated since 1984, have sought to impose cultural and 'moral' controls on various aspects of social and cultural life.[43]

In contrast to social issues, where its conservatism remains profound, the Brotherhood has become more moderate on democracy and political pluralism. With growing frequency and emphasis, they have asserted the need to respect democratic freedoms in Egypt.[44] They espouse, at least in their official discourse, the fundamental principles of democracy as defined by international law. More specifically, they call for free and fair elections, the liberalisation of laws on political parties and professional associations, the right to demonstrate, hold meetings and publish newspapers and the lifting of the emergency laws that have been in force in Egypt since 1981.[45] They have increasingly cooperated with other opposition movements, including leftist ones.[46] On this evidence, a number of authors and commentators have argued that the Brotherhood has undergone an ideological 'transformation'.[47]

But the Brotherhood's acceptance of democratic and human rights principles remains circumscribed and formal and is not necessarily underpinned by the internalisation of liberal values. It supports democracy, pluralism and human rights at a rhetorical level, but its old guard continues to call for the strict enforcement of traditional legal rulings, as did Deputy Supreme Guide Ma'moun Hudaybi in 1997, for example.[48] Although the Brotherhood has started to revise its position on democracy away from Hasan al Banna's ideas,[49] the break has not

---

[43] Author's interview with Bahey el Din Hassan, Cairo Institute for Human Rights Studies, Cairo, December 2005. The same argument is made by Magdi Khalil, although the evidence he furnishes is somewhat vague. Magdi Khalil, 'Egypt's Muslim Brotherhood and Political Power: Would Democracy Survive?', *The Middle East Review of International Affairs (MERIA)*, 10 (1) 2006.

[44] Mona el Ghobashy, 'The Metamorphosis of the Egyptian Muslim Brothers', *International Journal of Middle East Studies*, 37 (3) 2005, pp. 382–3.

[45] International Crisis Group, *Islamism in North Africa II*, Middle East and North Africa Briefing, 20 April 2004, p. 13.

[46] Maha Abdelrahman, '"With the Islamists? – Sometimes. With the State? – Never!" Cooperation between the Left and Islamists in Egypt', *British Journal of Middle Eastern Studies*, 36 (1) 2009, pp. 37–54.

[47] See, for example, el Ghobashy, 'The Metamorphosis of the Egyptian Muslim Brothers', pp. 373–95. See also Bruce Rutherford's description of an emerging 'Islamic constitutionalism' which he distinguishes, however, from liberalism. Bruce K. Rutherford, 'What Do Egypt's Islamists Want? Moderate Islam and the Rise of Islamic Constitutionalism', *Middle East Journal*, 60 (4) 2006, pp. 707–31.

[48] Carrie Rosefsky Wickham, 'The Path to Moderation: Strategy and Learning in the Formation of Egypt's Wasat Party', *Comparative Politics*, 36 (2) 2004, pp. 208–10.

[49] Krämer, 'The Integration of the Integrists', pp. 212–3.

been complete: loyalty to the movement's founder has remained a tacit condition of election to the leadership, which inhibits the Brotherhood from breaking with the illiberal aspects of his thought, particularly his opposition to multi-partyism.[50] There has not been a formal renunciation of Qutb's thought either. The divisions within the movement on all these issues remain profound. No internal consensus has emerged within the Brotherhood on applying to become a political party. Among other reasons, many are wary of the implications of a step of this kind, such as transparency in leadership election procedures and clarity about political objectives.[51] Despite the existence of different 'generations' within the movement, highlighted in the work of Khalil al Anani,[52] conservative hardliners continue to have a powerful role in the movement. More progressive and liberal members, such as Abd el Monem Abu el Fotouh, have been repeatedly sidelined in favour of conservative leaders and were totally ejected from the top echelons of the movement in the December 2009–January 2010 internal elections which placed a conservative leadership in power. All this has led to criticism that the Brotherhood would jettison democracy once they no longer needed it, because their main objective is still to establish an Islamic state.[53]

Where does this leave us in terms of understanding the evolution of the Brotherhood's political ideas? Evidently, the movement has changed, but the change is not complete.[54] Abu Elela Mady, the leader of Wasat party, was exactly right during our meeting in 2007, when he said that the Brotherhood had made positive but not complete changes.[55] To assess the movement's ideological evolution, we also need to consider the political and social context in which it operates. If moderation is always a relative concept, the Brotherhood is clearly 'moderate' in an Egypt which has become increasingly conservative and religious-minded over the last few decades. As analyst Maha Azzam has put it, 'in today's Egypt, the moderate interpretation of Islam is what was once considered extreme'.[56]

---

[50] ICG, *Islamism in North Africa II*, p. 15.
[51] Interview with Mady.
[52] Author's interview with Khalil al Anani, political analyst and specialist on Islamist movements, al Ahram Foundation, Cairo, November 2007. See his *Al-Ikhwan al-Muslimun (The Muslim Brotherhood)*, Cairo: Dar el Sorouk, December 2007.
[53] Khalil, 'Egypt's Muslim Brotherhood and Political Power'. Note, however, that the evidence in this article is not particularly strong or convincing.
[54] Author's interview with Mohamed el Sayed Said, specialist on Islamist movement, Center for Political and Strategic Studies, Al Ahram Newspaper, Cairo, November 2005.
[55] Interview with Mady.
[56] Azzam, 'Egypt', p. 120.

None of this uncertainty and ambiguity applies to terrorism and violence, which the Brotherhood has consistently renounced and stayed away from for the last forty years. Of course, sceptics would also question this statement. When I first started visiting Egypt in the 1990s, it was repeatedly put to me by political analysts and ordinary people that the Brotherhood was the 'political arm' of the Gamaa Islamiya, and that Islamist 'moderates' and 'radicals' were not substantially different, sharing common objectives if not necessarily strategies. Another long-standing criticism has been that the Brotherhood supports terrorism and violence tacitly by not condemning terrorist acts stringently enough, for example or by implication in terms of friendliness towards Sudan's Islamic regime despite its repressive and violent practices.[57] Be that as it may, there is no *evidence* in the public domain that the Brotherhood has perpetrated any terrorist acts directly over the last few decades. Even the public demeanour of the movement is cautious and conciliatory: in the late 1990s–early 2000s, the Brotherhood's popular demonstrations have tended to be more 'tame' than those organised by Egypt's left-wing organisations. There is no necessary connection between this observation and the renunciation of terrorism, but it arguably indicates a determination on the part of the Brotherhood to play within the established rules.

Participation and Repression as Causes of Moderation

Did the Muslim Brotherhood's inclusion and political participation in the post-1970 period contribute to its real, albeit limited, ideological change? Or was moderation the outcome of the movement's continuing, if intermittent, repression under the regimes of Sadat and Mubarak? In fact, both inclusion and repression played a role in the movement's shift to moderation.

After the severity of the Nasser years, a more mutually beneficial relationship with Anwar Sadat's government improved the fortunes of the Islamist movement as a whole. As Islamist student associations expanded in Egypt's universities in the 1970s, 'the regime erected no obstacles to their freedom of expression' and they, in return, 'refrained from attacking the regime too openly'.[58] With respect to political participation, there were gradual but important shifts as Egypt moved from a single-party system to a (restricted) multi-partyism after 1975–6.[59] Brotherhood candidates

---

[57] Magdi Khalil, 'Egypt's Muslim Brotherhood and Political Power'.

[58] Gilles Kepel, *The Prophet and Pharaoh: Muslim Extremism in Egypt*, trans. Jon Rothschild, London: Al Saqi Books, 1985, p. 146.

[59] Interestingly, Mady argues that the Brotherhood was in a position of weakness in the 1970s. Interview with Mady. A different but intriguing argument is made by Kepel who

participated in national elections as independents from the 1980s. They did so in alliance with the new Wafd party in 1984 and then with the Liberal and Labour parties in 1987. Electoral participation continued in the 1990s and 2000s, during which time the Muslim Brotherhood's concern with state recognition shaped their discourse and attitudes.[60] The Brotherhood was also active in student unions and professional associations, dominating the latter in the 1990s. Increasingly, some – albeit guarded – links of mutual support formed between the Brotherhood and secular liberal and social democratic opposition forces.[61]

Partial integration and the intermittent appearance of the 'carrot' of further participation ensured that the Brotherhood acquired and retained a stake in the system. For Mona el Ghobashy, the Brotherhood's 'energetic capitalization of Egypt's sliver of electoral competition for seats in Parliament, the professional unions, and municipal councils has had a profound effect on their political thought and organization'. In her view, the Brotherhood's case confirms that 'it is the institutional rules of participation rather than the commandments of ideology that motivate political parties. Even the most ideologically committed and organizationally stalwart parties are transformed in the process of interacting with competitors, citizens, and the state. Ideology and organization bow to the terms of participation.'[62] Recent developments confirm this view if only by default. The hard-line conservatives who emerged triumphant in the leadership contest in the Muslim Brotherhood in December 2009– January 2010 mentioned earlier advocate a renewed concentration on preaching and social reform.[63] They sidelined the more pragmatic or reformist elements who favoured continued political participation and

writes that the Muslim Brotherhood organisation was destroyed by Nasser in 1954, and that the role of the reconstituted Brotherhood, which coalesced around the magazine called *Dawa* in the 1970s, remained marginal. According to Kepel, the tendency around *Dawa* should be called neo-Muslim Brethren and the Jama'at al Ikhwan al Muslimin, the Islamist student associations, were the Muslim Brethren proper. Ibid., p. 107.

[60] This argument resonates with the view of Holger Albrecht that the existence of opposition in Egypt, including Islamist opposition, strengthens rather than weakens authoritarianism. Holger Albrecht, 'How Can Opposition Support Authoritarianism? Lessons from Egypt', *Democratization*, 12 (3) 2005, pp. 1–20.

[61] Interview with Mohamed el Sayed Said.

[62] El Ghobashy, 'The Metamorphosis of the Egyptian Muslim Brothers', pp. 374 and 390 for the respective quotes.

[63] Fawaz Gerges, 'The Muslim Brotherhood: New Leadership, Old Politics' *guardian. co.uk*, 20 January 2010, http://www.guardian.co.uk/commentisfree/belief/2010/jan/20/muslim-brotherhood-egypt, accessed 3 June 2010; and Issandr el-Amrani, 'Brothers Take a Step Back from Politics', *Middle East International*, 2 (5), 8 January 2010.

contestation. On such evidence, it seems that politicisation does entail greater moderation and that only by legalising the Brotherhood would such moderation be further encouraged.[64]

These arguments are convincing but they constitute only one aspect of a bigger and very mixed picture. I previously alluded to the fact that moderation followed the severe repression that the Brotherhood experienced under Nasser. Although not the only reason for the shift, repression undoubtedly played an important role in it. The Sadat and Mubarak regimes, along with including and co-opting the Brotherhood in the political process, also subjected it to periodic, and often severe, bouts of repression. However, this did not radicalise the movement or push it to take up terrorism. Sadat courted the Islamists in the early 1970s but then suppressed them harshly when they rejected his peace overtures with Israel in 1977. Hosni Mubarak distinguished between Islamist 'moderates' and 'radicals' in the 1980s, using the former against the latter, but then switched to a policy of suppressing both in the 1990s. Brotherhood leaders have been periodically imprisoned and the movement's activities banned, particularly around the sensitive time of elections. The regime has also tried to circumscribe the Brotherhood's dominant position in professional associations. Finally, even if the Brotherhood were to apply for legalisation as a political party, the regime would almost certainly not approve it.

This is clear from the regime's policy towards the Wasat, a political formation which broke away from the Brotherhood in 1996 and has subsequently repeatedly applied for – and been refused – legalisation as a political party. Although the Wasat still has some way to go in being described as an Islamist liberal party, especially on the question of women, its positions are considerably more liberal and progressive than the Brotherhood's.[65] In contrast to the Brotherhood, Wasat does not see *sharia* as fixed and unchanging and argues for its constant revision using

---

[64] This was the view expressed by Saad Eddin Ibrahim; interview with the author, Ibn Khaldun Centre for Political Studies, Cairo, November 2005. International Crisis Group also emphasises the view that the most politicised element of the Islamists is the least fundamentalist. International Crisis Group, *Understanding Islamism*, Middle East/North Africa Report 37, 2 March 2005, p. 5.

[65] The relationship between the Brotherhood and Wasat has been subject to considerable debate over the years since the latter's establishment. For some, Wasat was the product of the Brotherhood's lack of deep ideological transformation which forced some members, who were dissatisfied with its internal practices, to abandon the parent organisation. For others, the creation of the Wasat was instigated by the Brotherhood itself as a 'trial balloon' for the legalisation of an Islamist political party. Be that as it may, the split became deep and entrenched in subsequent years.

the method of reinterpretation (*ijtihad*). It claims to fully accept the concepts of popular sovereignty, pluralism and sexual equality and is in favour of complete equality between Muslims and Copts. It describes itself as a civil party with an Islamic background.[66]

Wasat emerged from the ranks of middle-generation Muslim Brotherhood activists who had been able, since the partial political liberalisation of the 1970s, to participate in Egyptian public life. In the course of their careers, these individuals assumed positions of responsibility in professional associations and interacted with leaders of parties and non-governmental organisations, human rights activists, academics and journalists, inside and outside the Islamist camp. They entered 'into sustained interaction with leaders of parties and nongovernmental organizations, human rights activists, academics, and journalists outside the Islamist camp, including Coptic Christians and unveiled, assertive women' and, in the words of Abu Elela Mady, these experiences gradually made them realise that 'they don't monopolise the Truth'.[67] However, according to political analysts Joshua Stacker and Carrie Rosefsky Wickham, the Wasat party was equally an outcome of repression, and in particular of the 1995 security operation against the Brotherhood which occurred in a period of intensified authoritarian rule.[68] Ultimately, the case of Egypt suggests that 'democratic learning in nondemocratic, non-western settings can be propelled by *a mix of regime accommodation and repression*' (my emphasis).[69] Wickham's conclusion on the Wasat party applies as much to the Muslim Brotherhood which, far from being radicalised by repression, has remained determined to avoid further confrontations with the regime and anxious to present itself 'as a moderate and responsible opposition that poses no threat to the public order.'[70]

Tunisia's Nahda

Islamist Politics in Tunisia

The seed for what eventually developed into Tunisia's Islamist movement was planted in the early 1970s by emissaries from the Dawa group who

---

[66] Wickham, 'The Path to Moderation', pp. 214–20.

[67] Ibid., pp. 219–20. The quote is from Wickham's interview with Mady in Cairo in July 1997.

[68] Ibid., p. 212; Joshua A. Stacher, 'Post-Islamist Rumblings in Egypt: The Emergence of the Wasat Party', *Middle East Journal*, 56 (3) Summer 2002, pp. 415–24.

[69] Wickham, 'The Path to Moderation', p. 224.

[70] Wickham, *Mobilizing Islam: Religion, Activism, and Political Change in Egypt*, New York: Columbia University Press, 2002, p. 225.

arrived in North Africa from India and Pakistan.[71] The Dawa found fertile ground in Tunisia, where the regime of Habib Bourguiba, in power since independence in 1956, was undergoing a process of 'retraditionalisation' to shore up its weakening legitimacy.[72] The government was confronted with growing secular opposition from leftist and liberal organisations and from the Tunisian General Labour Union (Union Générale Tunisienne du Travail, UGTT) which represented a dynamic labour movement. To counter them, it increasingly used religious themes in its official political discourse, even while it continued to be faithful to Islamist modernist principles which had been enshrined in the Personal Status Code of 1956.[73] Furthermore, as 'social engineering' and a centralised development model were gradually abandoned in the 1970s, and 'Arabisation' spread in education in the 1980s, the public appeal of Islamism increased.[74]

In the 1970s, the Islamists' concerns were largely cultural and apolitical. They were conservative, even hard-line, in their social and political ideology, rejecting equality of the sexes, democracy and human rights as un-Islamic. The movement then gradually came under the influence of the Egyptian Muslim Brotherhood and was given a decisive boost by the Iranian Revolution of 1979.[75] The politicisation of the movement was marked by the establishment of the Movement of the Islamic Tendency (Mouvement de la Tendance Islamique, MTI) in 1979. It alarmed the regime which, having hitherto tolerated the Islamists as a counter-balance to the left, now began to see them as a threat. As soon as the MTI applied for legalisation as a political party in 1981, its leadership was imprisoned. The initial period of repression lasted until 1984. As a result, a loose group called the 'Progressive Islamists', led by Salaheddine Jourchi and Ahmida Enneifer, which opted for a more liberal, intellectual Islamist approach, split off.[76] During the summer

---

[71] Douglas Kent Magnuson, *Islamic Reform in Contemporary Tunisia: A Comparative Ethnographic Study*, Unpublished PhD thesis, Department of Anthropology, Brown University, May 1987.

[72] Abdelkader Zghal, 'The Reactivation of Tradition in a Post-Traditional Society', *Daedalus*, 102 (1) 1973, pp. 225–37.

[73] On the basis of a modernist interpretation of Islam, the Tunisian Personal Status Code went further than any other in the Arab world in enhancing women's rights.

[74] Katerina Dalacoura, *Islam, Liberalism and Human Rights: Implications for International Relations*, revised edition, London: I. B. Tauris, 2003, p. 165.

[75] Muhammad Mahmoud, 'Women and Islamism: The Case of Rashid al-Ghannushi in Tunisia', Abdel Salam Sidahmed and Anoushiravan Ehteshami (eds.), *Islamic Fundamentalism*, p. 250.

[76] Alaya Allani, 'The Islamists in Tunisia: Between Confrontation and Participation', *The Journal of North African Studies*, 14 (2) 2009, p. 262.

of 1987, violent demonstrations and the planting of bombs in hotels in Sousse and Monastir were blamed on the MTI (though they denied it) and led to further arrests and trials of its members for plotting to over-throw the government.

In November 1987, soon after these events, the political situation in Tunisia was transformed when president Habib Bourguiba was replaced by his prime minister, Zine el Abidine Ben Ali, in what was effectively a coup d'état. The change led to a brief liberalisation and a thaw between the government and the Islamists. Alongside a wide range of secular opposition forces, the MTI signed the National Pact of reconciliation in 1988. It subsequently decided to participate in the April 1989 national elections, fielding its candidates as independents and winning 17 per cent of the total vote, with up to 30 per cent in some urban areas. Its strong performance alarmed the regime which clamped down on it once more. In June 1989, the Islamists' application to register as a political party under the name of Hizb al Nahda (Party of Renaissance) was rejected. Further alarmed by the rise of the FIS in neighbouring Algeria and its electoral (though aborted) success in the December 1991 elections, the Tunisian regime proceeded with a policy of sustained repression against the Islamists.[77]

Rachid Ghannouchi, the leader of the MTI/Nahda, fled abroad in 1989, first to Sudan and then to the United Kingdom where he was offered political asylum. Between 1990 and 1992, 8,000 Nahda sup-porters were arrested and mass trials took place in the summer of 1992 (in those trials, the regime asserted, without producing credible evidence, that Nahda was engaged in terrorist activities).[78] Individuals suspected of Islamist sympathies lost their jobs in the civil service. In an attempt to suppress all overt signs of Islamism, women were prohibited from wearing the *hijab* in official public spaces. Families of suspected Islamists suffered harassment and discrimination in what became, effec-tively, a policy of collective punishment.[79] Repression continued well into the 2000s which saw the release of almost all of the Islamist prisoners

---

[77] See also Fred Halliday, 'The Politics of Islamic Fundamentalism: Iran, Tunisia, and the Challenge to the Secular State', A. S. Ahmed and H. Donnan (eds.), *Islam, Globalization and Post-Modernity*, London: Routledge, 1994, p. 104.

[78] Noyon, *Islam, Politics and Pluralism*, pp. 105–8.

[79] Examples can be found in Amnesty International, *Tunisia: A Widening Circle of Repression*, June 1997, Report MDE 30/25/97, http://www.amnesty.org/en/library/asset/MDE30/025/1997/en/26a346c3-ea79-11dd-b05d-65164b228191/mde300251997en.pdf, accessed 7 March 2010. See also: Dalacoura, *Islam, Liberalism and Human Rights*, pp. 174–5.

but the continuing restriction of their civil and political rights and the banning of the Nahda movement. Ex-Nahda members continue to be restricted in their movements, access to healthcare, jobs and education, and subject to legal harassment.[80]

Moderation despite Repression

The repression of the Islamists in Tunisia has been part and parcel of the pervasive and severe authoritarianism of Ben Ali's regime. The country's secular leftist and liberal opposition has been crushed or co-opted; the UGTT, around which the country's labour movement centred, has become part of the state apparatus, losing all autonomy of action; and freedom of expression and association have been severely restricted. Despite the regime's attempt to keep up some appearances of pluralism and democracy, Tunisia under Ben Ali's ruling party, the Democratic Constitutional Rally (Rassemblement Constitutionnel Démocratique, RCD), exercises a monopoly of power.[81] The country's economic successes have been used to 'buy off' popular loyalties, despite rumblings about government corruption and crony capitalism. Opposition leader Nejib Chebbi, whom I interviewed in March 2007, describes Tunisia as a 'blocked' society suffocating under a ubiquitous, repressive governmental presence.[82]

The total eradication of political freedom and the severe repression experienced by Nahda have not pushed it in the direction of either terrorism or ideological extremism. On the contrary, Nahda has remained one of the most moderate Islamist movements in the Middle East and was described, again by Nejib Chebbi, as 'the most open-minded Islamist movement in the Middle East after Turkey'.[83] It had renounced the claim of being the sole guardian of Islam by the 1980s and implicitly accepted that its version of Islam was one choice among many.[84] In 1996, Nahda

---

[80] Amnesty International, *Tunisia: In the Name of Security: Routine Abuses in Tunisia*, report MDE 30/007/2008, http://www.amnesty.org/en/library/asset/MDE30/007/2008/en/b852a305-3ebc-11dd-9656-05931d46f27f/mde300072008eng.pdf, accessed 7 March 2010. There is no reliable survey data on Nahda's and Ghannouchi's support in Tunisia. Robert Lee, 'Tunisian Intellectuals: A Response to Islamism', *The Journal of North African Studies*, 13 (2) 2008, p. 158.

[81] Michele Penner Angrist, 'Parties, Parliament and Political Dissent in Tunisia', *The Journal of North African Studies*, 4 (4) 1999, p. 90.

[82] Author's interview with Nejib Chebbi, leader of the secular opposition movement, the Progressive Democratic Party (Parti Démocrate Progressiste, PDP), Tunis, March 2007.

[83] Ibid., His party, the PDP, has established informal links with Nahda activists in Tunisia.

[84] Dalacoura, *Islam, Liberalism and Human Rights*, p. 170.

organised its first congress abroad, in Belgium, to evaluate its policy towards the Tunisian regime in which it decided to give up the culture of confrontation and opted for a moderate policy. Its April 2001 conference in London decided to emphasise the policy of dialogue and create links with liberal and leftist opposition movements. In 2005, the movement cooperated with leftists, unionists and other opposition movements to demand greater political freedoms in Tunisia.[85] Although no Islamist liberal, Rachid Ghannouchi is touted as a paragon of moderation and (relative) openness of interpretation in terms of Islamist ideology.[86] In social terms, particularly on the sensitive question of the position of women, he steers a middle course between traditionalism and modernism.[87] Drawing on an interpretation of Islamic scripture, he endorses multi-party politics and the participation of Islamists in a non-Islamic government.[88] He argues that Islamic law should develop through the exercise of *ijtihad* and in accordance with public interest (*maslaha*).[89]

Tunisia experienced a series of terrorist incidents in the 2000s. In April 2002, an attack against a synagogue on the island of Djerba, in the south of the country, killed seventeen people.[90] In December 2006 and January 2007, Tunisia's police, army and secret service engaged in battles with armed radicals in Hammam Lif and Solimane, just south of Tunis, killing twelve of them.[91] The 2002 attacks were perpetrated by individuals loosely linked to al Qaeda. The later attacks were attributed to the Salafist Group for Preaching and Combat (GSPC) *cum* 'Al Qaeda in the Islamist Maghreb', which had allegedly crossed the border from Algeria to stir up trouble.[92] There is an argument that the emergence of Islamist terrorism in the country is at least in part caused by the regime's repression and policy of confrontation.[93] However, this policy

---

[85] Allani, 'The Islamists in Tunisia', p. 265.

[86] Azzam Tamimi, *Rachid Ghannouchi: A Democrat within Islamism*, Oxford: Oxford University Press, 2001.

[87] Mahmoud, 'Women and Islamism', pp. 249–65.

[88] Noyon, *Islam, Politics and Pluralism*, p. 101.

[89] Dalacoura, *Islam, Liberalism and Human Rights*, p. 170.

[90] Chris Hedges, 'A Nation Challenged: Tunisia: Explosion at Synagogue Tied to Jihad', *The New York Times*, 24 April 2002.

[91] Olivier Guitta, 'Terror in the Maghreb: Al Qaeda Linked Groups are Spreading from Algeria and Morocco into Tunisia', *The Daily Standard*, 14 February 2007, and 'Islamists from Algeria behind Recent Fire Exchange in Tunisia', *BBC Monitoring Middle East*, 5 January 2007.

[92] Craig S. Smith, 'Tunisia Is Feared as New Islamist Base: Qaeda-Linked Algerian Group Suspected of Using Country in Network', *International Herald Tribune*, 20 February 2007.

[93] Allani, 'The Islamists in Tunisia', p. 267. This argument was made to Allani by Abdelfattah Mourou, formerly the second in command of the Nahda movement.

has had the opposite effect on Nahda (or, more precisely, no effect at all in pushing it towards extremism). None of the terrorist activities in the 2000s had even the most tenuous link with Nahda, whose leader, Rachid Ghannouchi, has won libel cases against newspapers labelling him a terrorist on numerous occasions.[94]

Conclusion

Although political participation and inclusion can account for moderation in the case of Jordan, the evidence is ambiguous in the case of Egypt and contradictory in the case of Tunisia. If neither political participation nor repression explains Islamist moderation in these cases of Islamist movements in opposition, what other factors can account for it? The Jordanian, Egyptian and Tunisian case studies show that, on a basic level, moderation is the outcome of an instrumental calculation or strategic choice. Islamist movements adopt moderate ideological positions and abandon terrorist tactics because they estimate that a contest of strength against the regimes they confront is unwinnable.[95] However, focusing on strategic/instrumental factors still only offers us a partial explanation of Islamist moderation.

What more fully explains the shift towards moderation – and the steadfast adherence to it – is the changing nature of the social support given to those Islamist movements. The Jordanian, Egyptian and Tunisian Islamist movements examined in this chapter are staunchly middle-class entities which court the working classes and poorer sections of society through charity and social activism but do not challenge notions of private property and hierarchy in their respective societies in any substantial way.

The evidence in favour of this argument is plentiful. Jennifer Noyon describes the social support of Jordan's Muslim Brotherhood – a 'quintessentially middle class movement of older, established males'[96] – in some detail:

The Jordanian Muslim Brotherhood has long been dominated by a middle class and professional elite, such as doctors, lawyers, educators and some tribal figures. In Jordan's early years, its members comprised an important element of

---

94 See http://www.carter-ruck.co.uk/documents/newsletters/pdfs/newsletter%202003–2004.pdf, accessed 6 March 2010.

95 This indicates that the line between political explanations, such as repression, and strategic/instrumental explanations is in this instance very fuzzy. I will return to this point in the Conclusion.

96 Robinson, 'Can Islamists Be Democrats?', p. 384.

the kingdom's social and intellectual elite. Its leadership routinely met with the king socially and for political consultation. Its strength did not stem from an appeal to socially dislocated or uprooted urban masses. Blue-collar workers and peasants were not widely represented.[97]

Similar observations can be made about Tunisian Islamists. During their earlier history, they did not become involved in the vibrant Tunisian labour union politics of that time.[98] The Nahda leadership was 'drawn from an educated class which was largely traditionalist'; the movement had the makings of a counter-elite which sought to challenge the Westernised political class that had dominated Tunisia since independence.[99] The suppression of the movement makes it impossible to gauge how its sociological support base has evolved more recently, but the appeal to the middle classes is consistent with both its past and the more impressionistic information we have about it at present.

The case of the Egyptian Muslim Brotherhood is comparable, to some extent, to the Jordanian and Tunisian cases. In its early period, the Brotherhood appealed to, and was representative of, most social groups in Egypt.[100] In the post-Nasser period, the movement turned increasingly into a middle-class organisation. It supported Sadat's economic opening (*infitah*) and some of its members personally benefited from it. In a trend encouraged under the leadership of Umar al Tilmisani in the 1970s, the Brotherhood was gradually co-opted by the upper stratum of the merchant class. As we saw in the conclusion of Chapter 4, the Gamaa Islamiya challenge of the 1990s emerged partly as a response to this growing social trend in the Muslim Brotherhood. The 'divorce' between the Brothers and the poorer sections of society continued into the 2000s.[101] Even though ideological and class differences still separate the Brotherhood from Egypt's senior political and economic elites, the Brotherhood's ties to industrial workers and the urban and rural poor are sustained primarily through charitable activities.[102]

---

[97] Noyon, *Islam, Politics and Pluralism*, pp. 84–5.

[98] Magnuson, *Islamic Reform in Contemporary Tunisia*, pp. 175–8.

[99] Noyon, *Islam, Politics and Pluralism*, p. 99. See also Mohamed Elbaki Hermassi, 'La Société Tunisienne au Miroir Islamiste', *Maghreb-Machrek*, 103, Janvier-Février-Mars 1984. pp. 39–56.

[100] Mitchell, *The Society of Muslim Brothers*, pp. 12 and 38.

[101] Husam Tammam, 'Révisions douloureuses pour les Frères musulmans d'Egypte', *Le Monde Diplomatique*, Septembre 2005. The Brotherhood was also vehemently anti-communist.

[102] Wickham, *Mobilizing Islam*, pp. 209–10. On the complex issue of the Brotherhood's social support and economic policies, see also Sameh Naguib, 'Islamism(s) Old and

Ultimately, moderate Islamist movements reflect not just the values and interests of their middle-class supporters but also their wider societies on whose 'pulse' they rest a sensitive and expert finger.[103] There has been growing ideological convergence between the Jordanian and Egyptian Muslim Brotherhoods and Tunisian Nahda and their respective societies. I have argued elsewhere that Tunisia's Islamist movement is representative of the country's wider social development since independence.[104]

Earlier in this chapter, I pointed out how the Brotherhood's ideas appear increasingly 'mainstream' in the context of Egyptian society's growing religiosity and conservatism. A poignant example is the similarity between the Muslim Brotherhood ideas on the Coptic minority and the discriminatory way the Egyptian regime – despite the rhetoric of national unity – *actually* treats the Copts.[105] In the words of lawyer and activist Moheb Zaki, there exists a 'deeply entrenched widespread conviction among large sectors of the Muslim community that such discrimination as currently exists is in the natural order of things in a Muslim state, where it is unreasonable to expect strict equality between Muslims and non-Muslims'.[106] The convergence between the Brotherhood and Egyptian society is reinforced by the regime's long-standing effort to 'pull the rug' from under the Islamist opposition's feet by appearing respectful of Islamic values. The same applies in Jordan and even Tunisia, despite its regime's avowed Islamist modernism.

New', Rabab el Mahdi and Philip Marfleet (eds.), *Egypt: The Moment of Change*, London: Zed Books, 2009, 114–6.

[103] The moderation of Islamist movements is not due to the fact that their support derives from the middle classes in itself (after all, as we saw from the earlier discussion, most members of groups which employ terrorist tactics are middle-class, educated individuals). It is a product, rather, of the conservative values of these middle classes and the way the middle classes' relationship with their respective states has evolved. This is a complex issue which I cannot expound on here.

[104] Dalacoura, *Islam, Liberalism and Human Rights*, chapter 5.

[105] The Coptic minority in Egypt is the object of indirect discrimination, for instance, in suffering restrictions in church building. Copts do not enjoy political representation commensurate with their numbers. In the view of Mahmoud Nahla, if the Brotherhood ever came to power, the Copts would be slightly worse off than they are under the present regime. Author's interview with Mahmoud Nahla, lawyer, al Kalema organisation, Cairo, December 2005.

[106] Moheb Zaki, 'Strike Down the Hamayonic Decree', *Civil Society and Democratization in the Arab World*, 11 (131) 2005, p. 2.

6

Islamist Moderation and the Experience of Government: Turkey's Welfare and Justice and Development Parties and the Islamic Republic of Iran

The great majority of Islamist movements in the Middle East are opposition movements. Islamists who have held the reins of government are few and far between, but it is these cases that I will now consider and my focus here is Turkey and Iran.[1]

The case of Turkey is unique in that Islamist parties have alternated in power at various times in the country's recent political history. The Welfare Party formed the government in Turkey in 1996–7 and the Justice and Development Party (JDP) has held power since 2002.[2] Turkey's political system is not fully democratic but, compared to most regimes in the region, contains a long-established tradition of multi-party contestation

[1] The only other case in the Middle East where an Islamist movement took over power is in Sudan, where the National Islamic Front (NIF) ruled in alliance with the army between 1989 and 1999. In some ways, Saudi Arabia can also be described as an Islamist state. The Saudi state was founded in the 1930s partly on an alliance between the house of Saud and Wahhabism, a puritanical variant of Islam. To this day, Saudi leaders claim that the country is ruled by Islamic law.

[2] Some would question the description of the JDP as an Islamist party. As we shall see later in the chapter, in contrast to Welfare, the JDP has defined itself as a conservative party informed by Islamic values, not an Islamist party. However, I think the reasons for this self-description are instrumental in that the label 'Islamist' or 'Islamic' is a liability in the secular Turkish context. In my estimation, the JDP does have sufficient links with Islamism as a political ideology to merit considering it as an Islamist party. Some analysts have labelled the JDP as a 'post-Islamist' party. Ihsan Dağı defines post-Islamists as those who have Islamic views but do not prescribe construction of an Islamic society by means of state power. Ihsan Dağı, 'Rethinking Human Rights, Democracy, and the West: Post-Islamist Intellectuals in Turkey', *Critique: Critical Middle Eastern Studies*, 13 (2) Summer 2004, pp. 135–6. However, as I argued in the Introduction, I eschew the term 'post-Islamism' because it implicitly assumes that, once liberal and democratic values have been incorporated within it, Islamism has been 'transcended' – in other words, that an 'Islamist liberalism' is an oxymoron.

and political pluralism. As a result, Turkey offers a rare opportunity to investigate the effect not just of political but of (at least partially) democratic participation on Islamist movements. The case of Iran offers another unique perspective on the effects of political participation on Islamism. Following a popular revolution in Iran in 1979, an Islamist movement took power and captured not only the government, but the entire state apparatus which it put to work implementing an Islamist project.

The political experiences of Islamist movements in government are qualitatively different from those which continue to remain in opposition. For the former, the objective of attaining power has been achieved. They have been incorporated in the political process in their respective societies *and* burdened with the responsibilities of government. In the double sense of 'moderation' as used in this study (eschewing violent methods and having accepted, at least to a degree and on a formal level, democratic and pluralist values), can it be said that this type of political participation has led Islamist movements in a moderate direction? As in other case studies in this book, the evidence is inevitably mixed. Turkey's Welfare Party and the JDP did indeed become more ideologically moderate through political participation before arriving in government and even more so in their efforts to capture, exercise and retain political power. However, *repression* by the Turkish state also pushed them in this direction. I will consequently track how both participation and repression, alternately and sometimes simultaneously, produced Islamist moderation in Turkey. The case of Iran is also ambiguous, albeit for different reasons. After the Revolution's first radical decade, the Islamic Republic undeniably moved towards a more moderate interpretation of Islamism. This took the form of a move away from the use of terrorist methods abroad by the regime and some steps towards greater democratisation in terms of both regime practice and popular preferences. The responsibilities of government had clearly been an important cause behind these shifts, although many other factors were also at play, as we shall see in the conclusion of the chapter. However, the reassertion of the conservatives and the election of Mahmoud Ahmadinejad in 2005 made it very apparent that the shift towards moderation was partial and contested.

Turkey's Welfare and Justice and Development Parties

Islamist Politics until the 1980s
Islam has been important in the political history of Turkey since the Republic's establishment in 1923, when Mustafa Kemal Ataturk's

secularist revolution aspired to make a clean break with the Ottoman past in favour of an imagined Western future by distancing the nascent Republic from Islamic beliefs and institutions. Conventional wisdom holds that the clash between Kemalists and those favouring a greater role for Islam in public life was an important contest throughout the course of the Turkish Republic's political evolution. The ideological clash purportedly occurred between a secularist elite, formed initially around Ataturk and the army, and the people's 'natural' identification with Islam. Historical reality may or may not correspond to this depiction, and one must emphasise, at the very least, that the secularist-religious divide was only one of a number of cleavages in Turkey's political development and not always the most prominent or important one.[3]

In an apparent paradox, Islam has at times been used to legitimise and reinforce the secularist Kemalist state. Ataturk appealed to Islam as a means of rallying the people during the War of Independence of 1919–23, and in the 1980s, as we shall see later in this chapter, the military used Islam to strengthen social and political control. Islam, however, has mostly been linked to defiance against the state which has taken forms of a military rebellion in 1925 in the south-east of the country, which blended an ethnic (Kurdish) with a traditionalist religious discourse, and less overtly, of societal resistance to secular legislation and practices throughout the Republic's history. Islam also found political expression within the Democrat Party which won the elections of 1950 against Ataturk's own Republican People's Party shortly after the introduction of a multiparty system in 1946. Although not an Islamist party, the Democrat Party was more amenable to a greater role for Islam in public life. The Islamist trend continued to be represented within parties of the centre-right (such as the Motherland Party established by Turgut Özal in the 1980s) and remains so to the present day. At the same time, a series of more explicitly and exclusively Islamist political parties began to appear on the Turkish political scene from the 1970s onwards. These include the National Order Party (1970–1); the National Salvation Party (1972–80); the Welfare Party (1983–98); the Virtue Party (1998–2001); the Felicity Party (2001–present); and the Justice and Development Party (2001–present).

For more than thirty years, Turkey's Islamist movement in its various incarnations was closely linked with the political fortunes of Necmettin

---

[3] For instance Toprak, writing in 1981, notes that from the mid-1960s, the left-right cleavage became a major source of conflict and religion assumed a less prominent role in political polarisation. Binnaz Toprak, *Islam and Political Development in Turkey*, Leiden: E. J. Brill, 1981, p. 124.

Erbakan. He led Turkey's first and short-lived Islamist party, the National Order Party, which was closed down by Turkey's Constitutional Court in 1971 for exploiting religion for political purposes, but was promptly replaced by the National Salvation Party (NSP) in 1972. The NSP took active part in Turkish politics in the 1970s, becoming a junior partner in three coalition governments. Jennifer Noyon makes an interesting and revealing comment about Erbakan when she notes that his, 'background and political career indicate the striking extent, despite the denials of many of Turkey's own political observers, to which Islamist parties have formed part of the Turkish political mainstream from the beginning'.[4]

The NSP was conservative and traditionalist, reflecting the ideology of the 'National Outlook' (*Milli Görüş*), a manifesto published by Erbakan, which pervaded all Turkish Islamist movements until the early 2000s. As the term indicates, *Milli Görüş* was permeated by a strong sense of Turkish nationalism, but as Henri Barkey aptly put it, 'Erbakan is first and foremost a Turkish nationalist'.[5] This nationalism was not seen as the antithesis of Islamism but as being in a harmonious relationship with it. The NSP's stated policies included lifting the ban on wearing the headscarf in public places, facilitating the pilgrimage to Mecca (*hajj*) via an overland route, preventing the confiscation by semi-official organizations of the skins of religiously sacrificed sheep and mentioning the phrase 'spiritual growth' for the first time in the Fourth Development Plan.[6] It opposed democracy and argued that the polity must be ruled according to the Koran, not the people's value system.[7] It argued that Turkey, as a Muslim nation, must stand up to the culture of the West and emphasised the importance of the family and moral values. It favoured rapid industrialisation driven by the state and prioritised social justice and education.[8] Turkish politics during the 1970s became increasingly turbulent. The extreme left and the nationalist right became engaged in political violence which mostly took the form of clashes both with the Turkish state and between themselves. The NSP also took part. An

---

[4] Jennifer Noyon, *Islam, Politics and Pluralism: Theory and Practice in Turkey, Jordan, Tunisia and Algeria*, London: The Royal Institute of International Affairs, Middle East Programme, 2003, p. 71.

[5] Henri Barkey, 'Turkey, Islamic Politics, and the Kurdish Question', *World Policy Journal*, 13 (1) 1996, p. 48.

[6] Ahmet Yıldız, 'Politico-Religious Discourse of Political Islam in Turkey: The Parties of National Outlook', *The Muslim World*, 93 (2) 2003, p. 191.

[7] Fulya Atacan, 'Radical Islamic Thought in Turkey', *Current Turkish Thought*, 64, Istanbul: Redhouse Press, 1991, pp. 15–16.

[8] Toprak, *Islam and Political Development in Turkey*, pp. 99–103.

Islamist youth movement (Akıncılar Derneği, 'Raiders' Association'), linked to the NSP, became active and militant during those years. The NSP used the youth organisation as a paramilitary force to counteract its political opponents, primarily on the extreme right.[9] However, there is no evidence that they used terrorist methods and it would be far-fetched to describe the NSP as an Islamist terrorist movement, despite is dabbling in other forms of political violence.

The Welfare Party

The coup d'état of 1980 – the third in the history of Republican Turkey, with previous ones having occurred in 1960 and 1971 – initiated a period of authoritarianism and direct military domination in Turkish politics. However, contrary to what one would expect given the army's tradition of staunch secularism, the coup did not give rise to a period inimical to Islamist trends. From the 1970s, an 'Islamic revival' could already be observed in Turkey, as elsewhere in the Middle East. It was discernible in the mushrooming of Islamic charities and associations of all types, the growing reference to Islam in public debates, the proliferation of Islamic cooperatives and other economic enterprises and so on. Mystical religious brotherhoods (*tarikats*) such as the Nakşibendis and Nurcus became increasingly influential.[10] Segments of the political establishment demonstrated Islamist sympathies and the conception of Turkish national identity started being increasingly 'Islamised'.[11] Ironically, the Islamic revival was boosted by the military's pursuit of an anti-leftist agenda, which made it sympathetic to a blending of Turkish nationalism and Islam, the so-called Turkish Islamist synthesis.

The 1980 military coup abolished existing political parties and banned their leaders from politics, including the NSP and Erbakan, but this did not eliminate the Islamist trend in Turkish politics. Former NSP activists and supporters, particularly its middle and lower-tier cadres, were quick to join the Motherland Party of Turgut Özal and organise within it as a distinct and influential faction.[12] Özal was the strongman of Turkish

[9] Ronnie Margulies and Ergin Yildizoğlu, 'The Political Uses of Islam in Turkey', *Middle East Report*, 153, July–August 1988, p. 15; Gareth Jenkins, *Political Islam in Turkey: Running West, Heading East?*, New York: Palgrave Macmillan, 2008, p. 184.

[10] An offshoot of the Nurcus is the currently widely prominent and increasingly powerful Fethullah Gülen movement. The literature on Fethullah Gülen is extensive and growing, reflecting the intense debate and interest in the movement.

[11] M. Hakan Yavuz, 'Political Islam and the Welfare (*Refah*) Party in Turkey', *Comparative Politics*, 30 (1) October 1997, p. 80.

[12] Margulies and Yildizoğlu, 'The Political Uses of Islam in Turkey', p. 16.

politics from 1983 until his death in 1993 and had himself been a parliamentary candidate for the NSP in the 1970s. The Welfare Party, a direct successor to the NSP, was established in 1983 by Erbakan and others when Turkey returned, at least nominally at first, to civilian rule.

Repression and the restriction of political space in the early 1980s, coupled with the desire of Islamist activists to re-enter the political fray, encouraged Welfare towards greater ideological moderation in comparison with the Islamist parties that preceded it (though moderation did not entail the weakening of the close connection between Islamism and Turkish nationalism which remained a *leitmotif* of Islamist discourse in Turkey[13]). As we saw, the NSP had dabbled in political violence, if not terrorism but Welfare shunned it altogether. A radical Islamist faction did appear in the universities at the turn of the 1980s but its appeal was very limited and it was not related to the Welfare Party.[14] Neither is there evidence that the party leadership had links to the radical Islamist organisations which emerged in the 1980s, mostly in the south-east of the country, and came to be given the generic name of Hizbullah.[15] On democratic principles, Welfare still gave mixed signals but, compared to the NSP, became overall more open to them and no longer appeared to seek the overthrow of Turkish democracy in favour of an Islamic Republic. Although it emphasised conservative moral and social values, it did not focus on the reintroduction of *sharia*. It started to appeal to human rights principles, specifically the freedoms of religion and conscience, if only to point out that the Turkish state violated those freedoms. The October 1993 Welfare Party Congress decided to open up the party to new groups in the electorate and adopt procedural rules of democracy and a more secular platform. This decision reflected the growing influence of the party's modernisers led by Recep Tayyip Erdoğan.[16]

Welfare's ideological message, combined with organisational efficiency and the creation of a nation-wide grassroots movement delivered electoral success.[17] In the 1994 municipal elections, the party captured

---

[13] Yıldız, 'Politico-Religious Discourse of Political Islam in Turkey', p. 197.

[14] Gilles Kepel, *Jihad: The Trail of Political Islam*, trans. Anthony F. Roberts, London: I. B. Tauris, 2002, pp. 346–7.

[15] Turkey's Hizbullah had no links with its Lebanese namesake or indeed any other such named movement outside Turkish borders. Jenkins, *Political Islam in Turkey*, p. 188.

[16] Metin Heper, 'Islam and Democracy in Turkey: Towards a Reconciliation?', *Middle East Journal*, 51 (1) 1997, p. 37.

[17] The role of women was critical in this grassroots movement. See Yeşim Arat, *Rethinking Islam and Liberal Democracy: Islamist Women in Turkish Politics*, Albany: State University of New York Press, 2005.

a majority of Turkey's governorates, including Istanbul and Ankara. In the 1995 parliamentary vote, it won a plurality of votes, 21.4 per cent. This electoral success also reflected an overall shift of the Turkish electorate to the right. As a result, the Welfare Party formed a coalition government with Tansu Çiller's True Path Party for one year, June 1996 to June 1997.

Welfare's experience of government accelerated its shift towards greater ideological moderation which occurred in many different areas (not just those that constitute the definition of 'moderation' in this study). Welfare's capacity for negotiation and compromise became apparent in the municipalities it controlled, when it backed away from enforcing unpopular measures such as segregated buses for men and women in Konya.[18] While heading the Turkish government in 1996–7, Erbakan had to endure the constant bargaining and political compromises of heading a parliamentary coalition. He was unable to sever links with the European Union (EU) and the North Atlantic Treaty Organisation (NATO), which he had advocated previously, and had to abandon his pro-Islamic stance in Turkey's foreign relations while presiding over the reassertion of its links with Israel.[19] Before taking over the reins of government, Welfare railed against charging interest and foreign capital and presented itself as the champion of economic justice. When in power, and being confronted with growing tensions between its different constituencies (namely the emerging Anatolian bourgeoisie's demands to open up Turkey's economy and its poorer supporters' desire for wealth redistribution), it opted for token populist measures which did not tamper with fundamental economic structures.[20]

Despite Welfare's proneness to compromise and pragmatism and its overall moderate tone and direction while in government, it did entertain plans to enhance the role of Islam in public life. For instance, Erbakan

[18] Noyon, *Islam, Politics and Pluralism*, p. 73.
[19] Before coming to power, Welfare had opposed the customs union with the EEC/EU and proposed instead an Islamic customs' union, led by Turkey. Its pronouncements were strongly anti-Zionist and even contained anti-Semitic elements. Little came of its grand foreign policy designs, however. Erbakan's attempted openings abroad, in the form of official visits to Iran and Libya, caused embarrassment rather than a fundamental reorientation of Turkish policy which, steered by the army, initiated a period of military cooperation with Israel. Erbakan had to endorse the new relationship and ratify a series of trade agreements between the Turkish and Israeli military industries.
[20] Meliha Benli Altunışık and Özlem Tür, *Turkey: Challenges of Continuity and Change*, London and New York: Routledge, 2005, p. 57–8.

proposed changing civil servants' working hours to fit with Ramadan, hosted the leaders of Islamic sects during the breaking of the fast and was rumoured to be considering reinstating military officers expelled for suspected Islamist sympathies (expulsions he had been forced to go along with in the first few months of being in power). There were allegedly intentions to build a mosque in central Istanbul's Taksim square and relax the prohibition on wearing headscarves in public places. Most of these proposals were symbolically powerful and they alarmed the secular establishment and sections of the populace who feared that the tangible long-term implications would undermine Turkish secularism. A celebration of Jerusalem Day in Sincan, an Ankara suburb, in January 1997, where Islamist sloganeering was prominent, was the immediate cause for the National Security Council (NSC) to become mobilised against the Erbakan government. In what came to be called the 28 February 'process', powerful pressure was put on the government by elements of the Turkish state, primarily the army, behind the scenes with the purpose of removing it from power. This made the government's position untenable and led to its resignation in June 1997.[21]

The Justice and Development Party (JDP)

The 28 February 'process' – a coup d'état in all but name – initiated a period of repression of Turkish Islamism by a state apparatus keen to uphold Kemalist principles. This repression was covert, in the form of a series of drastic pro-secular policy measures such as expanded teaching on Ataturkism in school curricula, the closing of *imam hatip* (religious) schools, enforcing the headscarf ban in public places more strictly, teaching Kemalism to top bureaucrats and prayer leaders, and so on.[22] It was overt in that Turkey's Constitutional Court closed down the Welfare party in January 1998 and banned Erbakan from politics for five years. However, far from pushing Turkey's Islamists to extremes,

---

[21] Gareth Jenkins, *Context and Circumstance: The Turkish Military and Politics*, Adelphi Paper 337, Oxford University Press for the International Institute for Strategic Studies, 2001, pp. 61–3. The overthrow of the government was spearheaded by the military but involved a broader coalition of military and civilian groups, with the tacit acceptance of a large number of civil society organisations. Ziya Öniş, 'Political Islam at the Crossroads: From Hegemony to Co-existence', *Contemporary Politics*, 7 (4) 2001, pp. 285–6. See also Haldun Gülalp, 'Political Islam in Turkey: The Rise and Fall of the Refah Party', *The Muslim World*, 89 (1) January 1999, pp. 38–9.

[22] Ümit Cizre and Menderes Çınar, 'Turkey 2002: Kemalism, Islamism, and Politics in Light of the February 28 Process', *The South Atlantic Quarterly*, 102 (2/3) Spring/Summer 2003, p. 312.

repression made them even more moderate than previously, in different areas and on many levels.

The Virtue Party, which emerged in Welfare's stead, led by Recai Kutan, a close associate of Erbakan, exhibited a greater appreciation of democratic principles as a result of this repression. It adopted democratisation and individual rights as central planks of its political discourse. It sought alliances with its secular and liberal counterparts and appealed to democracy and human rights values. This change was part and parcel of a wider ideological shift which involved taking a less anti-Western stand in foreign policy and less confrontational stance on the headscarf issue, as well as a shift towards a social democratic message in socioeconomic areas. In other areas, however, Virtue's ideological shift to moderation was limited. With reference to the Kurdish and other minorities, Virtue retained Welfare's non-pluralist understanding of society. Its conception of democracy appeared somewhat self-serving and was restricted to the legal issues surrounding the closure of parties and the ban on Erbakan.[23]

One reason why Virtue's ideological evolution was limited was that it rested on a fragile internal compromise between conflicting ideological and generational factions, specifically between the so-called 'traditionalists' (or conservatives) and 'modernists' (or reformists). This uneasy coexistence eventually deepened into a rift which split the movement. With Virtue's disappointing electoral performance in the national poll of 1999 (15.4 per cent of votes), a fierce debate erupted within the party. The subsequent closure of Virtue in 2001 by the Constitutional Court speeded up and legitimised the split between traditionalists and modernists.[24] Two distinct parties emerged, Felicity and the Justice and Development Party (JDP, otherwise known with its Turkish acronym, AKP, which stands for Adalet ve Kalkınma Partisi). Felicity, led by Recai Kutan, continued to toe Erbakan's line, whereas the JDP, led by Recep Tayip Erdoğan and Abdullah Gül, broke ranks with the old guard. If repression, particularly after the 28 February 'process', had been behind Virtue's shift to moderation, the Turkish electorate's signal in 1999 was that it had not gone far enough. Simply put, the Islamists realised that,

---

[23] Menderes Çınar, 'Turkey's Transformation Under the AKP Rule', *The Muslim World*, 96 (3) 2006, p. 473. Recai Kutan denied that there was a Kurdish problem in Turkey, and when he did accept its existence, he upheld the same solution, namely that the real source of Turkish identity is Islam. Cizre and Çınar, 'Turkey 2002', p. 325.

[24] Ihsan Dağı, 'Transformation of Islamic Political Identity in Turkey: Rethinking the West and Westernization', *Turkish Studies*, 6 (1) 2005, p. 29.

with their previous positions, they would only ever secure a minority of the popular vote and that to win a majority, they had to move further towards the political centre.[25]

The JDP represented the most profound ideological transformation of Turkish Islamism since the 1970s and a dramatic break with the past. The new party traced its political ancestry to the Democrat Party of the 1950s and the Motherland Party of the 1980s. Distancing itself from the ideology of previous Turkish Islamist parties, it described itself as a 'conservative democratic party' and refrained from describing itself as 'Islamist' or even 'Muslim democrat'.[26] Erdoğan maintained that he did not intend to establish an Islamic state because, in his estimation, the Koran did not offer guidance on how a state should be run, only on how rulers should act. This was a far cry from his previous statements such as 'Thank God I am for *Sharia*', 'For us democracy is a means to an end' and 'One cannot be a secularist and a Muslim at the same time'.[27] As late as March 2008 when I visited Turkey for fieldwork, Turkish analyst and civil society activist Hakan Altınay could argue that Erdoğan was still a 'work in progress'.[28]

If the JDP's political programme arguably moved in a moderate, even liberal direction, the party continued to express its conservatism most clearly on social issues.[29] However, even in this area, important changes could be observed. The headscarf issue was a central concern for the party. Even more explicitly than Virtue before it, the JDP described the wearing of the headscarf as a right and justified it on the basis of internationally recognised human rights principles, specifically freedom of religion and conscience.[30] In what constituted essentially an ideological

[25] Author's interview with Hakan Altınay, Open Society Institute Assistance Foundation, Istanbul, March 2008.

[26] William Hale and Ergun Özbudun, *Islamism, Democracy and Liberalism in Turkey: The Case of the AKP*, Abingdon, Oxon: Routledge, 2010, p. 20.

[27] Metin Heper and Şule Toktaş, 'Islam, Modernity, and Democracy in Contemporary Turkey: The Case of Recep Tayyip Erdoğan', *The Muslim World*, 93 (2) 2003, p. 176. In a sympathetic analysis, Heper and Toktaş argue that Erdoğan moved away from such statements and that in his policies and general comportment he always showed flexibility and pragmatism. For instance, he did not expect women around him in official circles to cover their hair. As mayor of Istanbul (1994–8), he banned alcohol from municipal establishments but not in restaurants; and his municipality helped to renovate churches and synagogues as well as mosques (see pp. 157–85).

[28] Interview with Altınay.

[29] Ahmet İnsel, 'The AKP and Normalizing Democracy in Turkey', *The South Atlantic Quarterly*, 102 (2/3) Spring/Summer 2003, p. 304.

[30] The human rights NGO 'Organisation of Human Rights and Solidarity for Oppressed People' (Mazlumder) defends women's right to wear the headscarf on the basis

volte face, it portrayed secularism as the best available guarantee of freedom of religion and conscience as well as an indispensable condition of
democracy. The JDP began to ardently support Turkey's accession to the
EU because it saw the latter as a potential guarantor of these freedoms.
Happily for the new party, most Turks also favoured accession, which
ensured that that it was in sync with what the electorate wanted.

The broad and flexible Islamist ideology put forward by the JDP
allowed it to capture the political centre without losing right-wing votes.
Its ideological message had wide appeal to the Turkish electorate and
ensured its success at the polls. The discrediting of alternative political
parties, partly though not wholly because of Turkey's 2001 financial
crisis, contributed to its success. In the 2002 elections, the JDP secured
34.28 per cent of the votes and two-thirds of the Parliament's seats and
was able to form a single-party government – a rare occurrence in recent
Turkish political history. The Felicity Party received a meagre 2 per cent
of the vote. In the 2007 national elections, the JDP won yet another
landslide victory with 46.6 per cent of the vote.

It is clear from the preceding discussion that the JDP experienced its
most profound ideological transformation *before* taking over power, but
once it did, it showed an even greater aptitude for realism and pragmatic
adaptation to existing political and economic realities. For critics, such
as Soli Özel, this was a sign of excessive opportunism; for Rona Aybay,
it was because the JDP had very little room for manoeuvre, especially
in economic affairs.[31] For the most part, the JDP had proclaimed a final
and clear break with the anti-capitalism of previous Islamist parties, but
its election campaign had still contained a vague populist message. Once
in government, however, its attempts to introduce populist economist
policies were half-hearted and ultimately thwarted by the constraints of
the International Monetary Fund (IMF) programme imposed after the
2001 crisis.[32] Its overall record was one of prudence and adherence to
the IMF prescriptions while attempting to cushion the poorer sectors of
Turkish society through charity.[33]

of freedom of religion. Author's interview with Ayşe Bilgen, Mazlumder, Ankara,
March 2008.

[31] Author's interviews with Rona Aybay, lawyer and human rights activist, Ankara,
March 2008; and Soli Özel, Bilgi University, Istanbul, March 2008.

[32] Ultimately the IMF programme was backed by the threat that funds would be with-
drawn if conditions were not met. Marcie J. Patton, 'The Economic Policies of Turkey's
AKP Government: Rabbits from a Hat?', *Middle East Journal*, 60 (3) Summer 2006,
pp. 513–36.

[33] Hale and Özbudun, *Islamism, Democracy and Liberalism in Turkey*, p. 118.

Whether by choice or by necessity, the JDP moved towards enhancing democratic and pluralist principles once it assumed power. As the government of Turkey, it had to carry out legal and political reforms to meet the Copenhagen Criteria for accession to the EU. In its first three years in government (2002–5), the JDP pursued these reforms actively. Constitutional amendments limited the grounds for conviction for 'hate speech'; the death penalty was abolished; international agreements were given precedence over domestic law; equality of the sexes was strengthened; and the State Security Courts were abolished. The political role of the military was limited, mainly through the restructuring of the National Security Council, and civilian controls were strengthened. There was an easing of restrictions on Kurdish culture. Despite its social conservatism, the JDP also pioneered important reforms to improve women's rights. The new Civil Code introduced in 2002 reinforced gender equality and granted equal rights to spouses on age of marriage, divorce, alimony, equal management of the marriage union and the exercise of parental rights over children.[34]

It would be inaccurate to claim that the JDP presided over the full democratisation and liberalisation of the Turkish polity. The reforms ground to a halt in mid-decade and the process of EU accession appeared to lose momentum (for many reasons, not all having to do with Turkey or the JDP). Kurdish rights remained restricted in various ways. Freedom of speech was still curtailed through the Criminal Code and the new anti-Terrorism Act which penalised insults to 'Turkishness' and the state – the novelist and Nobel laureate Orhan Pamuk being the most famous victim of the legislation.[35] Discrimination against Turkey's Alevi religious minority and difficulties for other minorities continued and were highlighted by the murder of Armenian journalist Hrant Dink in January 2007.[36] The JDP was not wholly responsible for these continuing restrictions on democracy and human rights – after all, it did not control the entire state apparatus and certainly not the judiciary[37] – but as the executive power, it arguably did not work hard enough to loosen these restrictions. For instance, it did little to defend the freedom of speech of the many writers and journalists who were persecuted on the basis of illiberal laws.[38] Although the JDP was arguably more open to ethnic

[34] Ibid., p. 62; see generally chapter 5.
[35] Ibid., pp. 57–8.
[36] Jenkins, *Political Islam in Turkey*, pp. 179–80. Jenkins mentions the continuing problems faced by the Greek Orthodox and Protestant communities.
[37] Author's interview with Ergun Özbudun, Bilkent University, Ankara, March 2008.
[38] Marcie J. Patton, 'Turkey's Tug of War', *Middle East Report*, 239, Summer 2006, p. 43.

and other types of diversity than other political parties (and, while in government, tried to establish better relations with the country's Kurds and Alevis), its ideas remained emblematic of a Turkish nationalism and political culture which was still illiberal in many ways.[39] In my meeting with him in Istanbul in March 2008, Turkish academic Ziya Öniş pointed out that in its second term in office, the JDP agenda was becoming progressively concentrated on freedom of religion issues and ignored other liberal reforms. As a result, the liberal constituency which initially supported the JDP became increasingly disillusioned with it.[40]

However, what has really incensed the secularist establishment and sections of society, and created deep divisions between Turkish citizens, is not the illiberal aspect of JDP ideology and policies (most of which they share, after all), but its perceived threat to secularist institutions and symbols through its policies of Islamisation. In its first term in office, the JDP was cautious in the pursuit of such policies, with the exception of its attempt to reinstate the *imam hatip* (secondary schools for prayer leaders and preachers) and to recriminalize adultery (a 'bad idea, badly managed', according to Hakan Altınay). Following its massive electoral victory in 2007, however, it became bolder and took steps to reverse the headscarf ban at university campuses. This move (a 'good idea, badly managed', according to the same analyst) backfired and the government was forced to back down in the face of strong opposition.[41] More generally, secularists charge that the JDP tacitly or explicitly encourages restrictions on the sale and consumption of alcohol and gender segregation, and that it favours a general conservatism in social mores. The profound divisions these issues have caused make it extremely difficult for the outside observer to assess them in any objective manner. This is all the more so because the JDP message is at times incoherent and contradictory, partly reflecting its nature as an umbrella organisation containing widely divergent views. The question of women is the most

---

[39] Simten Coşar, 'Liberal Thought and Democracy in Turkey', *Journal of Political Ideologies*, 9 (1) 2004, pp. 71–98. The relationship between the JDP and the Alevi minority is particularly complex and fascinating. Despite the strong secularism of the Alevi community, the JDP has courted it. They have also attempted to create links with the Kurdish minority. Interview with Murat Somer, Köc University, Istanbul, March 2008. In early 2009, the JDP government initiated a 'Kurdish opening' but it had dissipated by 2010. See Alexander Christie-Miller, 'The PKK and the Closure of Turkey's Kurdish Opening', *Middle East Report Online*, 4 August 2010, http://www. merip.org/mero/mero080410.html, accessed 22 August 2010.

[40] Author's interview with Ziya Öniş, Köc University, Istanbul, March 2008.

[41] Interview with Altınay.

poignant illustration of this incoherence. On the one hand, as I mentioned earlier in the chapter, the JDP passed the Civil Code in 2002 which constituted a tremendous step towards sexual equality.[42] It has empowered women through political and social activism, and in multiple ways.[43] On the other hand, women are not present in the party's upper echelons. In the view of Turkish academic Özlem Tür, leading JDP figures do actually have more conservative views about women and in this they are distinct from other political parties.[44]

None of these ambiguities, however, pertain to the question of terrorism and political violence, with which the JDP was never associated. There is no evidence of links between Turkish Hizbullah and the JDP. On the contrary, it was alleged that Hizbullah became the partial instrument of elements in the Turkish state – which were opposed to the JDP government – to counter the Kurdistan Workers' Party (Parti Karkerani Kurdistan, PKK). In November 2003, an organisation specifically formed for the purpose, consisting of graduates from Afghan and Pakistani training camps, carried out terrorist bomb attacks against the HSBC bank and the UK Consulate.[45] As the government of the land, the JDP naturally oversaw the trial and conviction of the perpetrators.

The Islamic Republic of Iran

Iranian Islamism under the Shah

In a slow but sure manner from the 1960s onwards, opposition to the shah's regime crystallised around Islamist ideas and political formations. The reasons why Islamism became the foremost ideological discourse of resistance to the shah were complex and multi-faceted; to some extent, it happened by default following the suppression of the communist Tudeh party in Iran after 1953–4 and of the National Front after 1963.[46] Iranian Islamism became increasingly associated with the figure

---

[42] Rona Aybay pointed out that the work on changing the Civil Code had started years before the JDP came to power and that there was no direct relationship between its religious ideas and the new Code. Interview with Aybay. It remains a reality, however, that the Code was passed while the JDP was in government.

[43] Author's interview with Gareth Jones, Reuters correspondent, Ankara, March 2008.

[44] Author's interview with Özlem Tür, Middle East Technical University, Ankara, March 2008. On the question of women and the JDP, see also Zana Çtak and Özlem Tür, 'Women between Tradition and Change: The Justice and Development Party Experience in Turkey', *Middle Eastern Studies*, 44 (3) May 2008.

[45] Gareth Jenkins, *Political Islam*, p. 206.

[46] Nikki Keddie, *Roots of Revolution: An Interpretive History of Modern Iran*, New Haven, CT: Yale University Press, 1981, pp. 180–1.

of Ruhollah Musavi Khomeini, who spearheaded the gradual politicisation of a hitherto quietist Shia clerical class.[47] Khomeini became a protagonist in the confrontation with the shah when the reforms collectively
dubbed the 'White Revolution' led to the bloody suppression of popular
riots in 1963. He was exiled to Turkey in October 1964 and moved to
Iraq the following year. By the time Khomeini moved from Iraq to Paris
in October 1978, his leadership of the Iranian opposition movement was
clearly established. It rested on his skilful combination of a steadfast
opposition to the regime, over a period of decades, with the propaga-
tion of an intentionally vague populist message which allowed him to
create a broad alliance of social forces against it.[48] In the words of Shaul
Bakhash: 'He [Khomeini] managed to be all things to all people. Islamic
fundamentalists and westernized intellectuals, bazaar merchants and
the urban masses, came to see in his vision of the Islamic state the chance
to realize their very disparate aspirations.'[49]

Following the Revolution of 1979, however, the disparate coalition
which had overthrown the shah disintegrated. Khomeini and his followers either emasculated or eliminated other groups, such as conservatives
and liberals of the National Front, the secular left; national minorities
(Sunni Kurds, Turkomans and Baluchis), and religious critics, for example Ayatollah Kazem Shariatmadari.[50] The fall of Mehdi Bazargan's
government in November 1979 was a defeat for the moderate elements in
the revolutionary coalition. In January 1980, Abolhasan Bani Sadr, who
represented a 'leftist' version of Islamism, was elected president with an
overwhelming majority – only to be ejected from power in June 1981
as the more conservative Islamist factions emerged triumphant. The
Revolution had entered a radical phase which was to last until the late
1980s, a period punctuated by the end of the war with Iraq in 1988 and
Khomeini's death in 1989.

Terrorism and the Islamic Republic

In a pattern reminiscent of the French Revolution, the radical phase of
the Iranian Revolution was marked by revolutionary 'Terror'. Newly

---

[47] Baqer Moin, *Khomeini: Life of the Ayatollah*, London: I. B. Tauris, 1999. I use
the terms 'clerical' and 'clergy' in this section loosely to refer to the Shia religious
hierarchy.
[48] Ervand Abrahamian, *Iran between Two Revolutions*, Princeton, NJ: Princeton
University Press, 1982, p. 479.
[49] Shaul Bakhash, *The Reign of the Ayatollahs: Iran and the Islamic Revolution*, London:
Unwin Paperbacks, 1985, p. 19.
[50] Keddie, *Roots of Revolution*, p. 258.

established committees and tribunals meted out summary revolutionary 'justice'. In 1979, 757 individuals, mostly associated with the *ancien régime*, were executed. Bani Sadr's time in office saw an intensification of internal struggles, and the eighteen months following his fall from power in June 1981 witnessed a renewed attack against the new regime's opponents. In 1981–5 and in 1988, respectively, 12,300 and then 2,000 members of the Mojahedin-e Khalq, a leftist-Islamist organisation which had turned against the new regime, were executed while they in turn had been responsible for killing some 2,000 members of the regime.[51] The year 1982 was the bloodiest of the Revolution overall.

Revolutionary Terror refers to the brutal consolidation of the Revolution through the suppression of its opponents, but in a regime which blurred the line between the domestic and the international as a matter of principle, Terror at home spilt over into Iran's foreign relations. In November 1979, radical revolutionary elements, who eventually secured Khomeini's backing, took over the US embassy in Tehran and held its staff hostage for 444 days. In February 1989, Khomeini issued a *fatwa* (religious edict) sanctioning the killing of a foreign national, British author Salman Rushdie, for insulting Islam in his book *The Satanic Verses*. As these two events demonstrate, revolutionary Terror became closely connected to – indeed in some ways gave rise to – terrorist tactics. Such tactics were used by the Islamic Republic abroad to pursue its political objectives and they constitute my focus in this section.

Iran's use of terrorist tactics abroad must be situated within the broader context of its post-1979 revolutionary foreign policy. A core objective of this foreign policy was to export the regime's radical Islamist ideology to the Middle East and possibly beyond. Either by example or subversion, the Islamic Republic sought to undermine all regimes it deemed 'un-Islamic', which meant, in effect, those regimes not made in its own image. Its challenge to the Arab Gulf conservative monarchies was particularly grave. In November 1979, the Grand Mosque in Mecca was taken over by radical Islamists. They were Saudi citizens, and nothing suggests that they had been in contact with Tehran. However, Iran was probably in some way involved in the Shia uprising in Saudi Arabia's

---

[51] Ervand Abrahamian, 'Why the Islamic Republic has Survived', *Middle East Report*, 250, Spring 2009, p. 11; Bakhash, *The Reign of the Ayatollahs*, pp. 56–64 and 219–24. The new regime was targeted by an ultraconservative Islamist group called Forghan which carried out assassinations. Jerrold D. Green, 'Terrorism and Politics in Iran', Martha Crenshaw (ed.), *Terrorism in Context*, University Park: The Pennsylvania State University Press, 1995, pp. 576–7.

Eastern Province which occurred at the same time as the Mecca siege. In December 1981, the Sunni regime in Bahrain suppressed an attempted military coup in which Iran was alleged to have been involved. From 1981 on, it caused constant trouble for Saudi Arabia in the annual *hajj* to Mecca, which was used by Iranian pilgrims for propaganda purposes and by the Iranian regime to embarrass and weaken its Saudi adversaries.[52]

Iran's revolutionary foreign policy, and the challenge it presented to neighbouring regimes and others in the wider Middle East, as previously described, did not make the use of terrorist tactics inevitable. However, although the former did not necessarily lead to the latter, it provided a permissive context: Both subversion and terrorism were means of promoting the Islamic Republic's radical ideology abroad in defiance of established international norms.

The evidence surrounding the use of terrorist tactics abroad by the Islamic Republic remains murky and contested to this day. Often such evidence is circumstantial. For example, as we saw in Chapter 3, it is most likely – but not certain – that Iran (amongst others) was involved in the April 1983 attack on the US embassy in Beirut and against the French and US marines' barracks in October of the same year. Similar uncertainty surrounds Iran's role in the Western hostage crisis in Beirut in the 1980s. The spate of hostage taking began with the kidnapping of David Dodge, the president of the American University of Beirut, following the taking hostage of four Iranians in a car with diplomatic plates by the Israeli-backed Christian militia in South Lebanon in July 1982.[53] However, although Iran was undeniably involved in the taking of hostages – and appeared to benefit from this involvement – the type of control and influence that it had over events and decisions remains unclear.[54]

---

[52] Gilles Kepel, *Jihad: The Trail of Political Islam*, London: I. B. Tauris, 2002, pp. 119 and 134–5. On the Mecca siege of 1979, see Yaroslav Trofimov, *The Siege of Mecca: The Forgotten Uprising in Islam's Holiest Shrine and the Birth of al Qaeda*, New York: Doubleday, 2007.

[53] Green, 'Terrorism and Politics in Iran', p. 586.

[54] Ibid., pp. 587–8. Also according to Kepel, hostage taking was 'the means whereby Tehran loosened the stranglehold imposed by the war with Iraq and the hostility of the Arab and Western states'. Kepel, *Jihad*, p. 129. For Hala Jaber, Iran was happy to participate only from a distance in hostage taking in Lebanon, having learnt the hard way that holding hostages in its own territory (David Dodge was abducted in Beirut but subsequently held in Iran) was not to its political advantage. The author argues that Iran did not want the West to have proof it was involved in terrorism and wanted to be able to argue that it could influence, not control, the kidnappers. Hala

Furthermore, Iran's use of terrorist tactics abroad is difficult and sometimes impossible to disentangle from the activities of its allies and proxies such as Islamic Jihad in Egypt and Palestine (whose establishment was partly due to the influence of the Iranian Revolution), Hizbullah (created with Iranian help as we saw in Chapter 3) and Hamas (which Iran is alleged to be supporting increasingly in recent years). In some instances, those carrying out terrorist acts were not guided by Iran but simply inspired by it. For example, in December 1983, the US and French embassies in Kuwait were attacked by members of the Dawa group who were subsequently arrested and tried for the crime; all were Shia – Iraqi, Lebanese and Kuwaiti – but none were Iranian.[55] The hijackings of French, Saudi and Kuwaiti planes in late 1984 appeared to be inspired by Iran', yet the hijackers spoke Arabic, and in the Saudi and Kuwaiti cases, the planes were stormed by Iranian security forces.

The evidence of the Islamic Republic's responsibility for the use of another terrorist tactic, the assassination of its opponents abroad, is more compelling.[56] These took place reportedly on the grounds of an Islamic Revolutionary Guards Corps's intelligence committee standing order, of the 1980s, to 'neutralize all armed opposition to the regime wherever it was'.[57] Targets fell into two categories. The first was former top officials under the Shah, such as former Iranian prime minister and opposition leader Shapour Bakhtiar, killed in Paris in August 1991. The second category was of armed opponents of the Islamic Republic, such as the Mojahedin-e Khalq, which had come to be based in Iraq, and the secular, leftist Iranian Kurdish factions, operating from Iraqi Kurdistan. The Kurdish leader Abdol Rahman Qasemlu was killed in Vienna in 1989.[58] Four Kurdish leaders were assassinated by the Iranian intelligence services in September 1992 at Mykonos, a Greek restaurant in Berlin.[59] It was

Jaber, *Hezbollah: Born with a Vengeance*, New York: Columbia University Press, 1997, pp. 106–7.

[55] Graham Fuller and Rend Rahim Francke, *The Arab Shi'a: The Forgotten Muslims*, New York: St Martin's Press, 1999, p. 162.

[56] See the Introduction to this book for the working definition of terrorism used throughout the study. Although not indiscriminate acts, assassinations can target civilians with a view to achieving a political purpose. They can therefore be considered as terrorist acts.

[57] Dilip Hiro, *Iran Today*, London: Politico's, 2005, pp. 265–6. The source of the information is Robert Fisk (Independent, 12 April 1997).

[58] Gary Sick, 'Iran: Confronting Terrorism', *The Washington Quarterly*, 26 (4) Autumn 2003, p. 86.

[59] Hiro, *Iran Today*, p.266. Hiro writes that the background to the Mykonos assassinations was the Kurdistan Democratic Party of Iran (KDPI) staging pin-prick attacks from Iraq in Iranian territory following the Gulf War of 1991.

estimated that by 1997, the Iranian regime had liquidated eighty militant opponents in Europe, Iraq and Turkey. In the spring of 1997, a German court found three Lebanese and one Iranian guilty of the Mykonos killings; the judge identified the Supreme National Security Council of Iran under President Akbar Hashemi Rafsanjani as the planning centre for the assassinations. [60]

The Islamic Republic's radical phase ended at the close of its first decade. The use of terrorist tactics abroad, however, appeared to continue. Iran's hand was seen behind the attacks in Argentina in 1992 and 1994 and the June 1996 Khobar Towers bombing in Saudi Arabia. In the case of the 1992 bombing, German and Argentinean courts found complicity at the highest levels of the Iranian government, including the intelligence minister Ali Fallahian and the Iranian embassy in Argentina.[61] The precise degree of Iranian involvement in Khobar is undetermined. Washington alleged that the perpetrators of the Khobar explosion, who belonged to the Hizbullah group in Saudi Arabia, were sponsored by Iran's Revolutionary Guards and trained in Tehran. However, those arrested and executed for the crime were Saudi citizens, and Wahhabis, who hold Shias in low esteem.[62]

Although Iran's terrorist activities in the 1990s appeared unabated on one level, a transformation was occurring underneath the surface. What came to be called the 'Second Republic' gradually became more reticent in its use of terrorist tactics abroad. The change happened in fits and starts, reflecting the fragmented nature of foreign policy decision making in the Republic, but the overall direction was clear. Iran may have halted its policy of assassinations as early as spring 1993.[63] In 1995, the Iranian government was arguing that although the *fatwa* against Rushdie could not be revoked, it would not take any steps to implement it (although the 15 Khordad Foundation still offered a bounty for Rushdie's assassination).[64] Following the election of Muhammad Khatami to the presidency in 1997, Iranian foreign policy decision makers sought more intently to integrate Iran into the international community. In his CNN interview of January 1998, Khatami condemned the killing of 'innocent men and women who are not involved in confrontations' in the streets of Israel as 'terrorism'.[65]

---

[60] Dilip Hiro, *Neighbors, Not Friends: Iraq and Iran after the Gulf Wars*, London: Routledge, 2001, pp. 218 and 221.

[61] Sick, 'Iran: Confronting Terrorism', p. 86.

[62] Hiro, *Iran Today*, pp. 263–5.

[63] Gary Sick, 'Rethinking Dual Containment', *Survival*, 40 (1) 1998, p. 13.

[64] Hiro, *Neighbors, Not Friends*, p. 214.

[65] Sick, 'Iran: Confronting Terrorism', p. 89.

From the late 1990s onwards, the description of Iran as a terrorist state has increasingly been based on its support for groups such as Hamas and Hizbullah (and we saw in Chapter 3 that Hizbullah gradually moved away, substantially though not completely, from terrorism in the 1990s, in conjunction with Iran). The allegation that Iran entertains links with al Qaeda is unrealistic and unconvincing.[66]

The Islamic Republic's gradual move away from the use of terrorist tactics abroad from the 1990s onwards occurred within the wider context of greater pragmatism in foreign relations and an overall toning down of its rhetoric both towards the West and its Arab and non-Arab neighbourhood (with the exception of Israel). The reasons for it were partly linked to the responsibilities of government. Once the early heady days of the Revolution had passed, those who ran the Islamic Republic, even the hard-liners among them, began to realise how costly and destructive the use of terrorism abroad had become.[67] Already in the course of the mid- to late 1980s, many in the government realised that Iran's image as a 'terrorist state' impeded the war effort in that an arms embargo, generalized isolation in the Middle East and increasing unpopularity as a pariah state made its search for support against Iraq costly, frustrating and unsuccessful. This led to an early attempt to curb extremist elements. Reflecting a conscious decision to de-emphasise the terrorist component of its foreign policy, Mehdi Hashemi, who was involved in exporting the revolution abroad, was arrested, tried and executed in October 1986.[68] Under the 'Second Republic', President Rafsanjani and Supreme Leader Ali Khamenei increasingly appreciated that diplomatic isolation had severe repercussions for the country's regional status and, more specifically, that the country's serious economic problems and need for reconstruction necessitated some cooperation with the West.[69] Iran began to seek closer integration into the world capitalist economy,

---

[66] Ibid., pp. 84–5 and 91–2. The US State Department describes Iran as 'the most active state sponsor of terrorism' with reference to its support of Hizbullah, Hamas and 'other Palestinian terrorist groups'. State Department Country Reports on Terrorism 2008, chapter 3: State Sponsors of Terrorism, http://www.state.gov/s/ct/rls/crt/2008/122436.htm, accessed 23 April 2010.

[67] Shahram Chubin, lecture on 'Iranian Domestic Reform and Foreign Policy', London School of Economics, 22 January 2002.

[68] Green, 'Terrorism and Politics in Iran' p. 590–1. Rafsanjani already argued in July 1988 that Tehran's uncompromising policies pushed those who may have remained neutral in the Iran-Iraq war to turn against it. David Menashri, *Post-Revolutionary Politics in Iran: Religion, Society and Power*, London: Frank Cass, 2001, p. 174.

[69] Anoushiravan Ehteshami, *After Khomeini: The Iranian Second Republic*, London: Routledge, 1995, p. 42.

hoping to invite greater foreign private participation to help post-war recovery.[70] All this was incongruent with the use of terrorist tactics abroad. In a typical Iranian foreign policy fashion, however, such use did not stop altogether. Rafsanjani's efforts to build commercial and political ties with the West 'were sabotaged repeatedly by a policy that appeared driven by revolutionary vengeance and executed by shadowy forces'.[71]

Democracy, Liberalism and Political Pluralism

The Iranian Revolution held an initial democratic promise for many of its participants. The expectation that the Revolution would give rise to some form of democratic government was not completely unrealistic given that it was a genuinely popular revolution. However, this democratic potential soon dissipated. The process of consolidation of the new regime through revolutionary Terror led to the emergence of authoritarian structures of governance, a trend that accelerated after the fall of Bazargan. Although the new Iranian constitution of 1981 contained many democratic elements, they were quickly overshadowed by the same constitution's authoritarian aspects.[72] Power became increasingly concentrated in the newly instituted office of the Supreme Leader, in keeping with Ayatollah Khomeini's doctrine of *velayat-e faqih* ('guardianship of the Islamic jurist').

Khomeini's ideas had been the culmination of a departure from the Shia apolitical tradition which had started, as we saw, in the 1960s and led to religious leaders assuming a central role in the Revolution. However, tensions within the clerical class remained and a contradiction between two notions of supreme authority, the *velayat-e faqih* (merging temporal and religious authority) and the *marja'iyat* (purely religious and spiritual authority), was increasingly evident as the Republic consolidated itself.[73] More broadly, it became apparent in the first few

---

[70] Ibid., pp. 101–2, and see generally chapter 5.

[71] Sick, 'Iran: Confronting Terrorism', pp. 87–8. I noted earlier that in the spring of 1997, a German court identified the Supreme National Security Council of Iran under President Akbar Hashemi Rafsanjani as the planning centre for the assassinations of Iranian dissidents at the Mykonos restaurant in Berlin in 1992. There seems to be a contradiction here between Rafsanjani's efforts to build ties with the West and his responsibility for the killings. Suffice it to say that the historical record about Rafsanjani's precise role is still unclear.

[72] Asghar Schirazi, *The Constitution of Iran: Politics and the State in the Islamic Republic*, trans. John O'Kane, London: I. B. Tauris, 1998, chapters 4–7.

[73] Ziba Mir-Hosseini and Richard Tapper, *Islam and Democracy in Iran: Eshkevari and the Quest for Reform*, London: I. B. Tauris, 2006, p. 19.

years of the Revolution that the conflict between 'reason of state' and 'religious considerations' that characterised the Islamic Republic would be resolved in favour of the former. In January 1988, Khomeini declared that the Islamic state had 'the authority to "destroy a mosque" should its survival be in jeopardy and the interest of the community (*maslaha*) require it',[74] thereby admitting that if he had to choose between the survival of the state and *sharia*, he would choose the former.[75] The 'Second Republic' saw an even clearer preponderance of reason of state over religious considerations.

An important aspect of the conflict between reason of state and religious considerations was the contradiction between Islamist and secular elements in the Islamic Republic's laws. That this would be resolved in favour of the secular elements was already apparent in the Iranian Constitution of 1981 which established the nascent Islamic Republic's fundamental political structures. As Asghar Schirazi states, the constitution was based on the claim that 'the *shari'a*, because of its relation to the divine source of knowledge and its perfection, is endowed with universality and possesses the vitality to solve all humankind's social and political problems in every time and place'. From the belief that the *sharia* is the best foundation of government followed the view that the state should be governed by those who are expert in it – in other words, the Islamic jurists. However, reality was rather different:

Despite this claim the Constitution of the Islamic Republic contains important elements which have been borrowed, not from the *shari'a*, but from Western secular sources and stand out as concepts that are alien to the *shari'a*. First and foremost among these is the very idea of a constitution. One could also single out concepts such as: 'law', 'sovereignty of the people', 'nation', 'the rights of the nation', 'the legislature', 'the judiciary', 'parliament', 'republic', 'consultation of the people', 'elections'. [...] Indeed the entire structure of the state – its separation into three separate branches with corresponding institutions, the division of each of these institutions into different councils, government offices and organisations, the rules regulating relations between these bodies as well as the clauses in the constitution allocating economic rights and functions of the state, the private and the co-operative sectors – had to be borrowed by the Assembly of Experts [which deliberated on the constitution] from foreign models.[76]

---

[74] Farhad Kazemi, 'Civil Society and Iranian Politics', Augustus Richard Norton (ed.), *Civil Society in the Middle East*, Leiden: E. J. Brill, 1996, Vol. 2, p. 123.

[75] Mir-Hosseini and Tapper, *Islam and Democracy in Iran*, p. 22.

[76] Schirazi, *The Constitution of Iran*, pp. 17–18. Note that Schirazi gives some terms in Farsi, which I have omitted from the quote.

That secular laws would predominate over *sharia* became evident, not just in the Constitution, but in the legal reforms of the Republic's early years. One of the important objectives of the prominent legalists in the Islamic Republic, Khomeini among them, was to Islamise the laws of the state through the application of the *ahkam* or 'Islamic laws'. In August 1981, Khomeini ordered all courts to 'throw out' all non-Islamic laws with a view to Islamising the country's law codes.[77] In practice, though, this Islamisation encountered tremendous obstacles and ultimately had to be abandoned. The main reason was that the *sharia* does not provide *akham* for regulating most problems which arise in governing a modern state.[78] Except for laws applying to public morals, family law and the penal code, much of the legislative heritage from the old regime was retained. New legislation was approved but it was alien to the *sharia*.[79] *Sharia* was also circumvented through the rule of emergency and state ordinances which based their legitimacy on the interests of the Islamic state.[80] In the words of Keyvan Tabari:

Attempts to Islamicize the laws – to enact the revolutionaries' claim that Shi'ite Islam was a total way of life and total ideology – could not go much beyond the incorporation of a few archaic measures of punishment from the *Shari'a* (notably retaliation of *qesas*) in the criminal code. Further Islamic codification was abandoned when it became apparent that the *Shari'a* lacked provisions to govern situations in modern Iran not contemplated by the traditional Islam.[81]

The resolution of the contradiction between secular and religious elements in favour of the former was not the product of a lack of will or of political resistance by the regime's opponents. The very project of an Islamic state was unattainable. The reason was that the nation-state, by virtue of its mere existence, rendered *sharia* law subordinate to it. Ironically, this was already apparent in Khomeini's political doctrine which, although refusing to make reference to Western political thought and concepts, and using the vocabulary of Shia Islam, had as its essential preconditions the modern concepts of the state and politics.[82] The Revolution may subsequently have enacted Islamic law in theory but,

[77] Bakhash, *The Reign of the Ayatollahs*, p. 227.
[78] Schirazi, *The Constitution of Iran*, p. 162.
[79] Sami Zubaida, *Law and Power in the Islamic World*, London: I. B. Tauris, 2003, pp. 202–10.
[80] Schirazi, *The Constitution of Iran*, chapters 8–12.
[81] Keyvan Tabari, 'Rule of Law', *International Sociology*, 18 (1) 2003, p. 106.
[82] Sami Zubaida, *Islam, the People and the State: Political Ideas and Movements in the Middle East*, London: I. B. Tauris, revised edition, 1993, chapter 1.

as Olivier Roy argues, in the Islamic Republic, 'the state is the source of law and the source of its own legitimacy'. The constitution determines the place of the *sharia* and the parliament legislates so even though the *sharia* is incorporated in the constitution and supposed to be the supreme law, the structure of the polity and the conception of the law are modern and secular.[83] Sami Zubaida concurs with this view and adds historical depth to it: With the arrival of the modern nation-state in the Middle East of the nineteenth century, the codification of the law, even of *sharia*, meant that the law was 'etatized' and as such divorced from its anchor in religious institutions.[84] It follows from this that the government can abrogate any requirements of the *sharia*, as became evident by Khomeini's 1988 announcement.

By contrast to 'secularism', which is a doctrine aiming to separate religion and politics, 'secularisation' is a process which involves 'the differentiation and separation of institutions and spheres of knowledge and culture from religion and its authorities'. It does not involve a decline of religious faith as such but an 'insulation of that faith within limited institutional and personal spheres'. On the basis of this definition, the Middle East has been irreversibly secularised and religious revivalism is a symptom of this secularisation rather than a sign of its reversal.[85] The Islamic Revolution was a heroic attempt to thwart the secularisation process. However, not only did it fail but ironically it intensified the process of secularisation while disguising its reality behind 'imposed symbols and empty rhetoric.'[86] It has even caused the decline of personal religiosity: A survey conducted in 2001–2 showed that Iranians are less religious on a personal level than equivalent Egyptians and Jordanians.[87] In the words of Azadeh Kian-Thiébaut, 'the rule of political Islam has secularized religion by politicizing it'.[88]

The Revolution's project of an Islamic state not only intensified the secularisation process in Iran but also led to the discrediting of the religion

[83] Olivier Roy, *The Failure of Political Islam*, London: I. B. Tauris, 1999, pp. 177–8.

[84] Sami Zubaida, 'Islam and Secularization' *Asian Journal of Social Science*, 33 (3) 2005, pp. 438–48, and *Law and Power*, pp. 130–5.

[85] Ibid., p. 438–40.

[86] Sami Zubaida, 'Is Iran an Islamic State?', Joel Beinin and Joe Stork (eds.), *Political Islam: Essays from Middle East Report*, London: I. B. Tauris, 1997, p. 105.

[87] Mansoor Moaddel and Taqhi Azadarmaki, 'The Worldviews of Islamic Publics: The Cases of Egypt, Iran and Jordan', http://www.worldvaluessurvey.org/Upload/5_Iran.pdf, accessed 10 April 2010.

[88] Azadeh Kian-Thiébaut, *Secularization of Iran: A Doomed Failure? The New Middle Class and the Making of Modern Iran*, Paris: Peeters, 1998, p. 257.

itself. Systemic pressures from above to create a more religious society gave rise to a popular reaction and the 'desacralization' of the religious establishment.[89] Because of the clerical class's day-to-day involvement in affairs of state, they are blamed when things go wrong. By weakening traditional Shia religious structures in favour of a political organisation, the Revolution led to a deep crisis within the clergy so that increasing numbers of them came to the conclusion that the only way to 'save' Islam is to separate it from politics.[90] The project of an Islamic state also discredited religious structures in the eyes of the people. A 2005 study showed that in Iran, trust in religious institutions is very low compared to other Muslim countries, such as Egypt, Indonesia and Kazakhstan, if not Pakistan.[91] When state and religion are integrated, and there is a deficit of trust towards the state, the religious institutions also suffer. In Nikki Keddie's succinct words, 'there is nothing like having a government that calls itself Islamic to discredit Islamism'.[92]

Although Islamism can take many forms and interpretations and is not necessarily undemocratic or illiberal, the version enshrined by the Islamic Revolution in its nascent institutions and structures was authoritarian and repressive despite the fact that some democratic elements survived. As discussed, this was mostly to do with the political trajectory of the early phases of the Revolution. As the enthusiasm of the first few years subsided and the failures of the Islamic Republic became more manifest, so the authoritarian version of Islamism embodied in the regime was also discredited.

Khomeini had refused to use the word 'democracy' either in the title of the Republic or its constitution, considering it a Western import.[93] He thought the word 'liberal' was an insult. However, the strong antipathy to liberalism in Iran in the 1960s and 1970s, which Khomeini partly represented, was transformed into an appreciation of liberal (and secular)

[89] Yousef Ali Abazari, Abbas Varij Kazemi and Mehdi Faraji, 'Secularization in Iranian Society', Mehdi Semati (ed.), *Media, Culture and Society in Iran: Living with Globalization and the Islamic State*, trans. Ali Hosenipour, London: Routledge, 2008, p. 252.

[90] Olivier Roy, 'The Crisis of Legitimacy in Iran', *Middle East Journal*, 53 (2) 1999, pp. 201–16.

[91] Riaz Hasan, 'The State and Religious Institutions in Muslim Societies', Working Paper 79, Institute of Defence and Strategic Studies, Singapore, June 2005, http://www3.ntu. edu.sg/rsis/publications/WorkingPapers/WP79.pdf, accessed 11 April 2010.

[92] Nikki Keddie, 'Ideology, Society and the State in Post-Colonial Muslim Societies', Fred Halliday and Hamza Alavi (eds.), *State and Ideology in the Middle East and Pakistan*, Basingstoke, Hampshire: Macmillan Education, 1988, p. 26.

[93] Keddie, *Roots of Revolution*, p. 252.

ideas by the early 1990s.[94] In the course of the three decades after 1979, there occurred a gradual but discernible shift of popular preferences in favour of democracy, political pluralism and human rights principles. Two major surveys carried out in 2000 and 2005 by Mansoor Moaddel showed that Iranians' values have moved towards liberal democracy and secularism, more specifically towards social individualism, liberal democracy, gender equality and nationalism.[95]

The many internal problems and contradictions of the Islamic Republic also led to a reinterpretation within Islamist thought and the emergence of a 'New Religious Thinking' in the 1990s, which constituted a 'tremendous transformation in religious and political discourse'.[96] A series of liberal reformist Islamist intellectuals, Abdolkarim Soroush most prominent among them but also others such as Mohsen Kadevar and Hasan Yousefi Eshkevari, challenged the Islamic system from within.[97] Grand Ayatollah Husayn Ali Montazeri, who had been one of the main architects of the *velayat-e faqih*, argued in November 1997 for a democratization of the institution and the separation of the clerical establishment from the state.[98] The election of the reformist Muhammad Khatami to the presidency in 1997 and then in 2001, with 70 and 77 per cent of the vote, respectively, was partly the product of these internal processes and to some degree reflected the liberal Islamist message. Khatami was voted into power by an electorate which, as we saw from the earlier discussion, had come increasingly to appreciate democratic, liberal and pluralist principles.[99]

Khatami spoke about democracy, civil society, women's rights, the rule of law and dialogue between civilisations. Nevertheless, he remained a

---

[94] Ahmad Ashraf and Ali Banuazzi, 'Iran's Torturous Path Toward "Islamic Liberalism"', *International Journal of Politics, Culture and Society*, 15 (2) 2001, p. 249.

[95] Mansoor Moaddel, 'The Iranian Revolution and its Nemesis: The Rise of Liberal Values among Iranians', *Comparative Studies of South Asia, Africa and the Middle East*, 29 (1) 2009, pp. 126–36.

[96] Asef Bayat, 'What is Post-Islamism?', *International Institute for the Study of Islam in the Modern World (ISIM) Review*, 16, Autumn 2005, p. 5. Bayat describes this tendency as 'post-Islamism'.

[97] Mahmoud Sadri and Ahmad Sadri (eds.), *Reason, Freedom, and Democracy in Islam: Essential Writings of 'Abdolkarim Soroush'*, Oxford: Oxford University Press, 2000.

[98] Mir-Hosseini and Tapper, *Islam and Democracy in Iran*, p. 35. Montazeri had been Khomeini's designated successor, but Khomeini himself removed him from this position in March 1989, shortly before his death.

[99] Ali Gheissari and Vali Nasr, *Democracy in Iran: History and the Quest for Liberty*, Oxford and New York: Oxford University Press, 2006, p. 133.

product of the Islamic Republic and, although seeking to curb its abuses, he did not challenge its clerical oligarchy or the basic framework of its structures of government.[100] His attempts at reform were also thwarted by conservative opposition. Khatami's failed experiment made many in Iran conclude that the existing system was impervious to change. It led to the emergence of critics, such as journalist Akbar Ganji and Nobel laureate Shirin Ebadi, who moved away from Islamic reformism to advocate democratic and liberal values through a separation of religion and politics.[101]

The reformist drive under Khatami reached its pinnacle around the year 2000 and was followed by a conservative counter-offensive. In the Majlis (parliament) elections of February 2004, conservatives won a majority because the Council of Guardians blocked the candidacy of a great number of reformists.[102] The culmination of the counter-offensive was the election of Mahmoud Ahmadinejad to the presidency in 2005 and again in 2009. It would be wrong, however, to interpret the election of Ahmadinejad as a sign that the Iranian electorate rejected democratic and liberal values. The 2005 result was the culmination of a conservative resurgence which enjoyed the support of authoritarian state institutions and appealed to an electorate disillusioned with the reformist project through nationalist and populist slogans stressing economic equality and social justice.[103] To ensure electoral success for Ahmadinejad in 2009, there was a need for more blatantly dictatorial measures by the conservative establishment, including a hefty dose of electoral fraud.

Conclusion

Turkey's Islamist movements were moulded by the gradual opening and democratisation of the Turkish political process in the course of many

---

[100] Ladan Boroumand and Roya Boroumand, 'Reform at an Impasse', *Journal of Democracy*, 11 (4) 2000, p. 123.

[101] Ali Gheissari and Vali Nasr, 'Iran's Democracy Debate', *Middle East Policy*, 11 (2) 2004, see especially pp. 102–4.

[102] Farhad Khosrokhavar, 'The New Conservatives Take a Turn', *Middle East Report*, 233, Winter 2004, p. 24. In this very interesting piece, Khosrokhavar notes that the conservatives tailored their political message to the electorate in order to court its votes. Political participation has therefore affected even the conservative faction (pp. 24–7).

[103] Ali M. Ansari, *Iran Under Ahmadinejad: The Politics of Confrontation*, Adelphi Paper 393, Abingdon, Oxon: Routledge for the International Institute for Strategic Studies, 2007; see especially chapter 3; and International Crisis Group, *Iran: What Does Ahmadi-Nejad's Victory Mean?*, Middle East Briefing 18, 4 August 2005, pp. 4–6.

decades. Political inclusion, and in particular the experience of government, demonstrated that abstract Islamist theories had little relevance to real social and political problems.[104] However, by the same token, the ideological transformation of Turkish Islam was also the outcome of repression by the state which, through the military and the judicial system, upheld a strict interpretation of Kemalism. Pressure to conform to secular constitutional laws and norms, rather than democratic participation, constrained the ideological choices of Turkish Islamism and pushed them towards increasing moderation.[105]

A number of strategic/instrumental calculations by Turkey's mainstream Islamist parties also explain their shift towards moderation. Turkey's Islamists never engaged in terrorism, though they did dabble in political violence in the 1970s. The military coup of 1980 led to the realisation that these methods would not work, and they were subsequently shunned. Instrumental calculations were also behind Islamists' gradual shift towards the adoption of democratic and human rights principles. The repeated bans of Islamist parties and the restrictions on their activities made them realise how much they depended on human rights and the rule of law for their own protection.[106] By the late 1990s–early 2000s, they judged that an appeal to human rights and democratic principles through the European Union's institutions and international human rights instruments would be helpful in their confrontation with the Turkish state. The Muslim thinker Ali Bulaç openly stated that Islamic groups' support for and appreciation of the EU is due to the pressures brought to bear on Turkish Islamism by the 28 February 'process' measures.[107] Welfare appealed (though unsuccessfully) to the European Court of Human Rights against its closure in 1998. As we saw, the JDP argued against the headscarf ban on the basis of human rights principles, and specifically freedom of religion. It also made frequent reference to

---

[104] Dağı, 'Rethinking Human Rights, Democracy, and the West', p. 141. On this general development, see also M. Hakan Yavuz, *Islamic Political Identity in Turkey*, Oxford and New York: Oxford University Press, 2003.

[105] An alternative view is offered by Ziya Öniş who, in his discussion of the 28 February 'process', argues that the shift to the ideological centre could have been achieved by more subtle methods. Öniş 'Political Islam at the Crossroads', p. 294. The implication of this important insight is that although repression, in this instance as well as others in the political history of Turkey, appears to have 'worked', an alternative scenario based on engagement and the respect of liberal principles may have led to a more profound and long-term transformation. I will take this point up again in the Conclusion.

[106] Dağı, 'Transformation of Islamic Political Identity in Turkey', p. 31.

[107] Dağı, 'Rethinking Human Rights, Democracy, and the West', p. 146.

the United Nations Charter of Human Rights and the European Charter for the Protection of Human Rights and Basic Liberties.[108]

Over and above such strategic/instrumental calculations, there was yet another, arguably more profound cause of Turkey's Islamists' ideological evolution: the changing basis of their social support which occurred in the context of the broader economic transformation of the country. Here the shift from the NSP in the 1970s to Welfare in the 1980s and 1990s was the most critical. The ideology of the NSP in the 1970s championed 'independent industrial development' in relative isolation from the world economy. The party offered a political voice to lower and middle classes; artisans, small traders and other persons of low income from rural areas; and large numbers of small capitalists mostly in Central and Eastern Anatolia.[109] The typical NSP supporter was older, not highly educated (the NSP had no support among university graduates in Ankara, for instance) and probably a rural inhabitant or a rural migrant in large cities.[110] In contrast, Welfare began to attract the emerging Islamist business community from the 1980s, the so-called 'Anatolian tigers', which was becoming a dynamic sector in the new export-oriented economy. They also started to attract young professionals, an emerging Islamist counter-elite symbolised by the bearded engineer and veiled female student.[111] The emerging Islamist business class had much to lose through direct confrontation with the state, which goes a long way in explaining Welfare's accommodationist stance.[112] It therefore started emphasising that Islam was compatible with capitalism, favouring private instead of state initiative and opening up to the international market.[113] At the same time, Welfare tried to retain the support of the 'losers' of neo-liberal reforms,

---

[108] Heper and Toktaş, 'Islam, Modernity, and Democracy in Contemporary Turkey', p. 176.

[109] Margulies and Yildizoğlu, 'The Political Uses of Islam in Turkey', pp. 14–5.

[110] Toprak, *Islam and Political Development in Turkey*, pp. 108–17.

[111] Kepel, *Jihad*, pp. 349. Welfare developed links with the Independent Association of Industrialists and Businessmen (Müstakil Sanayici ve İşadamları Derneği, MÜSIAD), which was founded in 1990 to represent small- and medium-scale employers and represented the rise of 'Anatolian capital'. This was industrial activity in inner Anatolian towns based on small and medium-sized enterprises which until the 1990s had been neglected economically – because important businesses were institutionalised around big and diversified holding companies – and received little state subsidy. Ayşe Buğra, 'Class, Culture, and State: An Analysis of Interest Representation by Two Turkish Business Associations', *International Journal of Middle East Studies*, 30 (4) 1998, pp. 524–5.

[112] Öniş, 'Political Islam at the Crossroads', p. 290.

[113] Jenny White, *Islamist Mobilization in Turkey: A Study in Vernacular Politics* Seattle: University of Washington Press, 2002, pp. 123–4.

mainly the urban poor, through populism, the politics of identity and ultimately charity.[114] Welfare tried to resolve the contradictions between those two demands by emphasising the notion of mutual trust and, generally, the 'ethical' dimension of its policies. For instance, there was an assumption that in 'Islamic' labour markets, there is not really a need for a labour code because there is harmony and peace as opposed to conflict and controversy; strikes are therefore clearly not permitted.[115] The social underpinnings of Islamism further widened with the JDP. It encroached on the True Path Party and the Motherland Party constituencies to claim representation of a 'new middle class' which, in contra-distinction to the traditional republican bourgeoisie, was culturally conservative, politically nationalist, moderately authoritarian and espoused free enterprise.[116]

The case of the Islamic Republic of Iran is significantly different from that of Turkey. There, an Islamist movement captured the entire state apparatus as opposed to the government. However, the attempt to administer a complex state and society on the basis of an authoritarian Islamist model also pushed the Islamic Republic in a more moderate direction. Following the radical first decade of the Revolution, during which the new Iranian regime showed no hesitation in using terrorist tactics abroad, the Iranian government realised in the 1990s that the costs of being labelled a 'terrorist state' far exceeded the benefits. Domestic developments following the Revolution also led the Republic in a moderate direction. The attempt to implement the Islamist project was never attained, and in fact proved unattainable, with the exception of reforms in the 'moral' sphere, women's rights and family law and the penal code. The process of secularisation in Iran proved irreversible. The many failures of the Islamic Republic led to a reaction against the authoritarian version of Islamism which the Revolution had come to represent and had attempted to impose. That reaction took two forms: an internal ideological mutation within Islamist thinking which led to the emergence of a reformist movement; and disillusionment among the population with the Republic's structures of government. However, the shift to moder-

---

[114] Haldun Gülalp, 'Globalization and Political Islam: The Social Bases of Turkey's Welfare Party', *International Journal of Middle East Studies*, 33 (2) 2001, pp. 436–41.

[115] Buğra, 'Class, Culture, and State', p. 533.

[116] İnsel, 'The AKP and Normalizing Democracy in Turkey', p. 298. For an interesting discussion of the similarities and differences between the secular elites and Islamist counter-elites, see Nilüfer Göle, 'Secularism and Islamism in Turkey: The Making of Elites and Counter-Elites', *Middle East Journal*, 51 (1) 1997, pp. 46–58.

ation in the Islamic Republic was thwarted by a conservative counter-reaction.

I have previously emphasised the importance of strategic/instrumental factors in accounting for Islamist movements' shift to moderation. I have presented such factors as alternative explanations of moderation to political participation. However, in the case of the Islamic Republic as previously summarised, strategic/instrumental explanations intermesh with political explanations.[117] Attempting to administer an entire state apparatus forces one to make practical and down-to-earth decisions and abandon one's maximalist ideological positions. Controlling the fate of an entire population and seeking at the same time to stay in power – eminently political tasks – makes one's cost-and-benefit calculations more strategic and instrumental, and encourages pragmatism on all fronts.

Over and beyond these strategic/instrumental or political explanations (however one prefers to describe them), socio-economic reasons also played a hugely important role in the Islamic Republic's shift to greater moderation, incomplete and imperfect though it may have been. The turning point in the post-1989 period under Rafsanjani, to a more conciliatory policy abroad and more pragmatism at home, served the interests of an emerging mercantile bourgeoisie which had too much to lose from the Republic's confrontational policies.[118] The turn to moderation, however, should not be associated only with the rise of a particular class. The thirty years since the Revolution have witnessed a broad and profound socio-economic transformation in Iran. This transformation can be seen in the acceleration in the process of urbanisation (from 46 per cent in 1976 to 66 per cent in 2001) and the expansion of primary education.[119] The middle class has grown tremendously as can be seen by the rise of income per capita (from $3,400 in 1980 to $10,840 in 2007) and the expansion of tertiary education (from a gross enrolment figure

---

[117] I will take up this point again in the Conclusion.

[118] Ali M. Ansari, *Iran, Islam and Democracy: The Politics of Managing Change*, London: The Royal Institute of International Affairs, 2000.

[119] Zohreh Fanni, 'Cities and Urbanisation in Iran after the Islamic Revolution', *Cities*, 23 (6) 2006, p. 408. Net primary school enrolment increased from 60 per cent in 1970–5 to 90 per cent in 1993–8. World Bank Report no. 22050 IRN accessed 12 April 2010. Gross secondary enrolment increased from 45 per cent in 1985 to 76 per cent in 2007, 'Education Trends and Comparisons', World Bank Country Profile of Iran (education), http://web.worldbank.org/WBSITE/EXTERNAL/TOPICS/EXTEDUCATION/EXTDATASTATISTICS/EXTEDSTATS/0,,contentMDK:2160 5891~menuPK:3409559~pagePK:64168445~piPK:64168309~theSitePK:3232764,00. html, accessed 12 April 2010.

of 4.6 per cent in 1985 to 36.1 per cent in 2008).[120] According to one estimate, Iran's middle class had doubled in 2009 from 1997, and, in that year's elections, constituted half of the electorate. People under thirty years of age – a new, sophisticated, educated generation enjoying high Internet access and demanding of change – accounted for 40 per cent of the electorate.[121] In Schirazi's words:

In a complex, highly differentiated society such as that of Iran, with its exceptionally large urban population, its modern middle class, its academics, experts, and students, and a bourgeois movement that has already been under way for decades, the suppression of freedoms in general, and of an opposition press in particular, cannot be maintained in the long run.[122]

[120] Statistics compiled using The World Bank's World Development Indicators Database, http://ddp-ext.worldbank.org/ext/DDPQQ/member.do?method=getMembers&userid=1&queryId=13, accessed 12 April 2010, and the World Bank's Counry Profile of Iran (education).

[121] 'Middle class' is defined on the basis of $10 per person per day expenditures in PPP dollars and at least a basic education for the household head. Djavad Salehi-Isfahani, 'Iran's Presidential Elections: A Surge of Reformists in Politics' Wolfensen Center for Development/Dubai School of Government Middle East Youth Initiative, http://www.shababinclusion.org/content/blog/detail/1380/, accessed 12 April 2010.

[122] Schirazi, *The Constitution of Iran*, p. 301.

Conclusion

Employing case study evidence, I have argued that there is no necessary causal link between the lack of democracy in the Middle East and Islamist terrorism. Although in some cases a link does exist, it is not consistent enough to establish a regular (that is, a theoretical) pattern. As the preceding pages have amply demonstrated, being conclusive or categorical about the 'causes of things' is a vain endeavour. There are no clear, decisive answers when it comes to social science questions such as those investigated here. However, the process of investigation and exploration has, hopefully, offered the reader the means of drawing his or her own conclusions.

At the book's start, I stated its central question, rationale and methodology, defined key terms and concepts, and outlined the main contours of US democracy promotion in the post-2001 period. Chapter 1 introduced the debate on the complex and multi-faceted relationship between democracy and terrorism and argued that it is not plausible to maintain that a lack of democracy gives rise to terrorism. On the contrary, terrorism can even be encouraged by democratic politics and increase in periods of democratic transition. Political explanations of repression and political exclusion were the book's primary focus, but I divided the causes of terrorism into two broad categories: ideational and material/structural. I explained why my analysis of Islamist terrorism would focus on the latter category which was sub-divided into socio-economic and strategic/instrumental explanations.

The rest of the book (Chapters 2–6) explored the relationship between democracy and Islamist terrorism in the Middle East region. The argument unfolded in two parts. Chapters 2–4 investigated whether the three major types of Islamist terrorist movements – transnational, national liberation and domestic insurgency – were driven to adopt their methods by being excluded from the political process and repressed in their respective societies. The conclusions were mixed. In the case of al Qaeda, I argued that the movement's transnational mode of operation reinforced the lack of connectedness with political processes and led to an inability to compromise and negotiate. However, the counter-example of Hizb ut Tahrir showed that rootlessness, as a result of a transnational mode of existence and operation, did not necessarily lead to the adoption of terrorist tactics. The link between repression and political exclusion and Islamist terrorism was even more tenuous in the cases of Hamas and Hizbullah. Hamas's inclusion or exclusion in Palestinian political processes was not related to its adoption or abandonment of terrorist practices, and these practices were only partly related to repression. Although exclusion and repression of the Lebanese Shia were a factor in the creation of Hizbullah, the gradual abandonment of the movement's terrorist methods was linked only indirectly to its incorporation into the country's political system. Finally, repression and political exclusion played a role but were not the decisive factors behind the emergence and turn to terrorism of the Algerian GIA and the Egyptian Gamaa Islamiya. These movements expanded when political exclusion and repression caused disillusioned moderate Islamists to join them, especially in Algeria, but the existence of their radical core memberships, which gave the decisive 'push' towards terrorism, predated this expansion.

If a consistent causal link between political factors and Islamist terrorism cannot be established, answers must be sought elsewhere. Although it was not the purpose of the book to answer the question of what causes Islamist terrorism, some tentative answers could be offered. In all three types of Islamist terrorist movements examined, and especially in the cases the GIA and Gamaa Islamiya which led domestic insurgencies against their respective states, socio-economic reasons did play a role in the emergence of terrorism, although, similarly to political explanations, they were not decisive. Strategic/instrumental explanations, however, appeared on balance to be the most potent: In every case, and especially al Qaeda, Hizbullah and Hamas, Islamist movements were highly instrumental in their approach and used terrorist methods when their leaderships concluded that they delivered the results they sought.

Chapters 5 and 6 further developed the argument by looking at the other side of the metaphorical coin – moderation as a result of political participation. I asked whether Islamist movements eschewed terrorist tactics, and moved to (at least partial) acceptance of democracy and political pluralism, as a result of inclusion and participation in political processes. I looked at Islamist movements in opposition and in government. Once again, the findings were mixed. The inclusion of the Muslim Brotherhood in political processes from early on in Jordan's history led to a consistently moderate ideological stance. The Egyptian Muslim Brotherhood was influenced, albeit in a limited fashion, by its partial inclusion in the political process, but its initial major shift towards moderation had occurred largely as a result of repression under Nasser. Furthermore, the movement did not adopt terrorist tactics, even though it suffered intermittent repression by the Sadat and Mubarak regimes. In the case of the Tunisian Nahda movement, repression and political exclusion did not lead to terrorism or any other form of radicalism. Nahda maintained a consistently moderate stance.

The shift towards moderate ideological positions by Turkey's Welfare and Justice and Development parties was already advanced when they took up the reins of government, and largely explains their electoral successes. It accelerated during their periods in office, when the responsibilities of governing brought about even greater compromises and concessions of principle. However, ideological moderation in the case of Turkey's Islamists was not only the product of political inclusion, either prior to or during their times in government; it was also the outcome of repression by the Turkish state. In the case of Iran, where an Islamist movement captured the entire state apparatus following the Revolution of 1979, implementing an Islamist ideology and attempting to establish an Islamic state also led to moderation in the form of more pragmatic policies. The Islamic Republic began to move away from the terrorist methods it had used abroad in its first decade when it became clear that they were damaging to its interests. Domestically, the Iranian polity and public moved towards greater moderation in the sense of a shift away from the Islamist authoritarianism of the Revolution's early period. However, this process ultimately came to a standstill in the face of conservative counter-reaction. The Islamic Republic's case shows, once again, that political participation does not necessarily lead to moderation and can only partly account for it.

If political participation is not the key to explaining moderation, what is? Again, I did not claim to offer a complete account of the causes of Islamist moderation, but the concluding parts of Chapters 5 and 6 suggested some tentative answers. Strategic/instrumental reasons – in other words, a calculation that terrorism would be counter-productive – were significant. Socio-economic developments, and more specifically the support given to Islamist movements (in opposition or in government) by a widening middle class with an interest in avoiding confrontational politics, accounted more fully for the shift to moderation. Overall, strategic/instrumental calculations are highly significant – perhaps the most significant – factors both in the adoption of terrorist tactics and in the decision to eschew them. Socio-economic factors can play a role in causing the resort to terrorism, but more crucially, they underpin the shift to ideological moderation. In all cases, political explanations relating to democracy and participation may play a role in accounting for an overall direction – whether moderate or terrorist – but they are not decisive.

In a number of case studies, especially the Muslim Brotherhood in Egypt and the Welfare and Justice and Development Parties in Turkey, I drew links between repression and moderation. Strategic/instrumental reasons for moderation can be difficult to distinguish from political reasons in such instances. It may be that by experiencing repression, an Islamist movement makes the rational and strategic assessment that it cannot win a confrontation and therefore retreats to more moderate positions. Alternatively, repression can also cause an appreciation of democratic and liberal principles and a realisation of the havoc terrorism and violence can wreak.[1] The line between the two is very fine and reading peoples' 'true' motives a hugely challenging, if not altogether futile, task. In either case, it is easy to conclude – and it is certainly the case on one level – that repression 'works' in forcing a group to become more moderate. However, the costs of such repression are often impossible to measure. Does it lead to only a tactical and superficial transformation in ideas and methods? Would alternative ways of dealing with Islamists, through inclusion and the application of the rule of law, have had more far-reaching effects and caused a more genuine and profound espousal of democratic and liberal principles on their part?[2]

---

[1] Political and strategic/instrumental explanations can also be difficult to disentangle in cases where a movement controls power. I pointed out, in the context of discussing Iran, that its Islamist regime was forced to opt for pragmatic, moderate solutions for instrumental reasons, namely to hold on to power more effectively. However, the process of governing also possibly demonstrated the value of greater pragmatism and led to a genuine appreciation of moderate ideological positions and policies by at least some parts of the Islamist establishment.

[2] This was the insight offered by Ziya Öniş with regards to the effect of the 28 February process on the Turkish Islamist parties, which I discussed in the Conclusion of Chapter 6. Ziya Öniş, 'Political Islam at the Crossroads: From Hegemony to Co-existence', *Contemporary Politics*, 7 (4) 2001, p. 294.

These questions remain hypothetical given the pervasiveness of author-itarianism in most of the Middle East region, but they are nevertheless interesting to ponder in considering the effects of repression or inclusion on Islamist movements.

Although it has not been my focus in this study, one can make a reason-able case that a pernicious effect of repression (and political exclusion), in the Middle East and especially the Arab world, is widespread de-politicisation in the sense of popular apathy and disillusionment with political processes.[3] De-politicisation has pushed Islamist movements to focus their attention on 'moral' and social issues such as the rights and status of women and non-Muslims, as well as freedom of expression and of conscience.[4] In internal contestations of power within Islamist movements, de-politicisation has benefited conservatives as opposed to pragmatists who favour political engagement.[5] Such developments are in the interests of authoritarian governments whose practices remain unchallenged. Democracy suffers as a result.

Throughout the course of this study, Islamism has been revealed as a dynamic, evolving phenomenon which is far from uniform or immu-table, either in its ideological objectives or *modus operandi*. Individual Islamist movements cannot be understood without reference to their par-ticular contexts. Some of the complex reasons for Islamist movements' shift in the direction of either terrorism or moderation were brought into relief in the preceding pages. Islamist terrorism is only one variant of Islamism, the product of a combination of factors pertaining in par-ticular circumstances. These conclusions can be useful starting points for the discipline of International Relations which has been struggling

---

[3] I have not been able to locate academic literature on the issue of de-politicisation in the Middle East. However, in a general sense, the term is taken to mean the lack of popular interest in political issues, the limited readership of newspapers and the absence of a properly developed political class. It is arguably the product of authoritarian govern-ment practices in Jordan, Egypt and Tunisia, such as the overwhelming power of the executive, the subjugation of the legislature and the judiciary to it and the prohibition of real debate on vital issues of the day. Author's interviews with Bahey el Din Hassan, Cairo Institute for Human Rights Studies, Cairo, December 2005, and with Hishem Kassem, journalist and political activist, Cairo, December 2005.

[4] Gudrun Krämer, 'The Integration of the Integrists: A Comparative Study of Egypt, Jordan and Tunisia', Ghassan Salamé (ed.), *Democracy Without Democrats? The Renewal of Politics in the Muslim World*, London: I. B. Tauris, 1994, pp. 208–9. See also Salwa Ismail, 'The Paradox of Islamist Politics', *Middle East Report*, 221, Winter 2001, pp. 34–9.

[5] This is, in a nutshell, what occurred in the December 2009–January 2010 leadership elections in Egypt's Muslim Brotherhood, which were described in Chapter 5.

to accommodate Islamist terrorism and Islamism in general at a theoretical level. Highlighting the complexity of a phenomenon which is sometimes simplistically described as 'Islam' also offers a corrective to the 'clash of civilisations' thesis which enjoys wide currency in public, if not necessarily academic, discourse.

The book's conclusions are also relevant to the study of terrorism and political violence. As I noted in the Introduction and Chapter 1, a lot of attention has been paid to the links between democracy and terrorism at a general level and in other parts of the world, but reference to the Middle East region often appears to be missing from these theoretical discussions. Similarly, Islam is either ignored or deemed to have one, unchanging 'essence' or interpretation (conducive to terrorism). By working against such 'exceptionalism' and incorporating the Middle East and Islamist terrorism into wider social scientific debates, this study has at least partly narrowed an important gap.

The book has theoretical implications for the study of democracy, and lack thereof, in the Middle East. It may not have directly addressed the causes of the region's democratic deficit, the debate about political systems and how to characterise them or the prospects of reform in the region. However, by exploring the relationship between democracy and terrorism, it has shed some light on the functioning of political systems in the region, which is also useful in making recommendations for policy.

The United States in the post–11 September 2001 period incorporated democratisation into the objective of winning the 'war on terror', but if the democratic deficit in the Middle East is not the main cause of Islamist terrorism, encouraging democracy will not necessarily ameliorate the problem. This does not, of course, mean that democracy should be entirely marginalised as a tool of combating terrorism because in some cases, there *is* a causal link. Therefore, it follows that a well-informed and case-by-case approach should guide policy making. For instance, pursuing democratisation in the Palestinian territories with a view to reducing the appeal of terrorism is a red herring if one accepts my argument that Hamas terrorism in the Oslo and al Aqsa Intifada years was not primarily caused by political exclusion (and only very partially by repression) but was the outcome of strategic/instrumental calculations by Hamas. However, an opening up of Algeria's authoritarian system of government, which would include a genuine opportunity for political participation, may contribute to further reducing the appeal of Islamist terrorism in Algeria, which persists in the form of al Qaeda in the Islamic Maghreb.

A case-by-case approach must be combined with a multi-pronged policy. There are many causes of Islamist terrorism, as the preceding pages have shown, and policy makers must take all of them on board. Socio-economic factors play an important, if partial, role in the emergence of Islamist terrorism, so the focus on development and welfare must continue. Strategic/instrumental explanations indicate that Islamist terrorists, far from being irrational actors, have made careful calculations that the benefits of their actions outweigh the costs and that terrorism is the most effective way of achieving their objectives. Treating Islamist terrorists as rational actors, and understanding and responding to the utilitarian way they use terrorist tactics, is the most vital element of a successful counter-terrorism policy.

Bibliography

The 9/11 Commission Report: Final Report of the National Commission on Terrorist Attacks Upon the United States, New York: W. W. Norton & Co, 2004

Abazari, Yousef Ali, Kazemi, Abbas Varij, and Faraji, Mehdi, 'Secularization in Iranian Society', Mehdi Semati (ed.), *Media, Culture and Society in Iran: Living with Globalization and the Islamic State*, London: Routledge, 2008, trans. Ali Hosenipour

Abdelrahman, Maha, '"With the Islamists? – Sometimes. With the State? – Never!" Cooperation between the Left and Islamists in Egypt', *British Journal of Middle Eastern Studies*, 36 (1) 2009

Abrahamian, Ervand, 'Why the Islamic Republic Has Survived', *Middle East Report*, 250, Spring 2009

Iran between Two Revolutions, Princeton, NJ: Princeton University Press, 1982

Abu-Amr, Ziad, *Islamic Fundamentalism in the West Bank and Gaza: Muslim Brotherhood and Islamic Jihad*, Bloomington: Indiana University Press, 1994

Achcar, Gilbert, 'Fantasy of a Region that Does Not Exist: Greater Middle East: The US Plan', *Monde Diplomatique*, April 2004

Addi, Lahouari, 'Algeria's Army, Algeria's Agony', *Foreign Affairs*, 78 (4) 1998

Alagha, Joseph Elie, *The Shifts in Hizbullah's Ideology: Religious Ideology, Political Ideology, and Political Programme*, Leiden: Amsterdam University Press, International Institute for the Study of Islam in the Modern World, (ISIM) Dissertations, 2006

Albrecht, Holger, 'The Nature of Political Participation', Ellen Lust-Okar and Saloua Zerhouni (eds.), *Political Participation in the Middle East*, Boulder, CO: Lynne Rienner, 2008

'How Can Opposition Support Authoritarianism? Lessons from Egypt', *Democratization*, 12 (3) 2005

Alhamad, Laila, 'Formal and Informal Venues of Engagement', Ellen Lust-Okar and Saloua Zerhouni (eds.), *Political Participation in the Middle East*, Boulder, CO: Lynne Rienner, 2008

Allani, Alaya, 'The Islamists in Tunisia: Between Confrontation and Participation', *The Journal of North African Studies*, 14 (2) 2009

Altunışık, Meliha Benli and Tür, Özlem, *Turkey: Challenges of Continuity and Change*, London and New York: Routledge, 2005

Amnesty International, *Occupied Palestinian Territories Torn Apart by Factional Strife*, MDE 21/02/2007, 24 October 2007

Tunisia: In the Name of Security: Routine Abuses in Tunisia, 2008, Report MDE 30/007/2008

Under Fire: Hizbullah's Attacks on Northern Israel, 2006, Report MDE 02/025/2006

Tunisia: A Widening Circle of Repression, June 1997, Report MDE 30/25/97

Amrani, Issandr, 'Brothers Take a Step Back from Politics', *Middle East International*, 2 (5) 8 January 2010

'Mubarak's Last Stand?', *Middle East International*, 742, 21 January 2005

al Anani, Khalil, *Al-Ikhwan al-Muslimun* (The Muslim Brotherhood), Cairo: Dar el Sorouk, December 2007

Angrist, Michele Penner, 'Parties, Parliament and Political Dissent in Tunisia', *The Journal of North African Studies*, 4 (4) 1999

Ansari, Ali M., *Iran under Ahmadinejad: The Politics of Confrontation*, Adelphi Paper 393, Abingdon, Oxon: Routledge for the International Institute for Strategic Studies, 2007

Iran, Islam and Democracy: The Politics of Managing Change, London: The Royal Institute of International Affairs, 2000

Ansari, Hamied N., 'The Islamic Militants in Egyptian Politics', *International Journal of Middle East Studies*, 16 (1) March 1984

Arat, Yeşim, *Rethinking Islam and Liberal Democracy: Islamist Women in Turkish Politics*, Albany: State University of New York Press, 2005

Ashour, Omar, 'Islamist De-Radicalization in Algeria: Successes and Failures', *Middle East Institute Brief*, 21, November 2008

'Lions Tamed? An Enquiry into the Causes of the De-Radicalization of Armed Islamist Movements: The Case of the Egyptian Islamic Group', *Middle East Journal*, 61 (4) 2007

Ashraf, Ahmad and Banuazzi, Ali, 'Iran's Torturous Path toward "Islamic Liberalism"', *International Journal of Politics, Culture and Society*, 15 (2) 2001

Atacan, Fulya, 'Radical Islamic Thought in Turkey', *Current Turkish Thought*, 64, Istanbul: Redhouse Press, 1991

al Awadi, Hesham, 'Mubarak and the Islamists: Why Did the "Honeymoon" End?', *Middle East Journal*, 59 (1) 2005

Azzam, Maha, 'Egypt: The Islamists and the State under Mubarak', Abdel Sidahmed and Anoushiravan Ehteshami (eds.), *Islamic Fundamentalism*, Boulder, CO: Westview Press, 1996

Bakhash, Shaul, *The Reign of the Ayatollahs: Iran and the Islamic Revolution*, London: Unwin Paperbacks, 1985

Barkey, Henri, 'Turkey, Islamic Politics, and the Kurdish Question', *World Policy Journal*, 13 (1) 1996

Bayat, Asef, 'What Is Post-Islamism?', *International Institute for the Study of Islam in the Modern World (ISIM) Review*, 16, Autumn 2005

BBC Monitoring Middle East, 'Islamists from Algeria behind Recent Fire Exchange in Tunisia', 5 January 2007

Bennhold, Katrin, 'Poverty in the Streets of Algiers, Breeding Ground for Terrorism', *International Herald Tribune*, 13 November 2007

Bergen, Peter, *The Osama Bin Laden I Know*, New York: Free Press, 2006

Berkouk, Mhand, *US-Algerian Security Cooperation and the War on Terror*, Carnegie Endowment Web Commentary, June 2009, http://www.carnegieendowment.org/publications/index.cfm?fa=view&id=23276

Bloom, Mia, *Dying to Kill: The Allure of Suicide Terror*, New York: Columbia University Press, 2005

Boisbouvier, Christophe, 'Otages: Business au Sahara', *Jeune Afrique*, 2512, 1–7 March 2009

Bokhari, Farhan and Fidler, Stephen, 'Rivalries Rife in Lair of Leaders', *Financial Times*, 5 July 2007

Bonanate, Luigi, 'Some Unanticipated Consequences of Terrorism', *Journal of Peace Research*, 3 (16) 1979

Boroumand, Ladan and Boroumand, Roya, 'Reform at an Impasse', *Journal of Democracy*, 11 (4) 2000

Brown, Nathan J., *Living with Palestinian Democracy*, Carnegie Endowment for International Peace, Policy Brief 46, June 2006

    Aftermath of the Hamas Tsunami, Carnegie Endowment for International Peace, Web Commentary, 2 February 2006, http://www.carnegieendowment.org/publications/index.cfm?fa=view&id=17975&prog=zgp&proj=zdrl, zme&zoom_highlight=brown+hamas+tsunami

    Evaluating Palestinian Reform, Carnegie Endowment for International Peace, Carnegie Paper 59, June 2005

Brown, Nathan J. and Hamzawy, Amr, *The Draft Party Platform of the Egyptian Muslim Brotherhood: Foray into Political Integration or Retreat into Old Positions?* Carnegie Endowment for International Peace, Middle East Series, 89, January 2008

Brumberg, Daniel, 'The Trap of Liberalized Autocracy', *Journal of Democracy*, 13 (4) 2002

Buğra, Ayşe, 'Class, Culture, and State: An Analysis of Interest Representation by Two Turkish Business Associations', *International Journal of Middle East Studies*, 30 (4) 1998

Burgat, François, *Face to Face with Political Islam*, London: I. B. Tauris, 2003

Burke, Jason, *Al-Qaeda: Casting a Shadow of Terror*, London: I. B. Tauris, 2003

    'Al Qaeda – A Meaningless Label', *The Guardian*, 12 January 2003

Byman, Daniel, *Deadly Connections: States that Sponsor Terrorism*, Cambridge: Cambridge University Press, 2005

Carothers, Thomas, 'Debating Democracy', *The National Interest*, 90, July/August 2007

'The Backlash against Democracy Promotion', *Foreign Affairs*, 85 (2) 2006

A Better Way to Support Middle East Reform, Carnegie Endowment for International Peace, Policy Brief 33, February 2005

'Democracy: Terrorism's Uncertain Antidote', *Current History*, 102 (668) December 2003

Carter-Ruck & Partners, London, *Get Carter-Ruck*, December/January 2004

Cederman, Lars-Erik, Hug, Simon, and Wenger, Andreas, 'Democratization and War in Political Science', *Democratization*, 15 (3) 2008

Chehabi, H. E. and Mneimneh, Hassan I., 'Five Centuries of Lebanese-Iranian Encounters', H. E. Chehabi (ed.), *Distant Relations: Five Centuries of Lebanese-Iranian Ties*, London: Centre for Lebanese Studies in Association with I. B. Tauris, 2005

Christie-Miller, Alexander, 'The PKK and the Closure of Turkey's Kurdish Opening', *Middle East Report Online*, 4 August 2010, http://www.merip.org/mero/mero080410.html

Çınar, Menderes, 'Turkey's Transformation under the AKP Rule', *The Muslim World*, 96 (3) 2006

Cizre, Ümit and Çınar, Menderes, 'Turkey 2002: Kemalism, Islamism, and Politics in Light of the February 28 Process', *The South Atlantic Quarterly*, 102 (2/3) Spring/Summer 2003

Clark, Janine A., 'The Conditions of Islamist Moderation: Unpacking Cross-ideological Cooperation in Jordan', *International Journal of Middle East Studies*, 38 (4) 2006

Coady, C. A. J., 'The Morality of Terrorism', *Philosophy*, 60 (231) 1985

Coşar, Simten 'Liberal Thought and Democracy in Turkey', *Journal of Political Ideologies*, 9 (1) 2004

Crenshaw, Martha, 'The Logic of Terrorism: Terrorist Behavior as a Product of Strategic Choice', Walter Reich (ed.), *Origins of Terrorism: Psychologies, Ideologies, Theologies, States of Mind*, New York: Woodrow Wilson Center, 1990

'The Causes of Terrorism', *Comparative Politics*, 13 (4) 1981

(ed.) *Terrorism, Legitimacy and Power: The Consequences of Political Violence*, Middleton, CT: Wesleyan University Press, 1981

Cronin, Audrey Kurth, *Ending Terrorism: Lessons for Defeating al-Qaeda*, Adelphi Paper 394, Abingdon, Oxon: Routledge for the International Institute for Strategic Studies, 2008

Çtak, Zana and Tür, Özlem, 'Women between Tradition and Change: The Justice and Development Party Experience in Turkey', *Middle Eastern Studies*, 44 (3) May 2008

Dağı, Ihsan 'Transformation of Islamic Political Identity in Turkey: Rethinking the West and Westernization', *Turkish Studies*, 6 (1) 2005

'Rethinking Human Rights, Democracy, and the West: Post-Islamist Intellectuals in Turkey', *Critique: Critical Middle Eastern Studies*, 13 (2) Summer 2004

Dalacoura, Katerina, 'US Democracy Promotion in the Arab Middle East since 11 September 2001: A Critique', *International Affairs*, 81 (5) 2005

Engagement or Coercion? Weighing Western Human Rights Policies towards Turkey, Iran and Egypt, London: Royal Institute of International Affairs, 2003

Islam, Liberalism and Human Rights: Implications for International Relations, revised edition, London: I. B. Tauris, 2003

Davies, James C., *When Men Revolt and Why*, New York: Free Press, 1971

Della Porta, Donatella, *Social Movements, Political Violence and the State: A Comparative Analysis of Italy and Germany*, Cambridge: Cambridge University Press, 1995

Diamond, Larry, *Winning the New Cold War on Terrorism: The Democratic-Governance Imperative*, Institute for Global Democracy, Policy Paper 1, March 2002

Dinmore, Guy, 'Critics of "Utopian" Foreign Policy Fail to Weaken Bush Resolve', *Financial Times*, 13 January 2006

Dolgoff, Sam (editor and translator), *Bakunin on Anarchism*, Montreal: Black Rose Books, 1980

Ehteshami, Anoushiravan, *After Khomeini: The Iranian Second Republic*, London: Routledge, 1995

Eickelman, Dale F., 'Bin Laden, the Arab "Street", and the Middle East's Democracy Deficit', *Current History*, 101 (651) January 2002

el Ghobashy, Mona, 'The Metamorphosis of the Egyptian Muslim Brothers', *International Journal of Middle East Studies*, 37 (3) 2005

Ellingsen, Tanja and Gleditsch, Nils Petter, 'Democracy and Conflict in the Third World', Ketil Volden and Dan Smith (eds.), *Causes of Conflict in the Third World Countries*, Oslo: PRIO, 1997

Engene, Jan Oskar, *Patterns of Terrorism in Western Europe, 1950–1995*, Bergen, Norway: University of Bergen, 1998, unpublished PhD Thesis

England, Andrew and Khalaf, Roula, 'Building Bridges to Destruction', *Financial Times*, 6 July 2007

Entelis, John P., 'Civil Society and the Authoritarian Temptation in Algerian Politics: Islamic Democracy vs. the Centralized State', Vol. 2, Augustus Richard Norton (ed.), *Civil Society in the Middle East*, Leiden: E. J. Brill, 1996

Eubank, William and Weinberg, Leonard, 'Terrorism and Democracy: Perpetrators and Victims', *Terrorism and Political Violence*, 13 (1) 2001

'Terrorism and Democracy: What Recent Events Disclose', *Terrorism and Political Violence*, 10 (1) 1998

Evans, Martin and Phillips, John, *Algeria: Anger of the Dispossessed*, New Haven, CT and London: Yale University Press, 2007

Fanni, Zohreh, 'Cities and Urbanisation in Iran after the Islamic Revolution', *Cities*, 23 (6) 2006

Fattahm, Hassan, 'Drive for Democracy Stalls in Arab World', *International Herald Tribune*, 10 April 2006

Filiu, Jean-Pierre, 'The Local and Global Jihad of al Qaʻida in the Islamic Maghreb', *Middle East Journal*, 63 (2) 2009

'Hizb ut-Tahrir and the Fantasy of the Caliphate', *Monde Diplomatique*, June 2008

Freedom House, *Freedom in the World Report 2007*, http://www.freedom-house.org/template.cfm?page=15

Friedman, Thomas, 'At least Iraq's got the Arabs talking', *International Herald Tribune*, 20 February 2004

Front de Libération Nationale (FLN), 'Declaration of 1 November 1954', http://www.milestonedocuments.com/documents/view/proclamation-of-the-algerian-national-liberation-front/

Fuller, Graham and Francke, Rend Rahim, *The Arab Shi'a: The Forgotten Muslims*, New York: St Martin's Press, 1999

Gause, Gregory F., 'Remarks', *Democratizing the Middle East?*, The Fares Center for Eastern Mediterranean Studies, Tufts University, Occasional Paper 2, 2006

'Can Democracy Stop Terrorism?', *Foreign Affairs*, 84 (5) 2005

Gerges, Fawaz A., 'The Muslim Brotherhood: New Leadership, Old Politics' *guardian.co.uk*, 20 Jan 2010, http://www.guardian.co.uk/commentisfree/belief/2010/jan/20/muslim-brotherhood-egypt

The Far Enemy: Why Jihad Went Global, New York: Cambridge University Press, 2005

Ghadbian, Najib, 'Political Islam: Inclusion or Violence?', Kenton Worcester, Sally Avery Bermanzohn, and Mark Ungar (eds.), *Violence and Politics: Globalization's Paradox*, New York: Routledge, 2002

Gheissari, Ali and Nasr, Vali, *Democracy in Iran: History and the Quest for Liberty*, New York: Oxford University Press, 2006

'Iran's Democracy Debate', *Middle East Policy*, 11 (2) 2004

Ghorbal, Samy, 'Attentat de Djerba: Les Liens du Sang', *Jeune Afrique*, 2507, Janvier 2009

Glain, Stephen, 'Mideast: The New Muslim Brotherhood', *Newsweek International*, 30 April 2007

Gleis, Joshua L., 'National Security Implications of Al-Takfir Wal-Hijra', *Al Nakhlah: The Fletcher School Online Journal for Issues Related to Southwest Asia and Islamic Civilization*, Spring 2005

Glennie, Alex, *Building Bridges, Not Walls: Engaging with Political Islamists in the Middle East and North Africa*, London: Institute for Public Policy Research, 2009

Göle, Nilüfer, 'Secularism and Islamism in Turkey: The Making of Elites and Counter-Elites', *Middle East Journal*, 51 (1) 1997

The Graduate Institute, Geneva, Transnational and Non-State Armed Groups Database, 'Palestinian Islamic Jihad', http://www.armed-groups.org/6/section.aspx/ViewGroup?id=69

Graham, Gordon, *Ethics and International Relations*, Oxford: Blackwell, 1997

Green, Jerrold D., 'Terrorism and Politics in Iran', Martha Crenshaw (ed.), *Terrorism in Context*, University Park: The Pennsylvania State University Press, 1995

Greenberg, Karen J. (ed.), *Al Qaeda Now: Understanding Today's Terrorists*, New York: Cambridge University Press, 2005

Gresh, Alain and Vidal, Dominique, *The New A-Z of the Middle East*, London: I. B. Tauris, 2004

Guitta, Olivier, 'Terror in the Maghreb: Al Qaeda Linked Groups are Spreading from Algeria and Morocco into Tunisia', *The Daily Standard*, 14 February 2007

Gülalp, Haldun, 'Globalization and Political Islam: The Social Bases of Turkey's Welfare Party', *International Journal of Middle East Studies*, 33 (2) 2001

'Political Islam in Turkey: The Rise and Fall of the Refah Party', *The Muslim World*, 89 (1) January 1999

Gunaratna, Rohan, *Inside Al-Qaeda*, London: Hurst, 2002

Gunning, Jeroen, *Hamas in Politics: Democracy, Religion, Violence*, London: Hurst, 2007

'Peace with Hamas? The Transforming Potential of Political Participation', *International Affairs*, 80 (2) 2004

Gurr, Ted Robert, 'Terrorism in Democracies: When It Occurs, Why It Fails', Charles W. Kegley Jr. (ed.), *The New Global Terrorism: Characteristics, Causes, Controls*, Upper Saddle River, NJ: Prentice Hall, 2003

Hafez, Mohammed M., *Why Muslims Rebel: Repression and Resistance in the Islamic World*, Boulder, CO: Lynne Rienner, 2003

Review: Camille al Tawil, Al Haraka Al Islamiyya Al Musalahafi Al Jazair: Min 'Al Inqadth' ila 'Al Jama'a' (The Armed Islamic Movement in Algeria: From the FIS to the GIA), Beirut: Dar al Nihar, 1998, *International Journal of Middle East Studies*, 35 (1) 2003

'Armed Islamist Movements and Political Violence in Algeria', *Middle East Journal*, 54 (4) 2000

Hafez, Mohammed M. and Wiktorowicz, Quintan, 'Violence as Contention in the Egyptian Islamic Movement', Quintan Wiktorowicz (ed.), *Islamic Activism: A Social Movement Theory Approach*, Bloomington: Indiana University Press, 2004

Hale, William and Özbudun, Ergun, *Islamism, Democracy and Liberalism in Turkey: The Case of the AKP*, Abingdon, Oxon: Routledge, 2010

Halliday, Fred, *International Relations and the Middle East: Power, Politics and Ideology*, Cambridge: Cambridge University Press, 2005

'The Politics of Islamic Fundamentalism: Iran, Tunisia, and the Challenge to the Secular State', A. S. Ahmed and H. Donnan (eds.), *Islam, Globalization and Post-Modernity*, London: Routledge, 1994

Hamad, Ghazi Ahmad, 'The Challenge for HAMAS-Establishing Transparency and Accountability', unpublished document, courtesy of the Geneva Centre for the Democratic Control of Armed Forces, Ramallah, West Bank, 2006, http://www.dcaf.ch/publications/kms/details.cfm?ord279=title&q279= hamas&lng=en&id=21665&nav1=4

Hamzawy, Amr, *The Key to Arab Reform: Moderate Islamists*, Carnegie Endowment for International Peace, Policy Brief 40, July 2005

Hamzawy, Amr and Bishara, Dina, *Islamist Movements in the Arab World and the 2006 Lebanon War*, Carnegie Endowment for International Peace, Carnegie Paper 75, November 2006

Hamzeh, A. Nizar, 'Lebanon's Hezbollah: From Islamic Revolution to Parliamentary Accommodation', *Third World Quarterly*, 14 (2) 1993

Harik, Judith Palmer, *Hezbollah: The Changing Face of Terrorism*, London: I. B. Tauris, 2004

Hasan, Riaz, *The State and Religious Institutions in Muslim Societies*, Working Paper 79, Institute of Defence and Strategic Studies, Singapore, June 2005

Hawthorne, Amy, 'The New Reform Ferment', Thomas Carothers and Marina Ottaway (eds.), *Uncharted Journey: Promoting Democracy in the Middle East*, Washington, DC: Carnegie Endowment, 2005

Hedges, Chris, 'A Nation Challenged: Tunisia: Explosion at Synagogue Tied to Jihad', *The New York Times*, 24 April 2002

Hegghamer, Thomas, 'Jihadi-Salafis or Revolutionaries? On Religion and Politics in the Study of Militant Islam', Roel Meijer (ed.), *Global Salafism: Islam's New Religious Movement*, London and New York: Hurst/Columbia University Press, 2009

'Global Jihadism after the Iraq War', *Middle East Journal*, 60 (1) Winter 2006

Hegre, Harvard, Ellingsen, Tanja, Gates, Scott, and Gleditsch, Nils Petter, 'Toward a Democratic Civil Peace? Democracy, Political Change and Civil War 1816–1992', *American Political Science Review*, 95 (1) 2001

Heper, Metin, 'Islam and Democracy in Turkey: Towards a Reconciliation?', *Middle East Journal*, 51 (1) 1997

Heper, Metin and Toktaş, Şule, 'Islam, Modernity, and Democracy in Contemporary Turkey: The Case of Recep Tayyip Erdoğan', *The Muslim World*, 93 (2) 2003

Hewitt, Christopher, 'The Political Context of Terrorism in America: Ignoring Extremists or Pandering to Them?', David Rapoport and Leonard Weinberg (eds.), *The Democratic Experience and Political Violence*, London: Frank Cass, 2001

Hewitt, Christopher and Kelley-Moore, Jessica, 'Foreign Fighters in Iraq: A Cross-National Analysis of Jihadism', *Terrorism and Political Violence*, 21 (2) 2009

Hicks, Neil, 'Our Friend the Autocrat', *Washington Post*, 16 February 2004

Hiro, Dilip, *Iran Today*, London: Politico's, 2005

Neighbors, Not Friends: Iraq and Iran after the Gulf Wars, London: Routledge, 2001

Hoffman, Bruce, *Inside Terrorism*, New York: Columbia University Press, 2006

Hoffman, Bruce and McCormick, Gordon, 'Terrorism, Signalling and Suicide Attacks', *Studies in Conflict and Terrorism*, 27 (4) 2004

Holmes, Stephen, 'Al-Qaeda, September 11, 2001', Diego Gambetta (ed.), *Making Sense of Suicide Missions*, Oxford: Oxford University Press, 2005

Horne, Alistair, *A Savage War of Peace: Algeria, 1954–1962*, London: Macmillan, 1977

Howeidy, Amira, 'Democracy's Backlash', *Al Ahram Weekly Online* 785, 9–15 March 2006, http://weekly.ahram.org.eg/2006/785/eg3.htm

Khaled Hroub, 'A "New Hamas" through Its New Documents', *Journal of Palestine Studies*, 35 (4) Summer 2006

Hamas: Political Thought and Practice, Washington, DC: Institute for Palestine Studies, 2002

Human Rights Watch (HRW), *Why They Died: Civilian Casualties in Lebanon During the 2006 War*, 19, 5 (E) September 2007

'Egypt: Reading between the "Red Lines": The Repression of Academic Freedom in Egyptian Universities', *Human Rights Watch*, 17 (6) June 2005

World Report 2002, New York: Human Rights Watch, 2002

Erased in a Moment: Suicide Bombing Attacks against Israeli Civilians, New York: Human Rights Watch, October 2002

Huntington, Samuel and Nelson, Joan (eds.), *No Easy Choice: Political Participation in Developing Countries*, Cambridge, MA: Harvard University Press, 1976

Ibrahim, Saad Eddin, 'The Changing Face of Islamic Activism', *Civil Society*, 4, 1995

'Egypt's Islamic Militants', *Merip Reports*, 103, February 1982

İnsel, Ahmet, 'The AKP and Normalizing Democracy in Turkey', *The South Atlantic Quarterly*, 102 (2/3) Spring/Summer 2003

International Crisis Group (ICG), *Iraq after the Surge I: The New Sunni Landscape*, Middle East Report 74, 30 April 2008

Hezbollah and the Lebanese Crisis, Middle East Report 69, 10 October 2007

Enter Hamas: The Challenges of Political Integration, Middle East Report 49, 18 January 2006

Jordan's 9/11: Dealing with Jihadi Islamism, Middle East Report 47, 23 November 2005

Iran: What Does Ahmadi-Nejad's Victory Mean?, Middle East Briefing 18, 4 August 2005

Understanding Islamism, Middle East/North Africa Report 37, 2 March 2005

After Arafat? Challenges and Prospects, Middle East Briefing, 23 December 2004

Saudi Arabia Backgrounder: Who Are the Islamists?, Middle East Report 31, 21 September 2004

Islamism, Violence and Reform in Algeria: Turning the Page, Middle East Report 29, 30 July 2004

The Broader Middle East and North Africa Initiative: Imperilled at Birth, Middle East and North Africa Briefing, June 2004

Islamism in North Africa II: Egypt's Opportunity, Middle East and North Africa Briefing, 20 April 2004

Hizbollah: Rebel without a Cause?, ICG Middle East Briefing, Amman/ Brussels, 30 July 2003

Old Games, New Rules: Conflict on the Israel-Lebanon Border, Middle East Report 7, 18 November 2002

Ismail, Salwa, 'The Paradox of Islamist Politics', *Middle East Report*, 221, Winter 2001

Jaber, Hala, *Hezbollah: Born with a Vengeance*, New York: Columbia University Press, 1997

Jenkins, Gareth, *Political Islam in Turkey: Running West, Heading East?* New York: Palgrave Macmillan, 2008

    Context and Circumstance: The Turkish Military and Politics, Adelphi Paper 337, Oxford: Oxford University Press for the International Institute for Strategic Studies, 2001

Juergensmeyer, Mark, *Terror in the Mind of God: The Global Rise of Religious Violence*, Berkeley, Los Angeles and London: University of California Press, 2003

Kalyvas, Stathis, 'Wanton and Senseless? The Logic of Massacres in Algeria', *Rationality and Society*, 11 (3) 1999

Kaplan, Robert, 'We Can't Force Democracy: Creating Normality Is the Real Mideast Challenge', *Washington Post*, 2 March 2006

Kazemi, Farhad, 'Civil Society and Iranian Politics', Augustus Richard Norton (ed.), *Civil Society in the Middle East*, Vol. 2, Leiden: E. J. Brill, 1996

Keddie, Nikki, 'Ideology, Society and the State in Post-Colonial Muslim Societies', Fred Halliday and Hamza Alavi (eds.), *State and Ideology in the Middle East and Pakistan*, Basingstoke: Macmillan Education, 1988

    Roots of Revolution: An Interpretive History of Modern Iran, New Haven, CT: Yale University Press, 1981

Kegley, Charles, (ed.) *The New Global Terrorism: Characteristics, Causes, Controls*, Upper Saddle River, NJ: Prentice Hall, 2003

Kepel, Gilles, *Jihad: The Trail of Political Islam*, trans. Anthony Roberts, London: I. B. Tauris, 2002

    The Prophet and Pharaoh: Muslim Extremism in Contemporary Egypt, trans. Jon Rothschild, London: Saqi, 1985

Kepel, Gilles and Milelli, Jean-Pierre (eds.), *Al Qaeda in Its Own Words*, trans. Pascale Ghazaleh, Cambridge, MA: The Belknap Press of Harvard University Press, 2008

Khalaf, Roula and Fidler, Stephen, 'From Frontline Attack to Terror by Franchise', *Financial Times*, 5 July 2007

    'Why Algerian Extremists "Rebranded" as al-Qaeda', *Financial Times*, 20 April 2007

Khalil, Magdi, 'Egypt's Muslim Brotherhood and Political Power: Would Democracy Survive?', *The Middle East Review of International Affairs*, 10 (1) 2006

Khamidov, Alisher, *Countering the Call: The U.S., Hizb-ut-Tahrir, and Religious Extremism in Central Asia*, The Saban Center for Middle East Policy at the Brookings Institution, Analysis Paper 4, July 2003

Khosrokhavar, Farhad, 'The New Conservatives Take a Turn', *Middle East Report*, 233, Winter 2004

Kian-Thiébaut, Azadeh, *Secularization of Iran: A Doomed Failure? The New Middle Class and the Making of Modern Iran*, Paris: Peeters, 1998

Klein, Menachem, 'Against the Consensus: Oppositionist Voices in Hamas', *Middle Eastern Studies*, 45 (6) November 2009

    'Hamas in Power', *Middle East Journal*, 61 (3) 2007

'Competing Brothers: The Web of Hamas-PLO Relations', *Terrorism and Political Violence*, 8 (2) 1996

Koppel, Ted, 'Gifts for Iran: Look What Spreading Democracy Can Do', *International Herald Tribune*, 22 July 2006

Krämer, Gudrun, 'Cross-Links and Double Talk? Islamist Movements in the Political Process', Laura Guazzone (ed.), *The Islamist Dilemma: The Political Role of Islamist Movements in the Arab World*, Reading, Berkshire: Ithaca Press, 1995

'The Integration of the Integrists: A Comparative Study of Egypt, Jordan and Tunisia', Ghassan Salamé (ed.), *Democracy without Democrats? The Renewal of Politics in the Muslim World*, London: I. B. Tauris, 1994

Krebs, Lutz, Senn, Dominic, and Vorrath, Judith, *Linking Ethnic Conflict and Democratization: An Assessment of Four Troubled Regions*, National Centre for Competence in Research Working Paper No. 6, June 2007, http://www.nccr-democracy.uzh.ch/publications/workingpaper/pdf/WP6.pdf

Kristianasen, Wendy, 'Who Is a Salafist?', *Monde Diplomatique*, February 2008

Krueger, Alan B. and Maleckova, Jitka, 'Education, Poverty, Political Violence and Terrorism: Is There a Causal Connection?', *Journal of Economic Perspectives*, 17 (4) 2003

Kuriansky, Judy, *Terror in the Holy Land: Inside the Anguish of the Israeli-Palestinian Conflict*, Westport, CT: Praeger Pulishers, 2006

Labat, Séverine, *Les Islamistes algériens entre les urnes et le maquis*, Paris: Seuil, 1995

bin Laden, Osama, 'Declaration of a World Islamic Front for Jihad against Jews and Crusaders', 23 February 1998, http://www.fas.org/irp/world/para/docs/980223-fatwa.htm

'Declaration of War against the Americans Occupying the Land of the Two Holy Places', August 1996, http://www.pbs.org/newshour/terrorism/international/fatwa_1996.html

Lai, Brian, 'Explaining Terrorism Using the Framework of Opportunity and Willingness: An Empirical Examination of International Terrorism', Research Paper (unpublished), Department of Political Science, University of Iowa, April 2004

Langohr, Vickie, 'Of Islamists and Ballot Boxes: Rethinking the Relationship between Islamisms and Electoral Politics', *International Journal of Middle East Studies*, 33 (4) 2001

Laqueur, Walter, *No End to War: Terrorism in the Twenty-First Century*, New York: Continuum, 2003

The New Terrorism: Fanaticism and the Arms of Mass Destruction, New York: Oxford University Press, 1999

Lawrence, Bruce, *Messages to the World: The Statements of Osama Bin Laden*, trans. James Howarth, London: Verso, 2005

Lee, Robert, 'Tunisian Intellectuals: A Response to Islamism', *The Journal of North African Studies*, 13 (2) 2008

Lester, David, Yang, Bijou, and Lindsay, Mark, 'Suicide Bombers: Are Psychological Profiles Possible?' *Studies in Conflict and Terrorism*, 27 (4) 2004

Levitt, Matthew, *Hamas: Politics, Charity, and Terrorism in the Service of Jihad*, New Haven, CT and London: Yale University Press, 2007

Li, Quan, 'Does Democracy Promote or Reduce Transnational Terrorist Incidents?', *Journal of Conflict Resolution*, 49 (2) April 2005

Lia, Brynjar, *Architect of Global Jihad: The Life of al-Qaida Strategist Abu Mus'ab al-Suri*, New York: Columbia University Press, 2008

Lia, Brynjar and Hegghammer, Thomas, 'Jihadi Strategic Studies: The Alleged al Qaida Policy Study Preceding the Madrid Bombings', *Studies in Conflict and Terrorism*, 27 (5) September/October 2004

Lia, Brynjar and Kjøk, Åshlid, *Islamist Insurgencies, Diasporic Support Networks and Their Host States*, Kjeller: Norwegian Defence Research Establishment, 2001

Islamist Insurgencies, Diasporic Support Networks and Their Host States, Kjeller: Norwegian Defence Research Establishment, 2001

Lia, Brynjar and Skjølberg, Katja, *The Causes of Terrorism*, Kjeller: Norwegian Defence Research Establishment, 2004

Lizardo, Omar A., 'The Effect of Economic and Cultural Globalisation on Anti-US Transnational Terrorism, 1971–2000', *Journal of World-Systems Research*, 12 (1) 2006

Lust-Okar, Ellen, 'Taking Political Participation Seriously', Ellen Lust-Okar and Saloua Zerhouni (eds.), *Political Participation in the Middle East*, Boulder, CO: Lynne Rienner, 2008

'Elections under Authoritarianism: Preliminary Lessons from Jordan', Frederic Volpi and Francesco Cavatorta (eds.), *Democratization in the Muslim World: Changing Patterns of Power and Authority*, London: Routledge, 2007

'Divided They Rule: The Management and Manipulation of Political Opposition', *Comparative Politics*, 36 (2) 2004

Lustick, Ian S., 'Terrorism in the Arab-Israeli Conflict: Targets and Audiences', Martha Crenshaw (ed.), *Terrorism in Context*, University Park: The Pennsylvania State University Press, 1995

Magnuson, Douglas Kent, *Islamic Reform in Contemporary Tunisia: A Comparative Ethnographic Study*, Unpublished PhD thesis, Department of Anthropology, Brown University, May 1987

Mahmoud, Muhammad, 'Women and Islamism: The Case of Rashid al-Ghannushi in Tunisia', Abdel Salam Sidahmed and Anoushiravan Ehteshami (eds.), *Islamic Fundamentalism*, Boulder, CO: Westview, 1996

Mann, Michael, *Incoherent Empire*, London: Verso, 2003

Manokha, Ivan, 'Al-Qaeda Terrorism and Global Poverty: New Social Banditry', *Journal of Global Ethics*, 4 (2) 2008

Margulies, Ronnie and Yildizoğlu, Ergin, 'The Political Uses of Islam in Turkey', *Middle East Report*, 153, July–August 1988

Martinez, Luis, *The Algerian Civil War 1990–1998*, trans. Jonathan Derrick, London: Hurst & Co., 2003

Marzouki, Moncef, "The US Project for Democracy in the Greater Middle East – Yes, But With Whom?" (Arabic), *Al Hayat*, 23 February 2004

Mazarr, Michael J., 'The Psychological Sources of Islamic Terrorism', *Policy Review*, 125, June–July 2004

Mazzetti, Mark and Rohde, David, 'The Doomed Hunt for Al Qaeda's Leaders', *International Herald Tribune*, 30 June 2008

McAuley, Denis, 'The Ideology of Osama Bin Laden: Nation, Tribe and World Economy', *Journal of Political Ideologies*, 10 (3) October 2005

McDougall, James, 'After the War: Algeria's Transition to Uncertainty', *Middle East Report*, 245, Winter 2007

Meijer, Roel, 'Jihadi Opposition in Saudi Arabia', *International Institute for the Study of Islam in the Modern World (ISIM) Review*, 15, Spring 2005

Menashri, David, *Post-Revolutionary Politics in Iran: Religion, Society and Power*, London: Frank Cass, 2001

Milton-Edwards, Beverley, 'Climate of Change in Jordan's Islamist Movement', Abdel Salam Sidahmed and Anoushiravan Ehteshami (eds.), *Islamic Fundamentalism*, Boulder, CO: Westview Press, 1996

   Islamic Politics in Palestine, London: I. B. Tauris, 1996

Mir-Hosseini, Ziba and Tapper, Richard, *Islam and Democracy in Iran: Eshkevari and the Quest for Reform*, London: I. B. Tauris, 2006

Mishal, Shaul and Rosenthal, Maoz, 'Al Qaeda as a Dune Organization: Toward a Typology of Islamic Terrorist Organizations', *Studies in Conflict and Terrorism*, 28 (4) 2005

Mishal, Shaul and Sela, Avraham, *The Palestinian Hamas: Vision, Violence and Coexistence*, New York: Columbia University Press, 2000

Mitchell, Richard P., *The Society of the Muslim Brothers*, London: Oxford University Press, 1969

Moaddel, Mansoor, 'The Iranian Revolution and Its Nemesis: The Rise of Liberal Values among Iranians', *Comparative Studies of South Asia, Africa and the Middle East*, 29 (1) 2009

Moaddel, Mansoor and Taqhi, Azadarmaki, 'The Worldviews of Islamic Publics: The Cases of Egypt, Iran and Jordan', http://www.worldvalues-survey.org/Upload/5_Iran.pdf

Moin, Baqer, *Khomeini: Life of the Ayatollah*, London: I. B. Tauris, 1999

Muslim Brotherhood (Egypt) Official website: http://www.ikhwanonline.com/ an-Nabhani, Taqiuddin, 'A Draft Constitution of the Islamic State', *The Islamic State*, New Delhi: Milli Publications, 2001

el Naggar, Said, 'The Alexandria Statement', *al Wafd*, 25 April 2004 (unofficial translation from the Arabic by Robert Springborg and Ahmed Ezzelarab).

Naguib, Sameh, 'Islamism(s) Old and New', Rabab el Mahdi and Philip Marfleet (eds.), *Egypt: The Moment of Change*, London: Zed Books, 2009

Norton, Augustus Richard, *Hezbollah: A Short History*, Princeton, NJ: Princeton University Press, 2007

   'Why Hizbullah Is Winning', *Middle East Journal*, 61 (1) Winter 2007

   'Hizballah: Through the Fog of the Lebanon War: An Interview with Augustus Richard Norton', *Journal of Palestine Studies*, 36 (1) Autumn, 2006

Noyon, Jennifer, *Islam, Politics and Pluralism: Theory and Practice in Turkey, Jordan, Tunisia and Algeria*, London: Royal Institute of International Affairs, 2003

Nüsse, Andrea, 'The Ideology of Hamas: Palestinian Islamic Fundamentalist Thought on the Jews, Israel and Islam', Ronald Nettler (ed.), *Studies in Muslim-Jewish Relations*, Chur: Harwood Academic Publishers, 1993

Öniş, Ziya, 'Political Islam at the Crossroads: From Hegemony to Co-existence', *Contemporary Politics*, 7 (4) 2001

Ottaway, Marina, 'The Problem of Credibility', Thomas Carothers and Marina Ottaway (eds.), *Uncharted Journey: Promoting Democracy in the Middle East*, Washington, DC: Carnegie Endowment for International Peace, 2005

Ottaway, Marina and Carothers, Thomas, *The Greater Middle East Initiative: Off to a False Start*, Carnegie Endowment for International Peace, Policy Report 29, March 2004

Ottaway, Marina, Carothers, Thomas, Hawthorne, Amy, and Brumberg, Daniel, *Democratic Mirage in the Middle East*, Carnegie Endowment for International Peace, Policy Brief 20, October 2002

Ouazani, Cherif 'Algérie: Jusqu'où Ira al-Qaïda?', *Jeune Afrique*, 2449, 16–22 Décembre 2007

'Mort d'un juste', *Jeune Afrique*, 2438, 30 Septembre – 6 Octobre 2007

Pape, Robert, *Dying to Win: The Strategic Logic of Suicide Terrorism*, New York: Random House, 2005

'The Strategic Logic of Suicide Terrorism', *American Political Science Review*, 97 (3) 2003

Patton, Marcie J., 'The Economic Policies of Turkey's AKP Government: Rabbits from a Hat?', *Middle East Journal*, 60 (3) Summer 2006

'Turkey's Tug of War', *Middle East Report*, 239, Summer 2006

Peretz, Don, *Intifada: The Palestinian Uprising*, Boulder, CO: Westview Press, 1990

Pipes, Daniel, 'God and Mammon: Does Poverty Cause Militant Islam?', *The National Interest*, 66, Winter 2001/02

Pluchinsky, Dennis, 'Terrorism in the Former Soviet Union: A Primer, a Puzzle, a Prognosis', *Studies in Conflict and Terrorism*, 21 (2) 1998

'Middle Eastern Terrorist Activity in Western Europe in 1985: A Diagnosis and Prognosis', Paul Wilkinson and A. M. Stewart (eds.), *Contemporary Research in Terrorism*, Aberdeen: Aberdeen University Press, 1987

Polka, Sagi, 'The Centrist Stream in Egypt and the Public Discourse Surrounding the Shaping of the Country's Cultural Identity', *Middle Eastern Studies*, 39 (3) 2003

Pollack, Josh, 'Saudi Arabia and the United States, 1931–2002', *Middle East Review of International Affairs*, 6 (3) September 2002

Porter, Patrick, 'Long Wars and Long Telegrams: Containing Al-Qaeda', *International Affairs*, 85 (2) March 2009

Qasim, Tal'at Fu'ad 'What Does the Gama'a Islamiyya Want? Tal'at Fu'ad Qasim Interview with Hisham Mubarak', Joel Beinin and Joe Stork (eds.), *Political Islam: Essays from Middle East Report*, London: I. B. Tauris, 1997

Qassem, Naim, *Hizbullah: The Story from Within*, trans. Dalia Khalil, London: Saqi, 2005

Ranstorp, Magnus, *Hizb'Allah in Lebanon: The Politics of the Western Hostage Crisis*, Basingstoke and London: Macmillan Press, 1997

Rapoport, David C. and Weinberg, Leonard, 'Elections and Violence', David C. Rapoport and Leonard Weinberg (eds.), *The Democratic Experience and Political Violence*, London: Frank Cass, 2001

Rasanayagam, Angelo, *Afghanistan: A Modern History*, London: I. B. Tauris, 2003

Rashwan, Diaa, *Transformations among the Islamic Groups in Egypt*, Strategic Papers, Cairo: Al Ahram Center for Political and Strategic Studies, 2000

Richards, Alan, *Socio-Economic Roots of Radicalism?: Towards Explaining the Appeal of Islamic Radicals*, Carlisle, PA: Strategic Studies Institute, Army War College, 2003

Ricolfi, Luca, 'Palestinians, 1981–2003', Diego Gambetta (ed.), *Making Sense of Suicide Missions*, Oxford: Oxford University Press, 2005

Roberts, Hugh, *The Battlefield Algeria, 1988–2002: Studies in a Broken Polity*, London: Verso, 2003

Robins, Philip, *A History of Jordan*, Cambridge: Cambridge University Press, 2004

Robinson, Glen E., 'Hamas as Social Movement', Quintan Wiktorowicz (ed.), *Islamic Activism: A Social Movement Theory Approach*, Bloomington: Indiana University Press, 2004

'Can Islamists Be Democrats? The Case of Jordan', *Middle East Journal*, 51 (3) 1997

Rosendorff, B. Peter and Sandler, Todd, 'The Political Economy of Transnational Terrorism', *Journal of Conflict Resolution*, 49 (2) April 2005

Roth, Kenneth, 'The Wrong Way to Combat Terrorism', *The Brown Journal of World Affairs*, 14 (1) Fall/Winter 2007

Roy, Olivier, *Globalised Islam: The Search for a New Ummah*, London: Hurst and Company, 2004

The Failure of Political Islam, London: I. B. Tauris, 1999

'The Crisis of Legitimacy in Iran', *Middle East Journal*, 53 (2) 1999

'Hazy Outlines of an Islamist International: Fundamentalists without a Common Cause', *Monde Diplomatique*, October 1998

Roy, Sara, 'Hamas and the Transformation(s) of Political Islam in Palestine', *Current History*, 102 (660) January 2003

Ruedy, John, *Modern Algeria: The Origins and Development of a Nation*, 2nd edition, Bloomington: Indiana University Press, 2005

Russett, Bruce, *Grasping the Democratic Peace: Principles for a Post-Cold War World*, Princeton, NJ: Princeton University Press, 1993

Rutherford, Bruce K., 'What Do Egypt's Islamists Want? Moderate Islam and the Rise of Islamic Constitutionalism', *Middle East Journal*, 60 (4) 2006

Saad-Ghorayeb, Amal, *Hizbu'llah: Politics and Religion*, London: Pluto Press, 2002

Sadri, Mahmoud and Sadri, Ahmad (eds.), *Reason, Freedom, and Democracy in Islam: Essential Writings of 'Abdolkarim Soroush*, Oxford: Oxford University Press, 2000

Sageman, Marc, *Leaderless Jihad: Terrorist Networks in the Twenty-First Century*, Philadelphia: University of Pennsylvania Press, 2008

Understanding Terror Networks, Philadelphia: University of Pennsylvania Press, 2004

el Said, Sabah, *Between Pragmatism and Ideology: The Muslim Brotherhood in Jordan, 1989–94*, Washington, DC: The Washington Institute for Near East Policy, Policy Paper 39, 1995

Salehi-Isfahani, Djavad, 'Iran's Presidential Elections: A Surge of Reformists in Politics' Wolfensen Center for Development/Dubai School of Government Middle East Youth Initiative, http://www.shababinclusion.org/content/blog/detail/1380/

Sambanis, Nicholas, 'What Is Civil War? Conceptual and Empirical Complexities of an Operational Definition', *Journal of Conflict Resolution*, 48 (6) 2004

Sayigh, Yezid, *Armed Struggle and the Search for State: The Palestinian National Movement, 1949–1993*, Oxford: Clarendon Press, 1997

al Sayyid, Mustapha Kamel, *The Other Face of the Islamist Movement*, Democracy and Rule of Law Project, Global Policy Program, Working Paper 33, January 2003

Sayyid-Marsot, Afaf Lutfi, *Egypt's Liberal Experiment, 1922–1936*, Berkeley: University of California Press, 1977

Schemm, Paul, 'Grand Gesture', *Middle East International*, 745, 4 March 2005

Schenker, David, *Hamas Weapons in Jordan: Implications for Islamists on the East Bank*, The Washington Institute for Near East Policy, Policy Watch, 1098, 5 May 2006

Schirazi, Asghar, *The Constitution of Iran: Politics and the State in the Islamic Republic*, trans. John O'Kane, London: I. B. Tauris, 1998

Schulze, Reinhard, *A Modern History of the Islamic World*, trans. Azizeh Azodi, London: I. B. Tauris, 2000

Schwedler, Jillian, *Faith in Moderation: Islamist Parties in Jordan and Yemen*, New York: Cambridge University Press, 2006

Semati, Hadi, 'Democracy in Retrograde' *Los Angeles Times*, 24 September 2004

Shahzad, Syed Saleem, 'Takfirism: A Messianic Ideology', *Monde Diplomatique*, July 2007

Shay, Shaul, *The Shahids: Islam and Suicide Attacks*, Somerset, NJ: Transaction Publishers, 2004

Shikaki, Khalil, *With Hamas in Power: Impact of Palestinian Domestic Developments on Options for the Peace Process*, Working Paper 1, February 2007, Brandeis University: Crown Center for Middle East Studies

Sick, Gary, 'Iran: Confronting Terrorism', *The Washington Quarterly*, 26 (4) Autumn 2003
    'Rethinking Dual Containment', *Survival*, 40 (1) 1998

Sidel, John, *The Islamist Threat in Southeast Asia: A Reassessment*, Washington, DC: East-West Center, 2007

Silke, Andrew, 'Contemporary Terrorism Studies: Issues in Research', Richard Jackson, Marie Breen Smyth, and Jeroen Gunning (eds.), *Critical Terrorism Studies: A New Research Agenda*, London: Routledge, 2009

Skjølberg, Katja, 'Ethnic Pluralism, Legitimacy and Conflict: Western European Separatism 1950–95', Paper presented at the ISA Conference, Los

Angles, March 2002, http://www.svt.ntnu.no/iss/fagkonferanse/IPkvant/Skjolberg.pdf

Smith, Barbara, 'Algeria: The Horror', *New York Review of Books*, XLV (7) 1998

Smith, Craig S., 'Tunisia Is Feared as New Islamist Base: Qaeda-Linked Algerian Group Suspected of Using Country in Network', *International Herald Tribune*, 20 February 2007

Snyder, Jack, *From Voting to Violence: Democratization and National Conflict*, New York: W. W. Norton, 2000

Soage, Ana Belén, 'Hasan al-Banna and Sayyid Qutb: Continuity or Rupture?', *The Muslim World*, 99 (2) 2009

Sprinkzak, Ehud, 'Rational Fanatics', *Foreign Policy*, 120, 2000

Stacher, Joshua A., 'Post-Islamist Rumblings in Egypt: The Emergence of the Wasat Party', *Middle East Journal*, 56 (3) Summer 2002

Stern, Jessica, *Terror in the Name of God: Why Religious Militants Kill*, New York: HarperCollins Publishers, 2003

Tabari, Keyvan, 'Rule of Law', *International Sociology*, 18 (1) 2003

Taji-Farouki, Suha, *A Fundamental Quest: Hizb al-Tahrir and the Search for the Islamist Caliphate*, London: Grey Seal, 1996

Tamimi, Azzam, *Hamas: Unwritten Chapters*, London: Hurst & Co., 2007
  Rachid Ghannouchi: A Democrat within Islamism, New York: Oxford University Press, 2001

Tammam, Husam, 'Révisions douloureuses pour les Frères musulmans d'Egypte', *Le Monde Diplomatique*, Septembre 2005

al Tawil, Camille, *Al Haraka Al Islamiyya Al Musalahafi Al Jazair: Min 'Al Inqadth' ila 'Al Jama'a'* (The Armed Islamic Movement in Algeria: From the FIS to the GIA), Beirut: Dar al Nihar, 1998

Tilly, Charles, *From Mobilization to Revolution*, Reading, MA: Addison-Wesley, 1978

Toprak, Binnaz, *Islam and Political Development in Turkey*, Leiden: E. J. Brill, 1981

Toros, Harmonie and Gunning, Jeroen, 'Exploring a Critical Theory Approach to Terrorism Studies', Richard Jackson, Marie Breen Smyth, and Jeroen Gunning, (eds.), *Critical Terrorism Studies: A New Research Agenda*, Abingdon, Oxon: Routledge, 2009

Toth, James, 'Islamism in Southern Egypt: A Case Study of a Radical Religious Movement', *International Journal of Middle East Studies*, 35 (4) 2003

Trofimov, Yaroslav, *The Siege of Mecca: The Forgotten Uprising in Islam's Holiest Shrine and the Birth of al Qaeda*, New York: Doubleday, 2007

United Nations Development Programme, *Arab Human Development Report*, 2002

United Nations Fact Finding Mission on the Gaza Conflict, *Human Rights in Palestine and Other Occupied Arab Territories* (the 'Goldstone Report'), 23 September 2009, http://www2.ohchr.org/english/bodies/hrcouncil/specialsession/9/docs/UNFFMGC_Report.pdf

US State Department, Country Reports on Terrorism 2008

Usher, Graham, 'The New Hamas: Between Resistance and Participation', *Middle East Report Online*, 21 August 2005, http://www.merip.org/mero/mero082105.html

Vaisse, Justin, *Transformational Diplomacy*, Challiot Paper 103, European Union Institute for Security Studies, June 2007

Vertigans, Stephen, *Militant Islam: A Sociology of Characteristics, Causes and Consequences*, London: Routledge, 2009

Vorrath, Judith and Krebs, Lutz, 'Democratization and Conflict in Ethnically Divided Societies', *Living Reviews in Democracy*, 1, 2009, http://www.lrd.ethz.ch/index.php/lrd

Waldman, Adir, *Arbitrating Armed Conflict: Decisions of the Israel-Lebanon Monitoring Group*, Huntington, NY: Juris Publishing, 2003

Weinberg, Leonard, 'Turning to Terror: The Conditions under Which Political Parties Turn to Terrorist Activities', *Comparative Politics*, 23 (4) July 1991

Whitbeck, John V., 'Life and Death in Saudi Arabia', *International Herald Tribune*, 3 June 2004

White, Jenny, *Islamist Mobilization in Turkey: A Study in Vernacular Politics*, Seattle: University of Washington Press, 2002

Whitlock, Craig, 'Al-Qaeda's Far-Reaching New Partner', *Washington Post*, 5 October 2006

Wickham, Carrie Rosefsky, 'The Path to Moderation: Strategy and Learning in the Formation of Egypt's Wasat Party' *Comparative Politics*, 36 (2) 2004

    Mobilizing Islam: Religion, Activism, and Political Change in Egypt, New York: Columbia University Press, 2002

Wieviorka, Michel, *The Making of Terrorism*, trans. David Gordon White, Chicago and London: University of Chicago Press, 1993

Wiktorowicz, Quintan, 'Introduction: Islamic Activism and Social Movement Theory', Quintan Wiktorowicz (ed.), *Islamic Activism: A Social Movement Theory Approach*, Bloomington: Indiana University Press, 2004

    'The Salafi Movement in Jordan', *International Journal of Middle East Studies*, 32 (2) 2000

    'Islamists, the State, and Cooperation in Jordan', *Arab Studies Quarterly*, 21, Fall 1999

Wiktorowicz, Quintan and Kaltner, John, 'Killing in the Name of Islam: Al-Qaeda's Justification for September 11', *Middle East Policy*, 10 (2) 2003

Wilkinson, Paul, *Terrorism versus Democracy: The Liberal State Response*, 2nd edition, London and New York: Routledge, 2006

    Terrorism and the Liberal State, Basingstoke: Macmillan, 1986

Willis, Michael, *The Islamist Challenge in Algeria: A Political History*, Reading, Berkshire: Ithaca Press, 1996

Wittes, Tamara Cofman and Yerkes, Sarah, *What Price Freedom? Assessing the Bush Administration's Freedom Agenda*, Saban Centre for Middle East Policy, Analysis Paper 10, September 2006

The World Bank, World Development Indicators Database, http://data.world-bank.org/data-catalog

    World Bank Country Profile: Iran, http://web.worldbank.org/WBSITE/EXTERNAL/COUNTRIES/MENAEXT/IRANEXTN/0,,menuPK:312962~pagePK:141159~piPK:141110~theSitePK:312943,00.html

Interim Assistance Strategy for the Islamic Republic of Iran, Report No. 22050 IRN, April 16, 2001

World Markets Research Centre, 'Global Terrorism Index: Key Findings' *guardian.co.uk*, 18 Aug 2003, http://www.guardian.co.uk/world/2003/aug/18/alqaida.terrorism1

Wright, Lawrence, *The Looming Tower: Al-Qaeda's Road to 9/11*, London: Penguin Books, 2006

Yacoubian, Mona, *Engaging Islamists and Promoting Democracy: A Preliminary Assessment*, United States Institute of Peace, Special Report 190, August 2007, http://www.usip.org/files/resources/sr190.pdf

Yavuz, M. Hakan, *Islamic Political Identity in Turkey*, Oxford: Oxford University Press, 2003

'Political Islam and the Welfare (Refah) Party in Turkey', *Comparative Politics*, 30 (1) October 1997

Yıldız, Ahmet, 'Politico-Religious Discourse of Political Islam in Turkey: The Parties of National Outlook', *The Muslim World*, 93 (2) 2003

Zaki, Moheb, 'Strike Down the Hamayonic Decree', *Civil Society and Democratization in the Arab World*, 11 (131) 2005

al Zayyat, Montasser, *The Road to al-Qaeda: The Story of Bin Laden's Right Hand Man*, trans. Sara Nimis, London: Pluto Press, 2004

Zemni, Sami, 'From Local Insurgency to Al-Qaida Franchise', *International Institute for the Study of Islam in the Modern World Review*, 21, Spring 2008

Zghal, Abdelkader, 'The Reactivation of Tradition in a Post-Traditional Society', *Daedalus*, 102 (1) 1973

Zollner, Barbara H. E., *The Muslim Brotherhood: Hasan al-Hydaybi and Ideology*, London: Routledge, 2009

'Prison Talk: The Muslim Brotherhood's Internal Struggle during Gamal Abdel Nasser's Persecution, 1954 to 1971', *International Journal of Middle East Studies*, 39 (3) 2007

Zubaida, Sami, 'Islam and Secularization', *Asian Journal of Social Science*, 33 (3) 2005

Law and Power in the Islamic World, London: I. B. Tauris, 2003

'Is Iran an Islamic State?', Joel Beinin and Joe Stork (eds.), *Political Islam: Essays from Middle East Report*, London: I. B. Tauris, 1997

Islam, the People and the State: Political Ideas and Movements in the Middle East, revised edition, London: I. B. Tauris, 1993

Author's Interviews

Abdennour, Ali Yahia, lawyer and human rights activist, Algiers, March 2007

Abu el Fotouh, Abd el Monem, Muslim Brotherhood activist, Cairo, October 2007

Abu Odeh, Adnan, sociologist and political analyst, Amman, May 2007

Abu Rumman, Abdullah, journalist and member of the office of the Prime Minister, Amman, October 2007

Abu Rumman, Muhammad, journalist and specialist on the Islamist movement in Jordan. Amman, October 2007

Altınay, Hakan, Open Society Institute Assistance Foundation, Istanbul, March 2008

al Anani, Khalil, political analyst and specialist on Islamist movements, al Ahram Foundation, Cairo, November 2007

Anonymous Hizb ut Tahrir activist, West Bank, October 2007

Anonymous former Islamic Jihad activist, West Bank, October 2007

al Arabiyat, Abd al Latif, leader of Islamist Action Front, Amman, October 2007

Assaf, Nizam, Amman Centre for Human Rights Studies, Amman, October 2007

Ayachi, Hamida, journalist and specialist on the Islamist movement, Algiers, March 2007

Aybay, Rona, lawyer and human rights activist, Ankara, March 2008

Barghouti, Muhammad, former minister of Local Government, (Palestinian National Authority), Ramallah, October 2007

Beydoun, Ahmed, journalist, Beirut, September 2009

Bilgen, Ayşe, Mazlumder (NGO), Ankara, March 2008

Blanford, Nicholas, journalist, Beirut September 2009

Boudjema, Mounir, journalist and political analyst, Algiers, March 2007

Breizat, Fares, Center for Strategic Studies, University of Jordan, Amman, October 2007

Charara, Wadah, journalist and author on Hizbullah, Beirut, September 2009

Chebbi, Nejib, leader of the secular opposition movement, the Progressive Democratic Party (Parti Démocrate Progressiste, PDP), Tunis, March 2007

Chourou, Bechir, University of Tunis, Tunis, March 2007

Cohen, Hillel, author and expert on Islamist movements, Hebrew University of Jerusalem, Jerusalem, October 2007

Dağı, Ihsan, Middle East Technical University, Ankara, March 2008

Daraghmeh, Ayman, member of the Palestinian Legislative Council, Ramallah, October 2007

el Deiri, Makarem, electoral candidate for the Egyptian Assembly, Cairo, December 2005

Delici, Fouad, former FIS activist, Algiers, March 2007

Djema, Mohammed, political activist ('Movement for the Society of Peace', MSP), Algiers, March 2007

Dwaib, Khaled, Hamas activist and Palestinian Legislative Council member, Bethlehem, West Bank, October 2007

el Erian, Essam, Islamic National Conference Coordinator and member of the Muslim Brotherhood, Cairo, November 2005

Fahs, Hani, Shia leader and commentator, Beirut, September 2009

al Ghizali, Abdel Hamid, Cairo University, Muslim Brotherhood activist, Cairo, October 2007

Göksel, Timur, former spokesperson for United Nations Interim Force In Lebanon (UNIFIL) and political analyst, Beirut, September 2009

Hadi, Mahdi F. Abdul, Chairman of the Palestinian Academic Society for the Study of International Affairs, Jerusalem, October 2007

Hamided, Mohamed, former FIS activist, Algiers, March 2007

Hassan, Bahey el Din, Cairo Institute for Human Rights Studies, Cairo, December 2005

Himeur, Mohamed Arezki, journalist, Algiers, March 2007

Houry, Nadim, Human Rights Watch, Beirut, September 2009

Hussain, Ghaffar, Quilliam Foundation, former activist within Hizb ut Tahrir, London, January 2009

Hussein, Magdi, political activist (Labour Party), Cairo, November 2005

Ibrahim, Saad Eddin, Ibn Khaldun Centre for Political Studies, Cairo, November 2005

Irsheid, Zaki Bany, IAF secretary general, Amman, October 2007

Ismail, Mamdouh, lawyer and political activist, Cairo, December 2005

Jenkins, Gareth, journalist and expert on Turkish Islamism, Istanbul, March 2008

Jones, Gareth, Reuters correspondent, Ankara, March 2008

Kalaycioğlu, Ersin, Sabancı University, Istanbul, March 2008

Kassem, Hishem, journalist and political activist, Cairo, December 2005 and November 2007

Khashana, Nejib, journalist, Tunis, March 2007

Keilani, Musa, journalist, Amman, October 2007

Keyman, Fuat, Köc University, Istanbul, March 2008

Kirişci, Kemal, Boğaziçi University, Istanbul, March 2008

Latif, Omayma Abdel, journalist, Beirut, September 2009

Mady, Abu Elela, leader of Wasat Party, Cairo, December 2005

Massalmeh, Hassan, Council Member, Bethlehem Municipality, Bethlehem, West Bank, October 1007

Mezrag, Madani, former leader of the AIS, Algiers, March 2007

al Momani, Mohammad H., Jordan Institute of Diplomacy and Yarmouk University, Amman, October 2007

Mudessir, Moheb, journalist, BBC World Service, London, July 2007

Nahla, Mahmoud, lawyer, al Kalema organisation, Cairo, December 2005

Öniş, Ziya, Köc University, Istanbul, March 2008

Özbudun, Ergun, Bilkent University, Ankara, March 2008

Özel, Soli, Bilgi University, Istanbul, March 2008

Rashwan, Diaa, expert on the Islamist movement, al Ahram Centre for Political and Strategic Studies, Cairo, November 2007

Roberts, Hugh, Islamist movements and Algeria expert, London, August 2009

Safa, Oussama, General Director, Lebanese Centre for Policy Studies, Beirut, September 2009

Saghieh, Hazem, journalist, Beirut, September 2009

Saleh, Miriam, former Minister for Women's Affairs (Palestinian National Authority), Ramallah, October 2007

Salem, Paul, Carnegie Endowment for International Peace, Beirut, September 2009

Saqer, Jamal, political activist, Ramallah, October 2007

el Sayed Said, Mohamed, specialist on Islamist movement, Center for Political and Strategic Studies, al Ahram Newspaper, Cairo, November 2005

Shamsidi, Hakimi, political activist (al Islah), Algiers, March 2007
Shbeilat, Laith, former political activist and independent Islamist, Amman, October 2007
Somer, Murat, Köc University, Istanbul, March 2008
Tameemee, Raef, Fatah activist, Hebron, October 2007
Temlali, Yassine, journalist and political analyst, Algiers, March 2007
Tür, Özlem, Middle East Technical University, Ankara, March 2008
Turabi, Hasan, former head of Sudanese National Islamic Front, Khartoum, February 2004
Wolcott, Kirk, Middle East Partnership Initiative, US Department of State, Tunis, March 2007
Zoubir, Arous, Centre de Recherche en Economie Appliquée pour le Développement (CREAD), University of Algiers, Algiers, March 2007
Zweiri, Majhoob, Center for Strategic Studies, University of Jordan, Amman, October 2007

Index

Note: page numbers with an 'n' suffix refer to a footnote on that page